Prentice Hall **Realidades 1**

Communication Workbook with Test Preparation

PEARSON

Boston, Massachusetts   Chandler, Arizona   Glenview, Illinois   Upper Saddle River, New Jersey

Acknowledgments

"Las mañanitas" by Manuel M. Ponce. Copyright © 1945 by Promotora Hispanoamericana de Música, S.A. Copyright renewed. Administered by Peer International Corporation. International copyright secured. Used by permission

"México lindo" by Chucho Monge. Copyright © 1949 by Promotora Hispanoamericana de Música, S.A. Copyright renewed. Administered by Peer International Corporation. International copyright secured. Used by permission.

"Mi cafetal" from *MI CAFETAL.* Copyright © Madacy Entertainment. Used by permission of Madacy Entertainment.

"La golondrina" from *LA GOLONDRINA.* Copyright © Madacy Entertainment. Used by permission of Madacy Entertainment.

"Viva Jujuy" from *VIVA JUJUY.* Copyright © Madacy Entertainment. Used by permission of Madacy Entertainment.

Art, Photo and Map Credits
Page 230: (map) Design Associates, (tr) © Navaswan/FPG, (bl) © David Young Wolff/PhotoEdit; **Page 236:** (map) Jennifer Thermes; **Page 248:** (map) Jennfer Thermes; **Page 254:** Eldon Doty/H.K. Portfolio, Inc.; **Page 260:** Ted Smykal; **Page 266:** (map) Design Associates, © Charles & Josette Lenars/CORBIS; **Page 272:** © Eldon Doty/H.K. Portfolio, Inc.; **Page 278:** © John Neubauer/PhotoEdit; **Page 279:** (t) © Sisse Brimberg/NGS Image Collection, (b) © Dave Albers/Illustration Works, Inc.; **Page 285:** Ted Smykal; **Page 291:** (t) © Michelle Chaplow/CORBIS, (b) © Patrick Ward/CORBIS; **Page 297:** (map) Ted Smykal, Geoffrey Clifford/ASA/IPN Stock; **Page 303:** (t) The Textile Museum, Washington, D.C., no. 91.192 detail, (b) The Textile Museum, Washington D.C., no. 91.99; **Page 309:** © Michael Krasowitz/FPG; **Page 315:** (map) Ted Smykal, Jack Parsons/Omni-Photo Communications, Inc.; **Page 316:** Glenn LeBlanc/Index Stock Imagery, Inc.; **Page 322:** (t) © Nik Wheeler/CORBIS, (b) © Robert Frerck/Odyssey/Chicago; **Page 328:** (t) © AFP/CORBIS, (b) © Univision Network 2000; **Page 334:** (both) Reuters Newmedia, Inc., Inc./CORBIS.

PEARSON

ISBN-13: 978-0-13-369262-4
ISBN-10:   0-13-369262-0

4 5 6 7 8 9 10 V016 14 13 12 11

Table of Contents

Prentice Hall Realidades 1

Writing, Audio & Video Activities

PEARSON

Boston, Massachusetts   Chandler, Arizona   Glenview, Illinois   Upper Saddle River, New Jersey

Table of Contents

Realidades ❶

Para empezar

Nombre _____

Fecha _____

Hora _____

AUDIO

Actividad 1

You are at a party with students visiting from Ecuador. You have practiced several responses to the things they might say when you meet them. Listen to each question or statement and write the letter of the best response in the blank. You will hear each statement or question twice.

a. Me llamo ...

b. Muy bien, gracias.

c. Regular.

d. Mucho gusto.

e. Igualmente.

f. Hasta mañana.

1. _____

2. _____

3. _____

4. _____

5. _____

6. _____

Actividad 2

You have lost your dog, so you put up signs in your neighborhood asking your neighbors to call you if they see him. You will hear six messages on your answering machine from neighbors who have seen your dog. You will not understand everything they say, but listen carefully to find out their house number and what time they called so that you can track down your dog. Write down each house number and time on the chart. You will hear each message twice.

	NÚMERO DE CASA (House number)	HORA DE LA LLAMADA (Time of call)
1.	_____	_____
2.	_____	_____
3.	_____	_____
4.	_____	_____
5.	_____	_____
6.	_____	_____

Nombre _____   Hora _____

Fecha _____   **AUDIO**

Actividad 3

A new student has come into your Spanish class. He seems lost when the teacher asks the students to take out certain items. As you listen to what the teacher says, help him by identifying the picture that matches the item the teacher is asking the students to get out for class. You will hear each command twice.

Modelo   __f__   1. _____   2. _____   3. _____   4. _____   5. _____

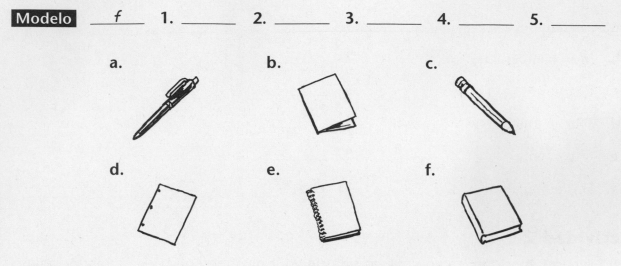

a.

b.

c.

d.

e.

f.

Actividad 4

Your teacher is using a map and an alphabet/number grid to plan a class trip to Spain. The five dots on the grid represent cities in Spain where your group will stop. Listen as you hear the first letter/number combination, as in the game of Bingo. Find that dot on the grid and label it "1." Next to it, write the name of the city. After you hear the second letter/number combination, find the second dot and label it "2," writing the name of the city next to it, and so on for the rest of the dots. Connect the dots to show the route of the class trip. You will hear each phrase twice.

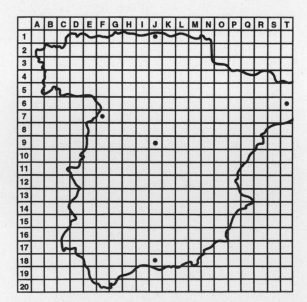

Realidades ❶

Para empezar

Nombre _____

Fecha _____

Hora _____

AUDIO

Actividad 5

While on vacation in Uruguay, your teacher visits an elementary school classroom. Each student in the class tells your teacher his or her birthday (**cumpleaños**) and what the weather is like at that time of the year in Uruguay. Remember, in South America the seasons are the reverse of those in the United States. In the first column write out each student's date of birth, and in the second column what season his or her birthday is in. You will hear each sentence twice.

	DATE OF BIRTH	SEASON
1. Juan	_____	_____
2. María	_____	_____
3. Miguel	_____	_____
4. Óscar	_____	_____
5. Carolina	_____	_____
6. Marta	_____	_____
7. Elena	_____	_____
8. Pedro	_____	_____

Realidades **1**

Nombre _____ Hora _____

Para empezar

Fecha _____ **WRITING**

Actividad 6

Describe the monster below, telling how many of each body part he has (**El monstruo tiene ...**). Each blank corresponds to one letter. Each letter corresponds to a number, which appears underneath the blank. Use these numbers to figure out which sentence refers to which body part. The first one has been done for you.

Modelo   El monstruo tiene $\underset{9}{D}\ \underset{15}{O}\ \underset{20}{S}$ $\underset{2}{C}\ \underset{10}{A}\ \underset{19}{B}\ \underset{1}{E}\ \underset{3}{Z}\ \underset{10}{A}\ \underset{20}{S}$.

1. El monstruo tiene $\underset{15}{\ }\ \underset{2}{\ }\ \underset{8}{\ }\ \underset{15}{\ }$ $\underset{15}{\ }\ \underset{17}{\ }\ \underset{15}{\ }\ \underset{20}{\ }$.

2. El monstruo tiene $\underset{6}{\ }\ \underset{22}{\ }\ \underset{10}{\ }$ $\underset{22}{\ }\ \underset{10}{\ }\ \underset{4}{\ }\ \underset{5}{\ }\ \underset{3}{\ }$ en cada cabeza.

3. El monstruo tiene $\underset{6}{\ }\ \underset{22}{\ }\ \underset{10}{\ }$ $\underset{19}{\ }\ \underset{15}{\ }\ \underset{2}{\ }\ \underset{10}{\ }$ en cada cabeza.

4. El monstruo tiene $\underset{2}{\ }\ \underset{6}{\ }\ \underset{10}{\ }\ \underset{11}{\ }\ \underset{4}{\ }\ \underset{15}{\ }$ $\underset{19}{\ }\ \underset{4}{\ }\ \underset{10}{\ }\ \underset{3}{\ }\ \underset{15}{\ }\ \underset{20}{\ }$.

5. El monstruo tiene $\underset{11}{\ }\ \underset{4}{\ }\ \underset{1}{\ }\ \underset{20}{\ }$ $\underset{9}{\ }\ \underset{1}{\ }\ \underset{9}{\ }\ \underset{15}{\ }\ \underset{20}{\ }$ en cada mano.

6. El monstruo tiene $\underset{20}{\ }\ \underset{1}{\ }\ \underset{5}{\ }\ \underset{20}{\ }$ $\underset{16}{\ }\ \underset{5}{\ }\ \underset{1}{\ }\ \underset{4}{\ }\ \underset{22}{\ }\ \underset{10}{\ }\ \underset{20}{\ }$.

Realidades 1

Para empezar

Nombre _____

Fecha _____

Hora _____

WRITING

Actividad 7

A. It is September and school is finally in session. You already have some important dates to mark on the calendar. To make sure you have the right day, write the day of the week that each date falls on.

SEPTIEMBRE						
lunes	**martes**	**miércoles**	**jueves**	**viernes**	**sábado**	**domingo**
		1	2	3	4	5
6	7	8	9	10	11	12
13	14	15	16	17	18	19
20	21	22	23	24	25	26
27	28	29	30			

1. el tres de septiembre _____

2. el veinte de septiembre _____

3. el primero de septiembre _____

4. el veinticuatro de septiembre _____

5. el doce de septiembre _____

6. el dieciocho de septiembre _____

7. el siete de septiembre _____

B. Now, write in what month the following holidays occur.

1. el Día de San Valentín _____

2. el Día de San Patricio _____

3. la Navidad _____

4. el Año Nuevo _____

5. el Día de la Independencia _____

Realidades ❶

Para empezar

Nombre _____

Fecha _____

Hora _____

WRITING

Actividad 8

Answer the questions below according to the map.

1. ¿Qué tiempo hace en el norte de México?

   _____

2. ¿Hace buen tiempo en el sur?

   _____

3. ¿Qué tiempo hace en el centro de México?

   _____

4. ¿Hace frío o calor en el este?

   _____

5. ¿Qué tiempo hace en el oeste?

   _____

6. ¿Qué estación es, probablemente?

   _____

Introducción

Actividad 1

Do you like the video so far? Did you enjoy meeting the characters? Are you curious to find out more about their home cities? Look at the map below. Then, write the names of the video friends that live at each location. As you are doing this exercise, begin to familiarize yourself with the names of these locations: Madrid, España; Ciudad de México, México; San José, Costa Rica; San Antonio, Texas.

| Esteban y Angélica | Ignacio y Ana | Claudia y Teresa | Raúl y Gloria |

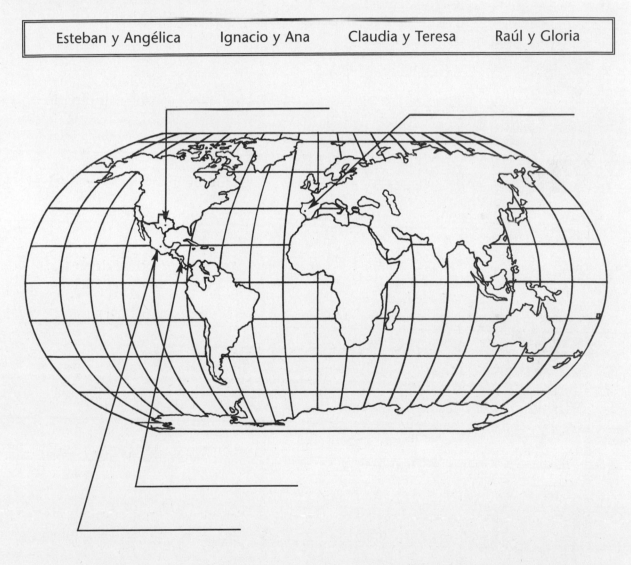

Realidades ①
Capítulo 1A

Nombre _____   Hora _____

Fecha _____

VIDEO

¿Comprendes?

Actividad 2

Match the characters with the activities they like to do or do not like to do.

1. Me llamo Ignacio y tengo 17 años. _____

a. Me gusta escuchar música también. Pero me gusta más hablar por teléfono.

2. Yo me llamo Ana y tengo 15 años. _____

b. Me gusta usar la computadora.

3. Me llamo Claudia y tengo 16 años. _____

c. A mí me gusta tocar la guitarra.

4. Y yo soy Teresa. Tengo 15 años. _____

d. Me gusta practicar deportes, correr y montar en bicicleta.

5. Soy Esteban. Tengo 15 años. _____

e. Me gusta leer libros y revistas.

6. Yo me llamo Angélica y tengo 16 años. _____

f. A mí me gusta ir a la escuela.

7. Soy Raúl y tengo 15 años. _____

g. Me gusta más jugar videojuegos.

8. Me llamo Gloria y tengo 14 años. _____

h. A mí no me gusta ni correr ni montar en bicicleta. A mí me gusta patinar.

8 *Video Activities* ▬ *Capítulo 1A*

Communication Workbook

© Pearson Education, Inc. All rights reserved.

Actividad 3

Decide whether response a, b, or c best describes the characters in each question.

1. When they are outside, what does Ana ask Ignacio? _____

    a. ¿Te gusta hablar por teléfono?

    b. ¿Qué te gusta hacer?

    c. ¿Te gusta tocar la guitarra?

2. Claudia and Teresa live in Mexico. What do they both like to do? _____

    a. pasar tiempo con amigos

    b. jugar videojuegos

    c. usar la computadora

3. What sports do Esteban and Angélica talk about? _____

    a. correr, montar en bicicleta y patinar

    b. esquiar, correr y nadar

    c. jugar al básquetbol, jugar al fútbol y montar en bicicleta

4. Does Raúl like to go to school? _____

    a. Sí. A Raúl le gusta mucho ir a la escuela.

    b. No. No le gusta nada.

    c. Pues... más o menos.

Y, ¿qué más?

Actividad 4

You have just seen and heard what these eight video friends like or do not like to do. Now fill in the blanks below to tell about things that you like to do and do not like to do.

1. Me gusta _____ .

2. A mí me gusta más _____ .

3. A mí no me gusta _____ .

4. A mí no me gusta ni _____ .

Actividad 5

You can learn a lot about a person from what he or she likes to do. You will hear two people from each group of three describe themselves. Listen and match the descriptions to the appropriate pictures. Put an *A* underneath the first person described, and a *B* underneath the second person described. You will hear each set of statements twice.

1. Luisa _____   Marta _____   Carmen _____

2. Marco _____   Javier _____   Alejandro _____

3. Mercedes _____   Ana _____   María _____

4. Carlos _____   Jaime _____   Luis _____

5. Isabel _____   Margarita _____   Cristina _____

Nombre _____   Hora _____

Fecha _____   **AUDIO**

Actividad 6

A group of students from Peru will visit your school. Since your class will be hosting the students, your teacher is trying to match each of you with a visiting student who likes to do the same things as you do. Listen to the questions and write the students' answers in the blanks. Then, write which of the activities you like better. Find out if the student has the same preferences as you do. Follow the model. You will hear each conversation twice.

Modelo   Guillermo: _____ *cantar* _____

A mí: _____ *Me gusta más bailar* _____.

1. Paco: _____
   A mí: _____.

2. Ana María: _____
   A mí: _____.

3. José Luis: _____
   A mí: _____.

4. Maricarmen: _____
   A mí: _____.

5. Luisa: _____
   A mí: _____.

Actividad 7

As one of the judges at your school's fall carnival, your job is to mark on the master tic tac toe board the progress of a live tic-tac-toe competition between Team X and Team O.

As each contestant comes to the microphone, you will hear "por X" or "por O" to indicate for which team he or she is playing. The contestant has to answer a question about activities in order to claim the square. Listen for the activity mentioned in each question, and put either an *X* or an *O* in the box under the picture of that activity.

At the end of this game round, see which team won! You will hear each statement twice.

Who won the game? _____

Realidades ①

Capítulo 1A

Nombre _____

Fecha _____

Hora _____

AUDIO

Actividad 8

Luisa, the host of your school's radio station talk show, is interviewing four new students. As you listen to the interview, write down one thing that each student likes to do, and one thing that each student does not like to do. You will hear the entire question and answer session repeated. You will hear this conversation twice.

	Armando	**Josefina**	**Carlos**	**Marta**
Likes				
Dislikes				

Actividad 9

As you turn on the radio, you hear a Spanish radio D.J. talking about the "Top Ten Tips" for being happy during this school year. As you listen, match the suggestion to one of the pictures and number them in the order the suggestions were given on the air. Remember to listen for cognates!

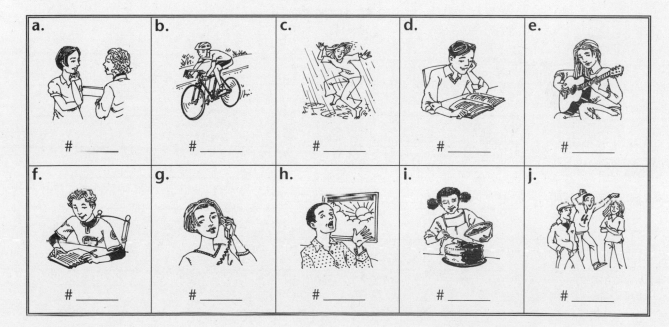

a. # _____

b. # _____

c. # _____

d. # _____

e. # _____

f. # _____

g. # _____

h. # _____

i. # _____

j. # _____

Realidades ❶

Capítulo 1A

Nombre _____

Hora _____

Fecha _____

WRITING

Actividad 10

Students like to do all sorts of activities during their free periods. Look at the picture below and write what each student is saying he or she likes to do. Then say whether or not you like to do those things. Follow the model.

Modelo	EL PROFESOR:	*A mí me gusta trabajar.*
	TÚ:	*A mí me gusta trabajar también.*

ESTUDIANTE #1: _____

TÚ: _____

ESTUDIANTE #2: _____

TÚ: _____

ESTUDIANTE #3: _____

TÚ: _____

ESTUDIANTE #4: _____

TÚ: _____

ESTUDIANTE #5: _____

TÚ: _____

ESTUDIANTE #6: _____

TÚ: _____

Realidades 1

Capítulo 1A

Nombre _____

Hora _____

Fecha _____

WRITING

Actividad 11

It is your first day at your new school, and your new friend Elena is interviewing you for the school newspaper. In the spaces provided, write your answers to the questions that Elena asks you.

ELENA: —Buenos días. ¿Cómo estás?

TÚ: —_____

ELENA: —¿Qué te gusta hacer?

TÚ: —_____

ELENA: —¿Te gusta ir a la escuela?

TÚ: —_____

ELENA: —¿Qué te gusta hacer en casa?

TÚ: —_____

ELENA: —¿Te gusta escribir o leer cuentos?

TÚ: —_____

ELENA: —¿Qué más te gusta hacer?

TÚ: —_____

ELENA: —Pues, muchas gracias por la entrevista. Buena suerte.

TÚ: —_____

Nombre _____

Hora _____

Fecha _____

WRITING

Actividad 12

A. Your classmates have signed up for different clubs. Look at the flyers below to see who signed up for which club. Then, decide how each student might answer the questions below based on the club that each one signed up for.

El Club Educativo

El club ideal para estudiantes a quienes les gusta ir a la escuela.

Actividades:

• usar la computadora
• leer y escribir cuentos
• estudiar

Eduardo _____
Eugenia _____
Esteban _____

El Club Deportista

El club ideal para estudiantes a quienes les gusta practicar deportes.

Actividades:

• nadar
• correr
• practicar deportes

Diana _____
Dolores _____
Diego _____

EL CLUB MUSICAL

El club ideal para estudiantes a quienes les gusta la música.

ACTIVIDADES:

• TOCAR EL PIANO O LA GUITARRA
• CANTAR
• BAILAR

MARICARMEN _____
MANOLO _____
MÓNICA _____

Modelo   Eduardo, ¿te gusta tocar la guitarra?

No, no me gusta tocar la guitarra. Me gusta estudiar.

1. Diana, ¿te gusta leer o escribir cuentos?

_____

2. Manolo, ¿qué te gusta hacer?

_____

3. Diego, ¿te gusta ir a la escuela para usar la computadora?

_____

4. Mónica, ¿te gusta nadar o correr?

_____

5. Eugenia, ¿qué te gusta hacer?

_____

B. Now, pick which club you would join and say why. Follow the model.

Modelo   _Prefiero el Club Educativo porque me gusta ir a la escuela._

Prefiero el Club _____ porque _____

_____

Communication Workbook

Actividad 13

A. Write two sentences about things that you like to do, and two sentences about things that you do not like to do. Follow the model.

Modelo   *A mí me gusta leer.*

   No me gusta correr.

1. _____

2. _____

3. _____

4. _____

B. Now, use your sentences from Part A to write a letter to your new penpal that will tell her a little bit about you.

29/9/2003

Saludos,

_____

_____

_____

_____

También _____

_____

_____

Un abrazo,

_____

VIDEO

Antes de ver el video

Actividad 1

During the video, Teresa, Claudia, Pedro, and Esteban describe each other in e-mails. How would you describe yourself? Below is a list of descriptive words. Check off the words that describe you.

Soy...
- ❑ artístico, -a
- ❑ atrevido, -a
- ❑ deportista
- ❑ desordenado, -a
- ❑ estudioso, -a
- ❑ gracioso, -a

- ❑ impaciente
- ❑ inteligente
- ❑ ordenado, -a
- ❑ paciente
- ❑ reservado, -a
- ❑ serio, -a

- ❑ simpático, -a
- ❑ sociable
- ❑ talentoso, -a
- ❑ trabajador, -ora

¿Comprendes?

Actividad 2

Fill in the blanks with the appropriate word or phrase from the bank. You may have to watch the video several times to remember each character well.

misteriosa	reservado	ordenados	inteligente
serio	trabajadora	sociable	
simpática	hablar por teléfono	buena	

1.  A Pedro no le gusta ni bailar ni cantar. Es _____.

Pero él escribe: "Soy muy gracioso. No soy muy _____."

Communication Workbook

Realidades **1**

Capítulo 1B

Nombre

Hora

Fecha

VIDEO

2. Teresa, desde un cibercafé en la Ciudad de México, escribe: "Yo soy *Chica*

_____."

3. Ella es la _____ amiga de Claudia.

4. Le gusta _____ , pero no le gusta ir a la escuela.

5. En la computadora, Claudia se llama *Chica* _____ .

6. A ella le gusta la escuela; es muy _____ , estudiosa

y _____ .

7. También le gustan los chicos inteligentes y _____ .

8. A Pedro le gusta *Chica misteriosa.* Ella también es una chica _____ .

Realidades ❶

Capítulo 1B

Nombre _____

Hora _____

Fecha _____

VIDEO

Actividad 3

According to Esteban, Pedro is quiet and reserved. Yet, in his e-mail, he writes the opposite. Read what he writes about himself in his e-mail. Then, write what he is really like by filling in the blanks.

> Me llamo Chico sociable. ¡Qué coincidencia! Me gusta pasar tiempo con mis amigos... Me gusta escuchar música. Según mis amigos soy muy gracioso. No soy muy serio. Escríbeme.

1. *Chico sociable*, el _____ de Esteban, se llama _____ .

2. Según Esteban, él no es un chico _____ . Él es _____ .

3. A Pedro no le gusta ni _____ ni _____ .

4. Pedro no es muy _____ . Él es muy _____ .

Y, ¿qué más?

Actividad 4

Describe people you know using each of the adjectives from the following list. Follow the model.

| paciente | inteligente | sociable | impaciente | deportista |

Modelo *La profesora de español es muy inteligente.*

_____

_____

_____

_____

Communication Workbook

Actividad 5

You are a volunteer for a service at your school that helps new students meet other new students in order to make the transition easier. People who are interested in participating in this program have left messages describing themselves. Listen as the students describe themselves, and put a check mark in at least two columns that match what each student says. Then write the names of the most well-matched students. You will hear each statement twice.

BUENOS AMIGOS

	CARMEN	PABLO	ANA	ANDRÉS	RAQUEL	JORGE
serio(a)						
reservado(a)						
deportista						
estudioso(a)						
talentoso(a)						
gracioso(a)						
atrevido(a)						
trabajador(a)						
artístico(a)						
sociable						
romántico(a)						

BUENOS AMIGOS:

1. _____ y _____

2. _____ y _____

3. _____ y _____

AUDIO

Actividad 6

What is your favorite season of the year? Your choice could say a lot about you. Listen as talk-show psychologist Doctor Armando describes people according to their preferred season (**estación preferida**) of the year. What characteristics go with each season? Listen and put a check mark in the appropriate boxes. By the way, is it true what he says about you and your favorite season? You will hear each statement twice.

Mi estación preferida es _____. Según el Dr. Armando, yo soy

_____.

Communication Workbook

Realidades ❶

Capítulo 1B

Nombre _____

Hora _____

Fecha _____

AUDIO

Actividad 7

Your Spanish teacher encourages you to speak Spanish outside of class. As you walk down the hall, you hear parts of your classmates' conversations in Spanish. Listen to the conversations and decide whether they are talking about a boy, a girl, or if you can't tell by what is being said. Place a check mark in the appropriate box of the table. You will hear each statement twice.

	#1	#2	#3	#4	#5	#6	#7	#8
?								

Actividad 8

Listen as Nacho describes his ex-girlfriend. How many things do they have in common? Put an *X* on the pictures that show ways in which they are very different and put a circle around the pictures that show ways they are very similar. You will hear each set of statements twice.

1. 2. 3. 4. 5.

Realidades ❶

Capítulo 1B

Nombre _____

Fecha _____

Hora _____

AUDIO

Actividad 9

Some people say we are what we dream! Listen as Antonieta calls in and describes her dream (**sueño**) to Doctor Armando, the radio talk show psychologist. Draw a circle around the pictures below that match what she dreams about herself.

After you hear Antonieta's call, tell a partner what kinds of things would be in a dream that reveals what you like to do and what kind of person you are. You might begin with "**En mi sueño, me gusta...**". You will hear this dialogue twice.

Realidades ①

Capítulo 1B

Nombre _____

Hora _____

Fecha _____

WRITING

Actividad 10

A. Fill in the words using the art as clues.

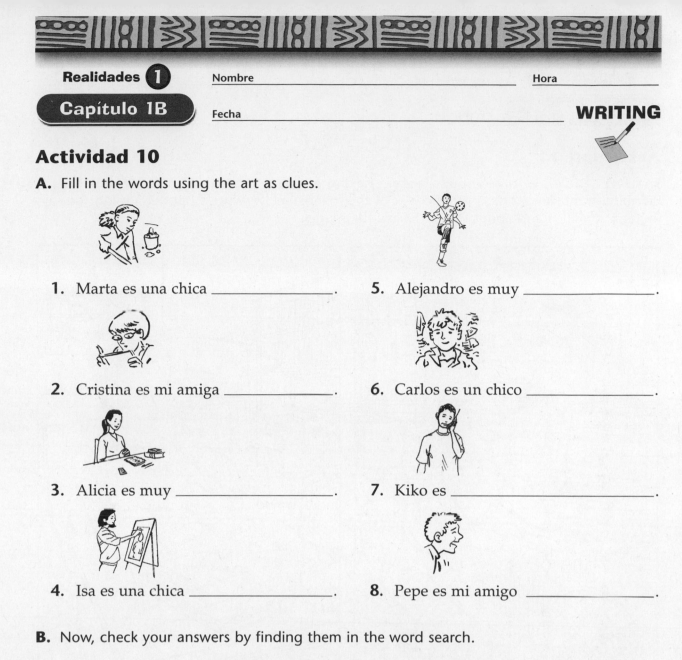

1. Marta es una chica _____.

2. Cristina es mi amiga _____.

3. Alicia es muy _____.

4. Isa es una chica _____.

5. Alejandro es muy _____.

6. Carlos es un chico _____.

7. Kiko es _____.

8. Pepe es mi amigo _____.

B. Now, check your answers by finding them in the word search.

```
N E P M V P I Q U U T D
T R A B A J A D O R A E
A S O I D U T S E D G S
L A K U X M A L E A R O
E M D I C Z P P O C A R
N T P A O X O J Z I C D
T I U M N R U F R T I E
O Q K I T E I T E S O N
S M X I E T D G P I S A
A O S L U R M R Y T O D
P T L A E U U J O R H O
A S O C I A B L E A E T
```

Actividad 11

Frida and Diego, who are opposites, are talking on the phone. Frida, the sociable one, is doing all the talking. Using the pictures of the friends below, write what Frida might be saying about herself and about Diego. Follow the models.

Modelo	_Yo soy deportista._		Modelo	_Tú eres paciente._
1.	_____		1.	_____
2.	_____		2.	_____
3.	_____		3.	_____
4.	_____		4.	_____
5.	_____		5.	_____

Actividad 12

Answer the following questions. Be sure to use the definite or indefinite article where appropriate. Follow the model.

Modelo ¿Cómo es tu mamá (*mother*)?

Ella es simpática y graciosa. _____

1. ¿Cómo eres tú?

   _____

2. ¿Cómo es tu profesor(a) de español?

   _____

3. ¿Cómo es tu mejor amigo(a)?

   _____

4. ¿Cómo es el presidente?

   _____

5. ¿Cómo es el director/la directora (*principal*) de tu escuela?

   _____

6. ¿Qué te duele?

   _____

7. ¿Cuál es la fecha de hoy?

   _____

8. ¿Cuál es la fecha del Día de la Independencia?

   _____

9. ¿Cuál es tu estación favorita?

   _____

10. ¿Qué hora es?

   _____

Actividad 13

A reporter for the school newspaper has asked you and several other students in your class-room to submit an article for the paper. The article is about personality traits and activities people like and dislike.

A. Think about your own personality traits. Write four adjectives that describe what you are like and four that describe what you are not like.

SOY	NO SOY
_____	_____
_____	_____
_____	_____
_____	_____

B. Now, write four things that you like to do and four things that you do not like to do.

ME GUSTA	NO ME GUSTA
_____	_____
_____	_____
_____	_____
_____	_____

C. Now, write your article using the information you have compiled about yourself.

_____

_____

_____

_____

_____

_____

_____

_____

_____

       Communication Workbook

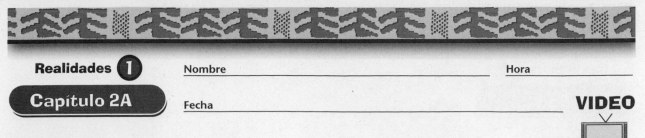

Realidades **1**

Capítulo 2A

Nombre _____

Hora _____

Fecha _____

VIDEO

Antes de ver el video

Actividad 1

Think of two of your favorite and two of your least favorite classes. Write the name of each class, when you have it, and why it is your favorite or least favorite.

Clase	Hora	Comentarios

¿Comprendes?

Actividad 2

Claudia had a bad day. Circle the correct answer to explain what happened to her.

1. Claudia tiene un día difícil en el colegio (*high school*). ¿Por qué?
   a. A Claudia no le gusta su colegio.
   b. Claudia no tiene amigos.
   c. Tiene problemas con el horario.
   d. A Claudia no le gustan las matemáticas.

2. ¿En qué hora tiene Claudia la clase de matemáticas?
   a. en la primera hora
   b. en la tercera hora
   c. en la quinta hora
   d. todas las anteriores (*all of the above*)

3. Claudia habla con la persona que hace el horario. ¿Cómo se llama?
   a. Sra. Santoro   b. Sr. López   c. Srta. García   d. Sr. Treviño

4. Para Teresa la clase de inglés es
   a. aburrida.   b. interesante.   c. fantástica.   d. difícil.

5. En la tercera hora Claudia piensa que las matemáticas son aburridas, porque
   a. es el primer día de clases.
   b. la profesora es muy divertida.
   c. tiene seis clases de matemáticas hoy.
   d. no entiende las matemáticas.

Nombre _____   Hora _____

Fecha _____   **VIDEO**

Actividad 3

Write **cierto** (*true*) or **falso** (*false*) next to each statement.

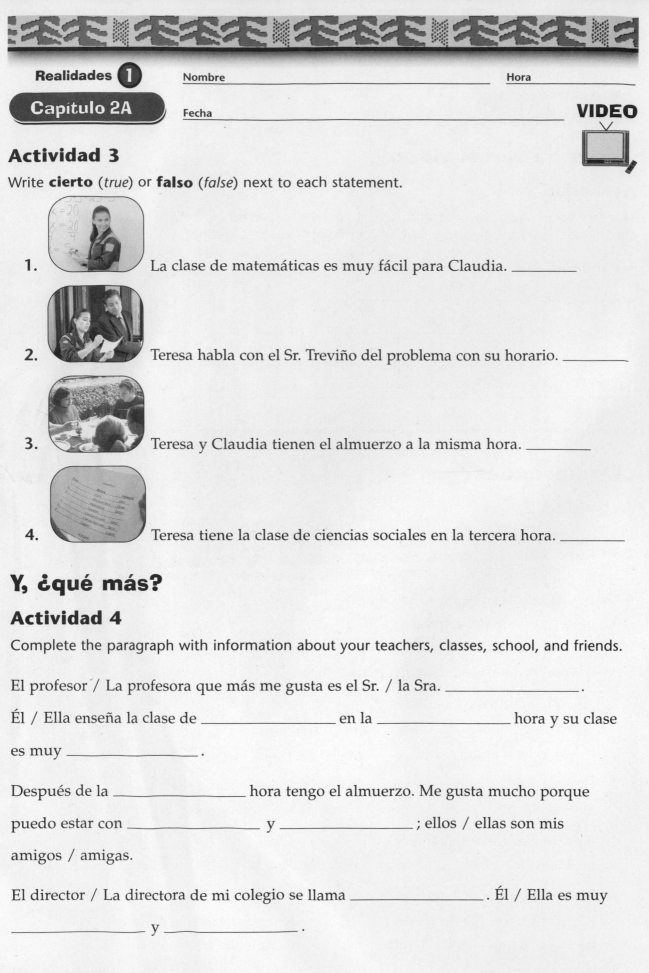

1. La clase de matemáticas es muy fácil para Claudia. _____

2. Teresa habla con el Sr. Treviño del problema con su horario. _____

3. Teresa y Claudia tienen el almuerzo a la misma hora. _____

4. Teresa tiene la clase de ciencias sociales en la tercera hora. _____

Y, ¿qué más?

Actividad 4

Complete the paragraph with information about your teachers, classes, school, and friends.

El profesor / La profesora que más me gusta es el Sr. / la Sra. _____.

Él / Ella enseña la clase de _____ en la _____ hora y su clase

es muy _____ .

Después de la _____ hora tengo el almuerzo. Me gusta mucho porque

puedo estar con _____ y _____ ; ellos / ellas son mis

amigos / amigas.

El director / La directora de mi colegio se llama _____ . Él / Ella es muy

_____ y _____ .

Actividad 5

You overhear several people in the hall trying to find out if they have classes together this year. As you listen to each conversation, write an *X* in the box under **SÍ** if they have a class together, or under **NO** if they do not. You will hear each conversation twice.

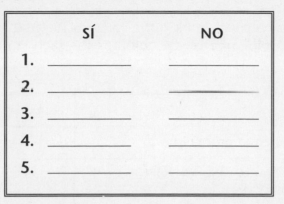

	SÍ	NO
1.	_____	_____
2.	_____	_____
3.	_____	_____
4.	_____	_____
5.	_____	_____

Actividad 6

As you stand outside the school counselor's office, you hear four students trying to talk to him. They are all requesting to get out of a certain class. From the part of the conversation that you hear, write in the blank the class from which each student is requesting a transfer. You will hear each statement twice.

	CLASE	PROFESOR(A)
1.	matemáticas	el profesor Pérez
2.	arte	la profesora Muñoz
3.	español	el profesor Cortez
4.	ciencias sociales	la profesora Lenis
5.	almuerzo	
6.	ciencias	el profesor Gala
7.	educación física	el profesor Fernández
8.	inglés	la profesora Ochoa

1. La clase de _____

2. La clase de _____

3. La clase de _____

4. La clase de _____

Actividad 7

Emilio, a new student from Bolivia, is attending his first pep assembly! He is eager to make friends and begins talking to Diana, who is sitting next to him. Listen to their conversation. If they have something in common, place a check mark in the column labeled **Ellos**. If the statement only applies to Emilio, place a check mark in the column labeled **Él**. If the statement only applies to Diana, place a check mark in the column labeled **Ella**. **Note:** Be sure you have placed a check mark in ONLY one of the columns for each statement. You will hear the conversation twice.

INFORMACIÓN	ÉL	ELLA	ELLOS
Tiene la clase de español en la primera hora.			
Tiene la clase de español en la segunda hora.			
Tiene una profesora simpática.			
Tiene una profesora graciosa.			
Tiene una clase de arte en la quinta hora.			
Tiene una clase de educación física en la quinta hora.			
Practica deportes.			
Estudia mucho en la clase de matemáticas.			
Es trabajador(a).			
Tiene mucha tarea.			
Tiene almuerzo a las once y media.			

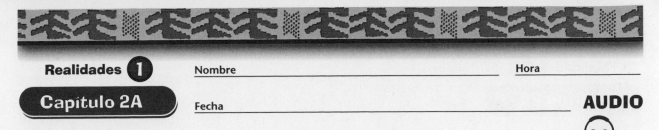

Realidades ❶

Capítulo 2A

Nombre _____

Fecha _____

Hora _____

AUDIO

Actividad 8

Listen as four people talk about what they do during the day. There will be some things that all four people do and other things that not all of them do. Fill in the grid with a check mark if the person says he or she does a certain activity. Also, fill in the **Yo** column with a check mark for the activities that you do every day. You will hear each set of statements twice.

	EVA	DAVID	RAQUEL	JOSÉ	YO

Realidades 1

Capítulo 2A

Nombre _____

Hora _____

Fecha _____

AUDIO

Actividad 9

You and your family are considering hosting a student from Costa Rica for a semester. Before you make the decision, you want to know a little about the student. Listen to part of a recording that the students from Costa Rica made for your class. Use the grid to keep track of what each of the students says. You will then use this information to decide which student would be the most compatible for you and your family. You will hear each set of statements twice.

Estudiante	Característica(s) de la personalidad	Clase favorita	Actividades favoritas
JORGE			
LUZ			
MARCO			
CRISTINA			

Which student is most like you? _____

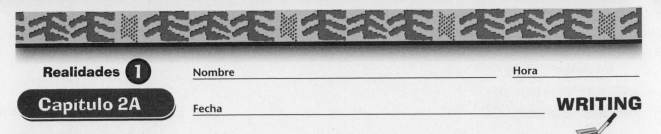

Realidades 1

Capítulo 2A

Nombre _____

Fecha _____

Hora _____

WRITING

Actividad 10

Your classmates are curious about your schedule at school. Using complete sentences, tell them what classes you have during the day. Follow the model.

| Modelo | _Yo tengo la clase de inglés en la segunda hora._ |

1. _____
2. _____
3. _____
4. _____
5. _____
6. _____
7. _____

Actividad 11

Answer the following questions using the subject pronoun suggested by the pictures. Follow the model.

¿Quiénes usan la computadora?

| Modelo | _Ellos usan la computadora._ |

¿Quién habla con Teresa?

1. _____ .

¿Quién habla con Paco?

2. _____ .

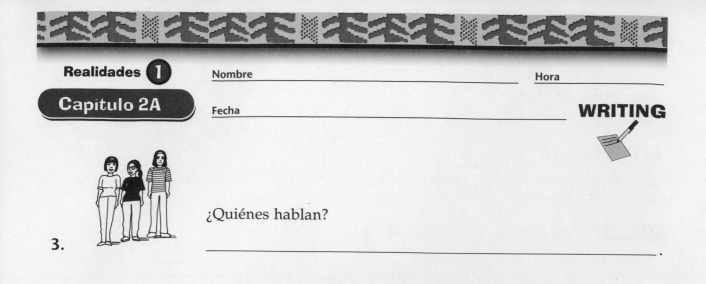

Realidades **1**

Capítulo 2A

Nombre _____

Fecha _____

Hora _____

WRITING

3.

¿Quiénes hablan?

_____ .

4.

¿Cómo es el Sr. García?

_____ .

5.

Ana

Ana, ¿tienes la clase de arte en la primera hora?

Sí, _____ .

6.

Cristina   Yo

¿Cristina y yo somos muy buenas amigas?

Sí, _____ .

Actividad 12

A new student at your school has come to you for information about how things work at your school and what your day is like. Answer the student's questions truthfully in complete sentences. Follow the model.

Modelo ¿La secretaria habla mucho por teléfono?

Sí, ella habla mucho _____.

1. ¿Estudias inglés en la primera hora?

   _____.

2. ¿Quién enseña la clase de matemáticas?

   _____.

3. ¿Necesito un diccionario para la clase de arte?

   _____.

4. ¿Cantas en el coro (*choir*)?

   _____.

5. ¿Pasas mucho tiempo en la cafetería?

   _____.

6. ¿Uds. practican deportes en la clase de educación física?

   _____.

7. ¿Los estudiantes usan las computadoras en la clase de ciencias naturales?

   _____.

8. ¿Uds. bailan en la clase de español?

   _____.

9. ¿Los profesores tocan el piano en la clase de música?

   _____.

10. ¿Los estudiantes hablan mucho en la clase de francés?

   _____.

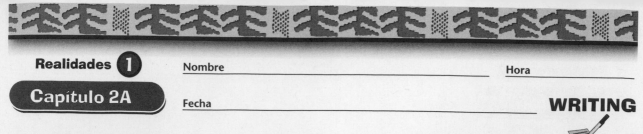

Realidades ❶

Capítulo 2A

Nombre _____

Fecha _____

Hora _____

WRITING

Actividad 13

A. List two classes that you have, when you have them, and who the teacher is.

Clase	Hora	Profesor(a)
1. _____	_____	_____
2. _____	_____	_____

B. Now, write complete sentences about whether or not you like each class from Part A. Make sure to tell why you do or do not like each class.

Clase 1: _____

_____

_____

_____

Clase 2: _____

_____

_____

_____

C. Now, using the information from Parts A and B, write a paragraph about one of the classes. Make sure to tell the name of the class, when you have it, and who the teacher is. You should also describe your teacher, tell what you do in class, and say whether or not you like the class.

_____

_____

_____

_____

_____

_____

_____

_____

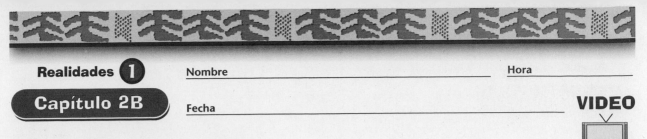

Realidades ①   Nombre _____   Hora _____

Capítulo 2B   Fecha _____   **VIDEO**

Antes de ver el video

Actividad 1

Look around your classroom and make a list of five items that you see. Then, describe their location. Follow the model.

COSA	DÓNDE ESTÁ
Modelo _la papelera_	_debajo del reloj_
1. _____	_____
2. _____	_____
3. _____	_____
4. _____	_____
5. _____	_____

¿Comprendes?

Actividad 2

Using the screen grabs as clues, answer the following questions with the correct information from the video.

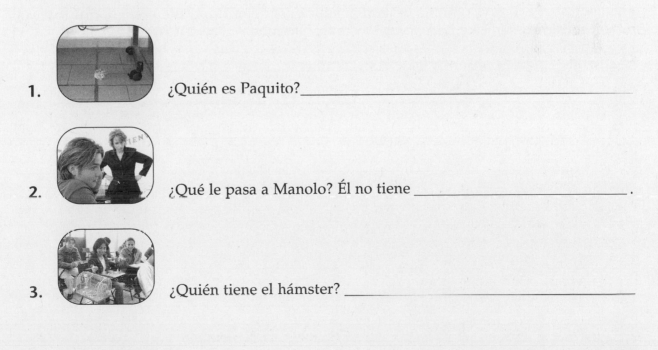

1. ¿Quién es Paquito?_____

2. ¿Qué le pasa a Manolo? Él no tiene _____.

3. ¿Quién tiene el hámster? _____

Realidades ①

Capítulo 2B

Nombre _____

Fecha _____

Hora _____

VIDEO

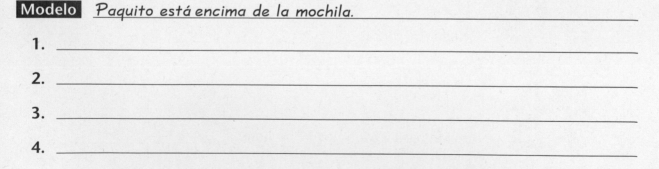

4. Los estudiantes están en _____.

5. ¿Para qué es el hámster? Es para _____.

Actividad 3

Next to each phrase, write the name of the character who said it in the video.

1. "¿Un ratón en la clase de ciencias sociales? ¡Imposible!"   _____

2. "¡No es un ratón! Es mi hámster."   _____

3. "Señorita, necesito hablar con usted más tarde."   _____

4. "Carlos, no tengo mi tarea."   _____

5. "¡Aquí está! Está en mi mochila."   _____

6. "Paquito, mi precioso. Ven aquí. ¿Estás bien?"   _____

Y, ¿qué más?

Actividad 4

Imagine that Paquito is running around in your classroom. Using the prepositions that you have just learned, indicate four places where he might be. Follow the example below.

Modelo   *Paquito está encima de la mochila.* _____

1. _____

2. _____

3. _____

4. _____

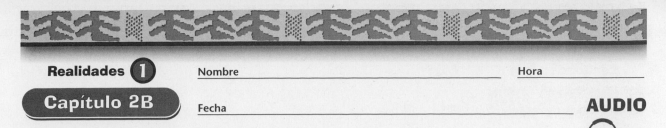

Actividad 5

As you look at the picture, decide whether the statements you hear are **ciertos** or **falsos**. You will hear each statement twice.

1. cierto   falso   6. cierto   falso   11. cierto   falso
2. cierto   falso   7. cierto   falso   12. cierto   falso
3. cierto   falso   8. cierto   falso   13. cierto   falso
4. cierto   falso   9. cierto   falso   14. cierto   falso
5. cierto   falso   10. cierto   falso   15. cierto   falso

Realidades 1

Capítulo 2B

Nombre _____

Hora _____

Fecha _____

AUDIO

Actividad 6

Tomás suddenly realizes in the middle of his science class that the diskette with his entire class project on it is missing! He asks several people if they know where it is. Listen as different people tell Tomás where they think his diskette is. In the timeline, write what classroom he goes to and where in the classroom he looks, in the order in which you hear them. You will hear this conversation twice.

	Susana	Antonio	Noé	Sr. Atkins
Classroom				
Location in room				

Where did Tomás eventually find his diskette?_____

Actividad 7

It's time to take the Spanish Club picture for the yearbook, but there are several people who have still not arrived. Andrés, the president, decides to use his cell phone to find out where people are. As you listen to the first part of each conversation, complete the sentences below with the information he finds out. For example, you might write:
Beto está en el gimnasio.
You will hear each dialogue twice.

1. Los dos profesores de español _____.

2. Javier _____.

3. Alejandra y Sara _____.

4. Mateo _____.

5. José y Antonieta _____.

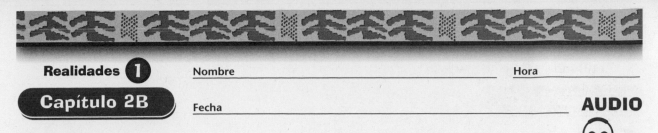

Actividad 8

One of your classmates from Spanish class is working in a store that sells school supplies. She overhears a customer speaking Spanish to his father, and decides to try out her Spanish. As she asks him what he wants to buy, she discovers that he never wants just one of anything. As the customer tells your classmate what he wants, write the items on the sales receipt below. Use the pictures below to calculate the price of his purchases. You will hear each conversation twice.

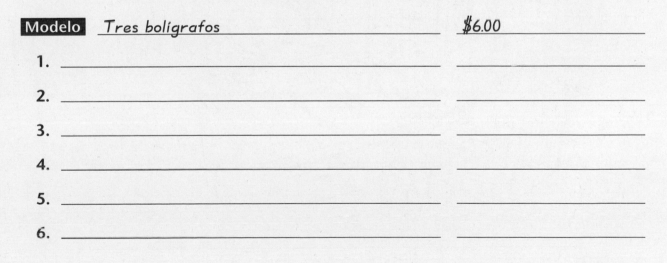

¿QUÉ NECESITA COMPRAR?	PRECIO
Modelo *Tres bolígrafos*	*$6.00*
1. _____	_____
2. _____	_____
3. _____	_____
4. _____	_____
5. _____	_____
6. _____	_____

Realidades 1

Capítulo 2B

Nombre _____

Hora _____

Fecha _____

AUDIO

Actividad 9

Listen to two friends talking outside the door of the Spanish Club meeting. They want to go to the meeting, but they are afraid they won't remember everyone's names. Look at the drawing. In the grid, write in the name of the person who is being described. You will hear each dialogue twice.

(A)	(B)	(C)
(D)	(E)	(F)

Realidades ①

Capítulo 2B

Nombre _____

Fecha _____

Hora _____

WRITING

Actividad 10

After your first day of school, you are describing your classroom to your parents. Using the picture below, tell them how many of each object there are in the room. Follow the model.

| Modelo | *Hay un escritorio en la sala de clases.* _____ |

1. _____

2. _____

3. _____

4. _____

5. _____

6. _____

7. _____

Realidades ①

Capítulo 2B

Nombre _____   Hora _____

Fecha _____

WRITING

Actividad 11

You are describing your classroom to your Spanish-speaking pen pal. Using complete sentences and the verb **estar**, tell what is in your room and where each item is located. Follow the model.

| Modelo | _Hay una mesa en la clase. Está al lado de la puerta._ |

1. _____

2. _____

3. _____

4. _____

5. _____

6. _____

7. _____

8. _____

Actividad 12

Answer the following questions about things you have for school. Use the pictures as a guide. Follow the model.

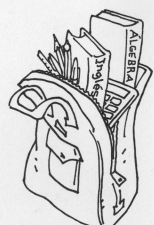

| Modelo | ¿Qué hay en la mochila? |

En la mochila hay unos lápices y bolígrafos. También hay una calculadora y dos libros: el libro de matemáticas y el libro de inglés.

46 *Writing Activities* ━ *Capítulo 2B*

Communication Workbook

Realidades **1**

Capítulo 2B

Nombre _____

Fecha _____

Hora _____

WRITING

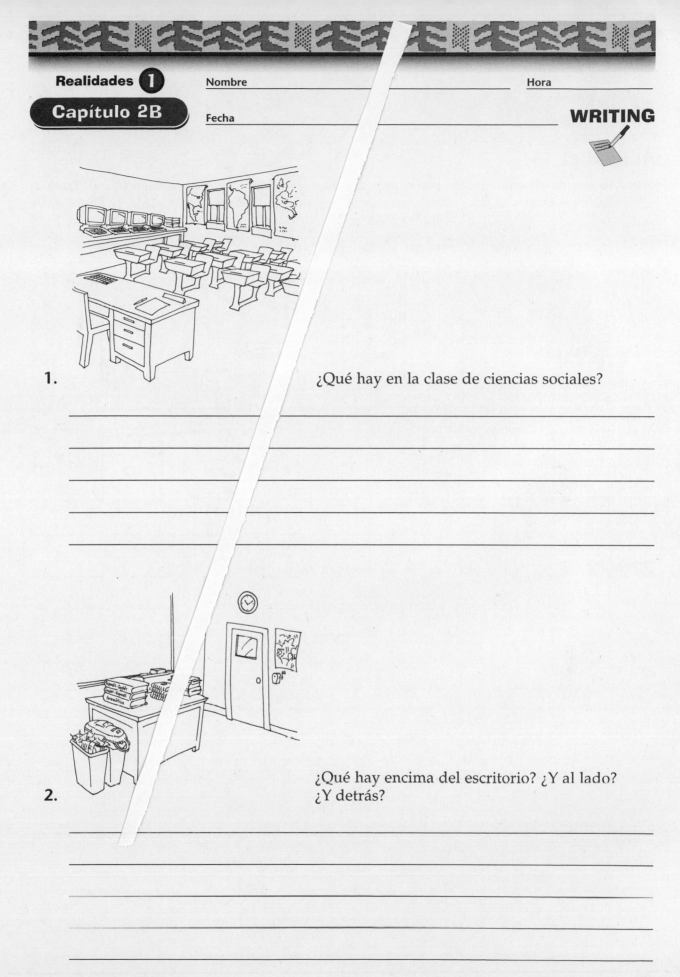

1. ¿Qué hay en la clase de ciencias sociales?

_____

_____

_____

_____

2. ¿Qué hay encima del escritorio? ¿Y al lado? ¿Y detrás?

_____

_____

_____

_____

Realidades ❶

Capítulo 2B

Nombre _____

Hora _____

Fecha _____

WRITING

Actividad 13

The two rooms pictured below were once identical, but Sala 2 has been rearranged. Look at each picture carefully. Circle seven items in Sala 2 that are different from Sala 1. Then, write sentences about how Sala 2 is different. Follow the model.

Sala 1   Sala 2

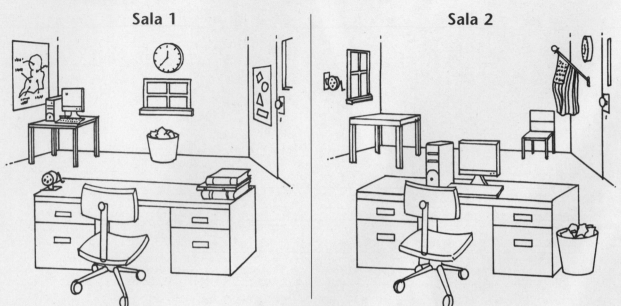

Modelo   *En la sala 2 no hay libros encima del escritorio.*

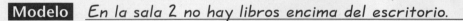

1. _____

_____

2. _____

_____

3. _____

_____

4. _____

_____

5. _____

_____

6. _____

_____

7. _____

_____

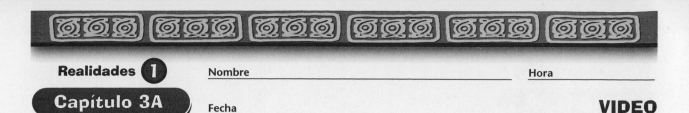

Antes de ver el video

Actividad 1

What do you like to eat for breakfast and lunch? Fill in the chart with that information.

Desayuno	Almuerzo

¿Comprendes?

Actividad 2

Think about the foods Rosa believes people in the United States eat for breakfast. What do Tomás and Raúl really eat?

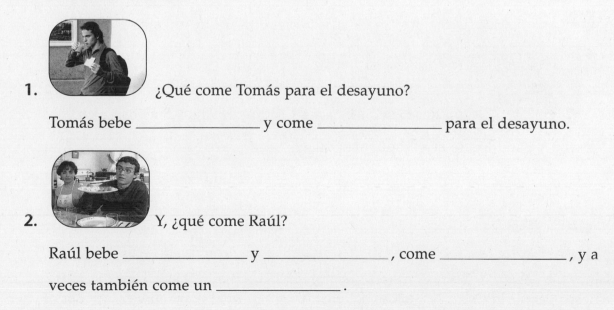

1. ¿Qué come Tomás para el desayuno?

   Tomás bebe _____ y come _____ para el desayuno.

2. Y, ¿qué come Raúl?

   Raúl bebe _____ y _____ , come _____ , y a

   veces también come un _____ .

Realidades **1**

Capítulo 3A

Nombre _____

Fecha _____

Hora _____

VIDEO

Actividad 3

Although Rosa makes a big breakfast for Tomás that day, the family does not eat very much regularly. Answer the questions below.

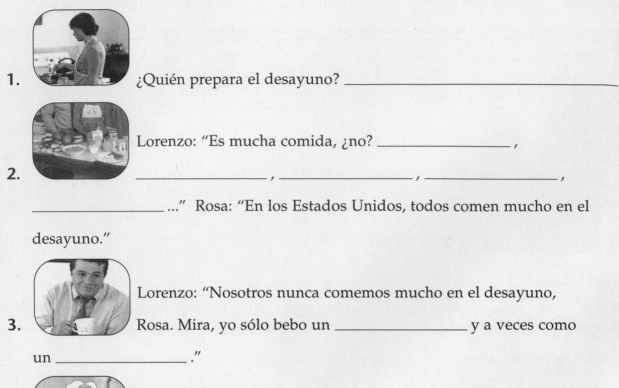

1. ¿Quién prepara el desayuno? _____

2. Lorenzo: "Es mucha comida, ¿no? _____ , _____ , _____ , _____ , _____ ..." Rosa: "En los Estados Unidos, todos comen mucho en el desayuno."

3. Lorenzo: "Nosotros nunca comemos mucho en el desayuno, Rosa. Mira, yo sólo bebo un _____ y a veces como un _____ ."

4.  Según Rosa, en los Estados Unidos comemos huevos, salchichas, tocino y pan tostado en el desayuno y _____ _____ en el almuerzo.

Y, ¿qué más?

Actividad 4

Do you recall what you wrote in **Actividad** 1 about foods that you like to eat? Now that you have heard people in Costa Rica talk about what they eat, write down three questions of your own to ask a classmate about food. With a partner, ask your questions and compare answers.

¿ _____ ?

¿ _____ ?

¿ _____ ?

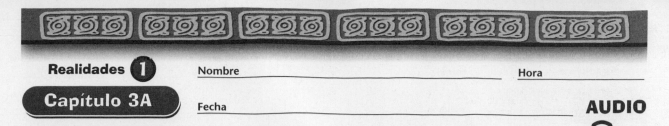

Realidades ❶

Capítulo 3A

Nombre _____

Hora _____

Fecha _____

AUDIO

Actividad 5

You are helping out a friend at the counter of Restaurante El Gaucho in Argentina. Listen to the orders and record the quantity of each item ordered by each customer in the appropriate box of the chart. You will hear each conversation twice.

RESTAURANTE EL GAUCHO

El almuerzo	Cliente 1	Cliente 2	Cliente 3	Cliente 4
Ensalada				
Hamburguesa				
Hamburguesa con queso				
Sándwich de jamón y queso				
Perro caliente				
Pizza				
Papas fritas				
Refresco				
Té helado				
Galletas				

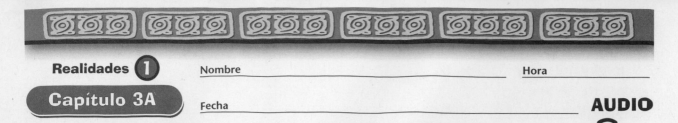

Realidades 1

Capítulo 3A

Nombre _____

Hora _____

Fecha _____

AUDIO

Actividad 6

While working at the Hotel Buena Vista, you need to record breakfast orders for room service. Use the grid to make your report. First, listen carefully for the room number and write it in the appropriate box. Then write in the time requested. Finally, put a check mark next to each item ordered by the person in that room. You will hear each set of statements twice.

HOTEL BUENA VISTA

Número de habitación (*room number*)				
Hora de servicio				
Jugo de naranja				
Jugo de manzana				
Cereal				
Pan tostado				
Huevos				
Jamón				
Tocino				
Salchichas				
Yogur de fresas				
Café				
Café con leche				
Té				

Realidades 1

Capítulo 3A

Nombre _____

Fecha _____

Hora _____

AUDIO

Actividad 7

You are waiting in line at a restaurant counter. You hear people behind you talking about your friends. Listen carefully so you can figure out whom they're talking about. Pay close attention to verb and adjective endings. Put a check mark in the column after each conversation. You will hear each set of statements twice.

	Carlos	Gabriela	Carlos y sus amigos	Gabriela y sus amigas
1.	_____	_____	_____	_____
2.	_____	_____	_____	_____
3.	_____	_____	_____	_____
4.	_____	_____	_____	_____
5.	_____	_____	_____	_____
6.	_____	_____	_____	_____
7.	_____	_____	_____	_____

Actividad 8

Listen as actors from a popular Spanish soap opera are interviewed on the radio program called **"Las dietas de los famosos"** (*Diets of the Famous*). As you listen, write **sí** if the person mentions that he or she eats or drinks something most days. Write **no** if the person says that he or she never eats or drinks the item. You will hear this conversation twice.

	Lana Lote	Óscar Oso	Pepe Pluma	Tita Trompo
(eggs)				
(drink)				
(sausages)				
(bacon)				

Nombre _____

Hora _____

Fecha _____

AUDIO

	Lana Lote	Óscar Oso	Pepe Pluma	Tita Trompo
🍓				
🍌				
🍔				
🍟				
🌭				
🍪				
🥗				
☕				
🍶				
☕				

Communication Workbook

Realidades ①

Capítulo 3A

Nombre _____

Hora _____

Fecha _____

AUDIO

Actividad 9

Listen as the woman at the table next to you tries to help a child order from the menu. As you listen, check off the items on the menu that the child says he likes and those he dislikes. Then in the space provided, write what you think would be an "acceptable" lunch for him. You will hear this conversation twice.

le gusta								
no le gusta								

Un almuerzo bueno para Beto es _____

_____ .

Realidades ❶   Nombre _____   Hora _____

Capítulo 3A   Fecha _____   W

Actividad 10

You have decided to help your parents by doing the food shopping for the week. Y ⟨
Rodrigo is helping you make the shopping list. Complete the conversation below ⟨
picture and your own food preferences.

RODRIGO: ¿Qué hay de beber?

TÚ: _____

RODRIGO: ¿Quieres (*do you want*) algo más?

TÚ: _____

RODRIGO: ¿Qué hay de comer para el desayuno?

TÚ: _____

RODRIGO: ¿Qué más quieres, entonces?

TÚ: _____

_____

RODRIGO: ¿Qué hay para el almuerzo?

TÚ: _____

RODRIGO: ¿Y quieres algo más?

TÚ: _____

_____

RODRIGO: ¿Y qué frutas necesitan?

TÚ : _____

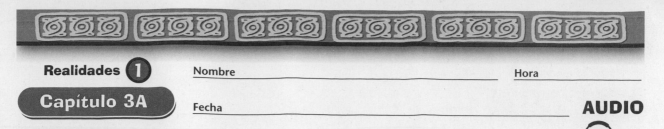

Actividad 9

Listen as the woman at the table next to you tries to help a child order from the menu. As you listen, check off the items on the menu that the child says he likes and those he dislikes. Then in the space provided, write what you think would be an "acceptable" lunch for him. You will hear this conversation twice.

le gusta								
no le gusta									

Un almuerzo bueno para Beto es _____

_____ .

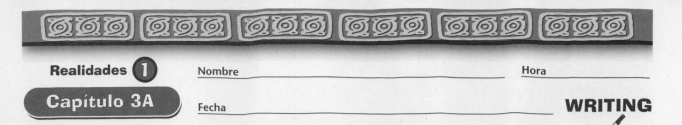
Actividad 10

You have decided to help your parents by doing the food shopping for the week. Your friend Rodrigo is helping you make the shopping list. Complete the conversation below using the picture and your own food preferences.

RODRIGO: ¿Qué hay de beber?

TÚ: _____

RODRIGO: ¿Quieres (*do you want*) algo más?

TÚ: _____

_____

RODRIGO: ¿Qué hay de comer para el desayuno?

TÚ: _____

RODRIGO: ¿Qué más quieres, entonces?

TÚ: _____

_____

RODRIGO: ¿Qué hay para el almuerzo?

TÚ: _____

RODRIGO: ¿Y quieres algo más?

TÚ: _____

_____

RODRIGO: ¿Y qué frutas necesitan?

TÚ : _____

WRITING

Actividad 11

Describe each of the following scenes using as many **-er** and **-ir** verbs as you can. Use complete sentences.

_____

_____

_____

yo   Ana y yo

tú   los estudiantes

_____

_____

_____

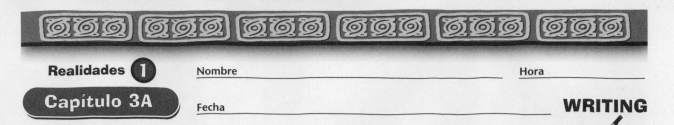

Realidades ①

Capítulo 3A

Nombre _____

Fecha _____

Hora _____

WRITING

Actividad 12

In anticipation of your arrival in Spain next week, your host sister writes to ask you about your favorite foods. Complete your response below with sentences using the verbs **gustar** and **encantar**.

Estimada Margarita:

Gracias por su carta. Hay muchas comidas que me gustan. Para el desayuno,

_____. También

_____. Pero no

_____.

Pero me encanta más el almuerzo. Por ejemplo, _____

_____. También

_____. Pero no _____

_____.

¿Y a ti? ¿Te gustan las hamburguesas? ¿ _____

_____? ¿ _____

_____? ¿ _____

_____?

Nos vemos en una semana.

Un fuerte abrazo,

Melinda

Realidades 1

Capítulo 3A

Nombre _____

Fecha _____

Hora _____

WRITING

Actividad 13

The school nurse is teaching a class on nutrition and asks everyone to fill out a survey about what he or she eats. Using complete sentences, write your responses below.

1. ¿Qué comes y bebes en el desayuno?

_____

_____

_____

_____

_____

2. ¿Qué come y bebe tu familia en el almuerzo?

_____

_____

_____

_____

_____

3. ¿Qué comida te encanta?

_____

_____

_____

_____

_____

Realidades ①

Capítulo 3B

Nombre _____

Fecha _____

Hora _____

VIDEO

Antes de ver el video

Actividad 1

Think about the typical diet of a teenager. Which foods are healthy choices and which ones are not? Make a list of five foods in each category.

Comida buena para la salud ☺

_____

_____

_____

_____

_____

Comida mala para la salud ☹

_____

_____

_____

_____

_____

¿Comprendes?

Actividad 2

Write the name of the person from the video who made each statement.

1. "El café de aquí es muy bueno."   _____

2. "No, no; un refresco no; un jugo de fruta."   _____

3. "En Costa Rica, un refresco es un jugo de fruta." _____

4. "Yo hago mucho ejercicio..."   _____

5. "Aquí en San José, todos caminamos mucho."   _____

6. "... aquí una soda no es una bebida; es un restaurante." _____

7. "Me encanta el gallo pinto."   _____

Nombre _____ Hora _____

Fecha _____

VIDEO

Actividad 3

Answer the questions.

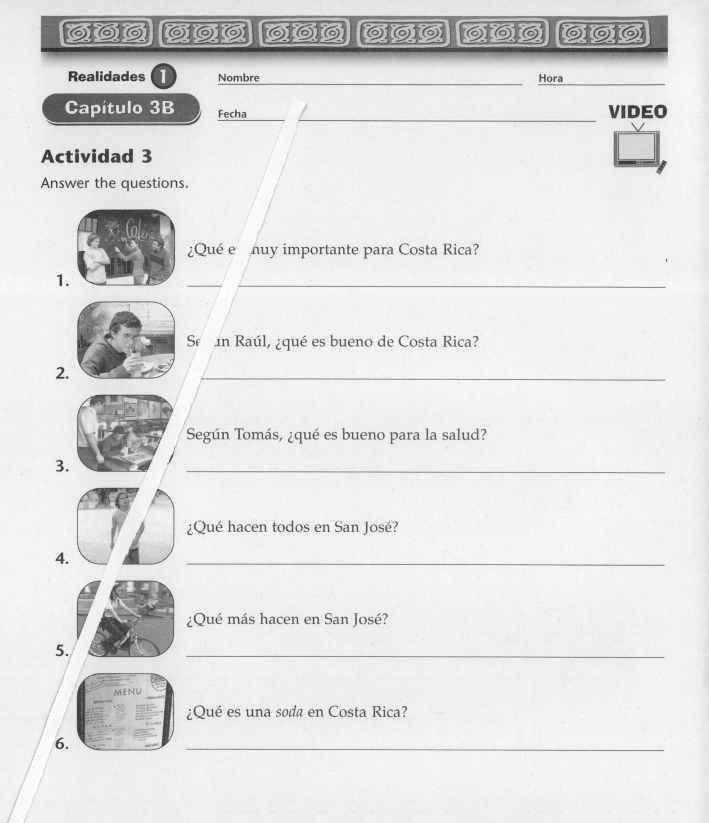

1. ¿Qué es muy importante para Costa Rica?

   _____

2. Según Raúl, ¿qué es bueno de Costa Rica?

   _____

3. Según Tomás, ¿qué es bueno para la salud?

   _____

4. ¿Qué hacen todos en San José?

   _____

5. ¿Qué más hacen en San José?

   _____

6. ¿Qué es una *soda* en Costa Rica?

   _____

Realidades 1

Capítulo 3B

Nombre _____ Hora _____

Fecha _____

VIDEO

Y, ¿qué más?

Actividad 4

Tomás was confused because he learned that **un refresco** was a soft drink. However, in Costa Rica **un refresco** is fruit juice. Can you think of any examples of English words that have a different meaning depending on where in the United States you go? What are their different meanings?

_____

_____

_____

_____

_____

_____

_____

Communication Workbook

Realidades **1**

Capítulo 3B

Nombre _____

Hora _____

Fecha _____

AUDIO

Actividad 5

Listen to a radio announcer as he interviews people at the mall about their lifestyles. Pay close attention to the things that they say they do and eat. What in their lifestyles is good or bad for their health? Match what they say to the pictures below. Then write the corresponding letter in the appropriate column. You will hear this conversation twice.

ACTIVIDADES

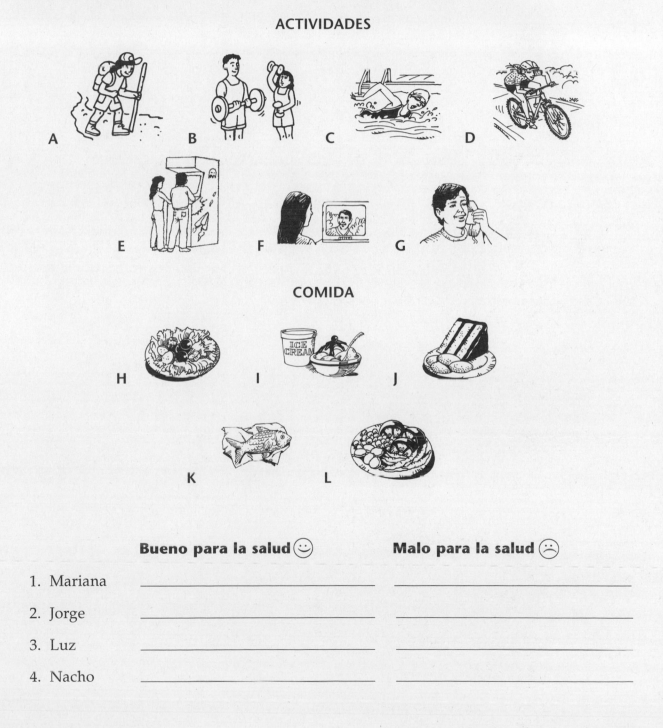

A   B   C   D

E   F   G

COMIDA

H   I   J

K   L

	Bueno para la salud ☺	**Malo para la salud** ☹
1. Mariana	_____	_____
2. Jorge	_____	_____
3. Luz	_____	_____
4. Nacho	_____	_____

Nombre _____ Hora _____

Fecha _____

AUDIO

Actividad 6

Listen as students in a health class in Costa Rica present a list of the "dos and don'ts" of staying healthy. Which are **consejos lógicos** (*logical advice*) and which are **consejos ridículos** (*ridiculous advice*)? Place a check mark in the appropriate box of the chart. You will hear each set of statements twice.

	1	2	3	4	5	6	7	8	9	10
Consejo lógico										
Consejo ridículo										

Actividad 7

A Spanish-speaking telemarketer calls your home to interview you about the food preferences of teens. He must have gotten your name from your Spanish teacher! He asks you to tell him whether you think certain food items are **malo** or **sabroso**. Be sure to listen carefully so that you will be able to use the correct form of the adjective for each item. Write what you would say in the spaces below. You will hear each question twice.

1. _____
2. _____
3. _____
4. _____
5. _____
6. _____
7. _____
8. _____
9. _____
10. _____

Realidades ①

Capítulo 3B

Nombre _____

Fecha _____

Hora _____

AUDIO

Actividad 8

In an effort to improve food in the school cafeteria, students are asked to anonymously call in their opinions about school food. You are asked to chart the responses of the Spanish-speaking students. As you listen to their opinions, fill in the grid. If they say something positive about a particular menu item, put a plus sign in the appropriate column; if they say something negative, put a minus sign in the column. You will hear each set of statements twice.

1										
2										
3										
4										
5										

Actividad 9

Listen as people call in to ask Dr. Armando their health questions on his radio program **"Pregunte al doctor Armando."** While you listen to their questions and Dr. Armando's advice (**consejo**), fill in the chart below. Do you agree with his advice? You will hear this conversation twice.

NOMBRE	¿LA PREGUNTA?	EL CONSEJO
1. Beatriz		
2. Mauricio		
3. Loli		
4. Luis		

Realidades 1

Nombre _____ Hora _____

Capítulo 3B

Fecha _____

WRITING

Actividad 10

A. The school nurse has compiled information on what everyone eats and is now telling you which foods are good for your health and which are not. Remember what you wrote for her survey? List the items you eat on a daily basis. Be sure to use words from the previous chapter as well as ones from this chapter.

_____ _____ _____
_____ _____ _____
_____ _____ _____
_____ _____ _____

B. Now, use the nutrition pyramid shown and what you know about a well-balanced diet to fill in what the nurse would say. Follow the model.

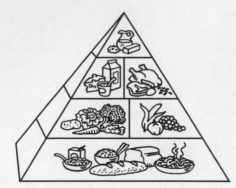

Modelo	_Los espaguetis son buenos para la salud. Ud. debe comer mucho pan y_

muchos cereales. _____

1. _____
   _____

2. _____
   _____

3. _____
   _____

4. _____
   _____

Communication Workbook

Nombre _____   Hora _____

Fecha _____   **WRITING**

Actividad 11

Write your opinions of the following foods. Use the correct forms of the following adjectives in your sentences.

bueno	malo	sabroso	divertido
malo para la salud		bueno para la salud	
interesante		horrible	

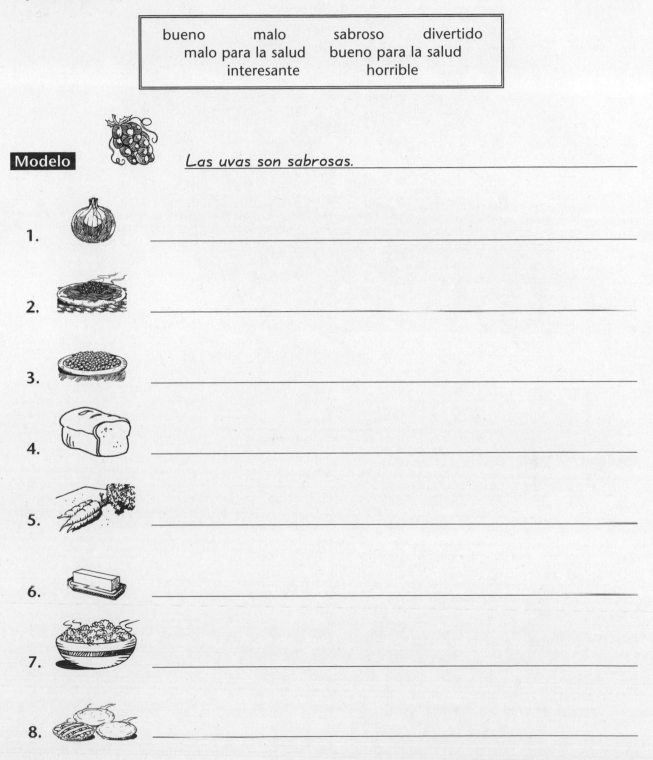

Modelo   _Las uvas son sabrosas._ _____

1. _____

2. _____

3. _____

4. _____

5. _____

6. _____

7. _____

8. _____

Actividad 12

Below you see three groups of friends sitting at tables in a cafeteria. Describe the people and items at each table.

Mesa 1:

_____

_____

_____

_____

Mesa 2:

_____

_____

_____

_____

Mesa 3:

_____

_____

_____

_____

Actividad 13

Write a letter to your Spanish-speaking pen pal about a restaurant that you and your parents like to go to for dinner. Tell what you and your family members normally eat and drink, what the food is like, and what the waiters (**camareros**) are like.

Estimado(a) _____ :

_____

_____

_____

_____

_____

_____

_____

_____

_____

_____

_____

_____

_____

_____

_____

_____

Un abrazo,

_____

Realidades ❶

Capítulo 4A

Nombre _____

Fecha _____

Hora _____

VIDEO

Antes de ver el video

Actividad 1

Think of activities you do at different times during the week. Make a list of four activities you do during the week and then four activities you do during the weekend.

Actividades durante la semana

_____

_____

_____

_____

Actividades durante el fin de semana

_____

_____

_____

_____

¿Comprendes?

Actividad 2

Javier has just moved to a new high school in Spain, and he is sitting by himself. Ignacio, Elena, and Ana try to find out more about him. What do they do, and what do they learn? Write **cierto** (*true*) or **falso** (*false*) next to each statement.

1. El estudiante nuevo es un poco reservado. _____

2. Él se llama Gustavo. _____

3. Él es de Salamanca. _____

4. Todos los días va a la biblioteca después de las clases. _____

5. Los tres amigos van a hablar con él. _____

6. A Javier le gusta practicar deportes. _____

Communication Workbook

Realidades ❶

Capítulo 4A

Nombre _____

Hora _____

Fecha _____

VIDEO

7. A veces, él prefiere ir al cine a ver películas. _____

8. A él no le gusta hablar con su amigo Esteban de San Antonio. _____

Actividad 3

What do the new friends do after class? Fill the blanks with complete sentences.

Nuevos amigos	¿Adónde va después de las clases?
1. Javier	
2. Ignacio	
3. Elena	
4. Ana	

Y, ¿qué más?

Actividad 4

What do you do after school every day? What do you sometimes do, and what do you never do at all? Write a short paragraph about your afterschool activities, following the example below.

Modelo *Yo voy a mi trabajo todos los días en el centro comercial. A veces, voy con una amiga al cine después del trabajo. Nunca voy al gimnasio durante la semana.*

_____

_____

Realidades 1

Capítulo 4A

Nombre _____

Fecha _____

Hora _____

AUDIO

Actividad 5

Listen as Lorena talks to Luis and Antonio about where they are going during the week. Under each picture in the grid, write in the name of Luis or Antonio if they tell Lorena they are going to that place. In some cases, you will fill in both of their names. After completing the grid, you will be able to complete the sentences under the grid. You will hear this conversation twice.

lunes							
martes							
miércoles							
jueves							
viernes							
sábado							
domingo							

1. Luis y Antonio van al (a la) _____ el _____.

2. También van al (a la) _____ el _____.

Realidades ①

Capítulo 4A

Nombre _____

Hora _____

Fecha _____

AUDIO

Actividad 6

You are volunteering as a tour guide during the upcoming Hispanic Arts Festival in your community. To make sure you would be able to understand the following questions if a visitor were to ask them, write the number of the question under the correct picture that would correspond to a logical response. You can check your answers to see if you're ready to answer visitors' questions during the Festival. You will hear each question twice.

Actividad 7

Your friend Miguel calls his mother from your house to give her an update on his plans for the day. Just from listening to his side of the conversation, you realize that his mother has LOTS of questions. What does she ask him, based on Miguel's answers? Choose from the following:

A. ¿Adónde vas?   **D.** ¿Cómo es tu amigo?

B. ¿Con quiénes vas?   **E.** ¿Por qué van?

C. ¿Cuándo vas?

You will hear each set of statements twice.

1. _____   2. _____   3. _____   4. _____   5. _____

Realidades ①

Capítulo 4A

Nombre _____

Fecha _____

Hora _____

AUDIO

Actividad 8

The yearbook staff is identifying students' pictures for the yearbook. Look at the pictures from the class trip to Mexico. Listen to the conversations and write the names of Arturo, Susi, Gloria, Martín, David, Eugenia, Enrique, and Lucía under the correct pictures. You will hear each dialogue twice.

Actividad 9

Listen as a radio interviewer talks to Maricela, a young woman from Spain, about her city that was once home to the **Reyes** Fernando and Isabel. You will learn why it is such a popular tourist spot. After listening, answer the questions below. You will hear this conversation twice.

1. Maricela es de
   a) Madrid.   b) Aranjuez.   c) Barcelona.

2. La ciudad es famosa por
   a) el pescado.   b) el helado.   c) las fresas.

3. Los turistas van
   a) al palacio.   b) a las montañas.   c) a la playa.

4. La ciudad de Maricela está a unos _____ minutos de Madrid.
   a) quince   b) treinta   c) cincuenta

5. Las comidas típicas son
   a) pizza y espaguetis.   b) fresas y pasteles de manzana.   c) pollo y judías verdes.

6. Maricela va _____ para pasar tiempo con los amigos.
   a) al parque   b) al cine   c) a las montañas

Realidades 1

Capítulo 4A

Nombre _____

Hora _____

Fecha _____

WRITING

Actividad 10

While on a hike one day, you stumble upon a "Wheel of the Future." When you spin this wheel, you will land on a picture of a place. The wheel will send you to that place if you tell it when you want to go and what you plan to do there. Write what you would tell the wheel for each place. Follow the model.

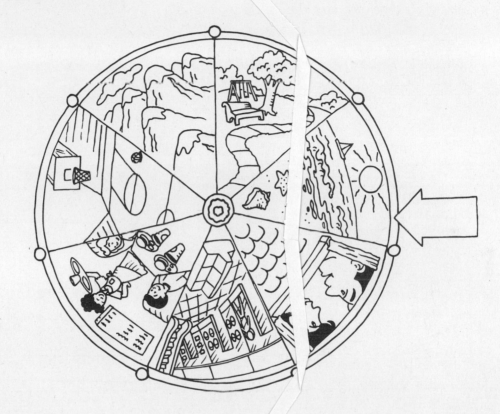

Modelo   *Voy a la playa el viernes para nadar*

1. _____

2. _____

3. _____

4. _____

5. _____

6. _____

7. _____

Realidades 1

Capítulo 4A

Nombre _____

Fecha _____

Hora _____

WRITING

Actividad 11

You are having a surprise party for your best friend next weekend, and you need to know where your family and friends are going to be this week so that you can get in touch with them to make plans. Below is a planner containing information on everyone's plans for the week. Using the pictures to help you, write where your friends and family will be and what they will be doing on that day. Use the model as a guide.

Modelo   Yo   Lunes: _El lunes yo voy a la biblioteca para hacer la tarea._

Tú   lunes _____
                             _____

Geraldo   martes _____

Mi familia y Yo   miércoles _____
                             _____

Juan y Tú   jueves _____
                             _____

Pedro y Claudia viernes _____
                             _____

Mariana   sábado _____

Anita y Lucita   domingo _____
                             _____

Actividad 12

You are a contestant on a game show. The host of the show has given you these answers. Write the corresponding questions.

Modelo   El catorce de febrero

¿Cuándo es el Día de San Valentín?

1. El primer presidente de los Estados Unidos

   _____

2. Al norte (*north*) de los Estados Unidos

   _____

3. Usamos esta cosa para conectar al Internet.

   _____

4. Muy bien, gracias. ¿Y tú?

   _____

5. Vamos a la tienda para comprar frutas.

   _____

6. Las personas que enseñan las clases

   _____

7. Usamos estas partes del cuerpo para ver.

   _____

Actividad 13

A. Write four complete sentences that tell about places you and a friend go to on the weekend.

1. _____

2. _____

3. _____

4. _____

Realidades 1

Capítulo 4A

Nombre

Hora

Fecha

WRITING

B. Now, use your sentences from Part A to write a paragraph telling with whom you go to these places, what the places are like, and what you do when you are there.

_____

_____

_____

_____

_____

_____

_____

_____

_____

_____

_____

_____

_____

_____

Realidades ①

Capítulo 4B

Nombre _____

Fecha _____

Hora _____

VIDEO

Antes de ver el video

Actividad 1

Think of activities you like to do. Here is a list of six activities. Rank them in order from your favorite to your least favorite, with 1 as your favorite and 6 as your least favorite.

_____ ir a bailar   _____ ir al cine a ver películas

_____ nadar   _____ montar en bicicleta

_____ estudiar en la biblioteca   _____ ir de compras al centro comercial

¿Comprendes?

Actividad 2

Ignacio, Javier, Elena, and Ana are playing soccer at the park. Who makes each statement? Write the name of the person who says each item on the line.

1. "Mañana juego al tenis con mis primos."   _____

2. "Yo también estoy muy cansada y tengo mucha sed."   _____

3. "Prefiero otros deportes, como el fútbol."   _____

4. "¿Sabes jugar también al vóleibol?"   _____

5. "También me gusta ir de pesca."   _____

6. "Puedes bailar conmigo..."   _____

7. "Lo siento. No sé bailar bien."   _____

8. "Voy a preparar un pastel fabuloso."   _____

Actividad 3

Look at the activities below, and circle the ones you saw or heard about while watching the video. Then, write the ones that Elena can do well on the lines below.

jugar al fútbol	jugar al tenis	ir de cámping	ir de pesca
ir a las fiestas	ver el partido	jugar al vóleibol	
caminar en el parque	jugar al fútbol americano		practicar deportes
ir al concierto	preparar un pastel	jugar al béisbol	jugar al golf
jugar al básquetbol	bailar y cantar	tomar refrescos	

_____

_____

Y, ¿qué mas?

Actividad 4

Imagine that Ignacio, Javier, Elena, and Ana want you to join them in their various activities. What answers might you give them? Respond to their invitations with some of the phrases from the video, or make up your own responses from what you have learned. Follow the model.

Modelo   ¿Quieres jugar al fútbol en el parque?

Sí, quiero jugar al fútbol en el parque, pero no juego muy bien.

1. ¿Puedes jugar al tenis mañana?

   _____

2. Oye, juegas muy bien al vóleibol. ¿Puedes jugar más tarde?

   _____

3. ¿Quieres ir con nosotros a la fiesta esta noche?

   _____

4. ¿Sabes bailar?

   _____

Actividad 5

There are not enough hours in the day to do everything we want to do. Listen to the following interviews. What do these people want more time to do? In the blanks provided, write the number of the statement that corresponds to each picture. You will hear each set of statements twice.

Actividad 6

After listening to each of the following statements, decide if you think the excuses given are believable (**creíble**) or unbelievable (**increíble**). Be prepared to defend your answers with a partner after making your decisions. You will hear each set of statements twice.

EXCUSAS, EXCUSAS

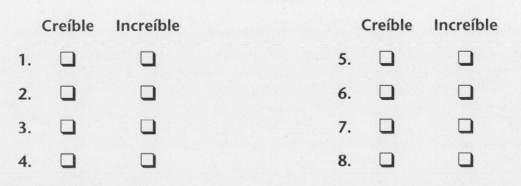

	Creíble	Increíble		Creíble	Increíble
1.	☐	☐	5.	☐	☐
2.	☐	☐	6.	☐	☐
3.	☐	☐	7.	☐	☐
4.	☐	☐	8.	☐	☐

Realidades ❶

Capítulo 4B

Nombre _____

Fecha _____

Hora _____

AUDIO

Actividad 7

Listen to the following couple as they try to decide what they are going to do tonight. Every time an activity is mentioned that one of the two people is going to do, draw a circle around the picture. If the other person is NOT going to do that activity, draw an *X* through the picture. The pictures with circles only should represent what both people finally decide to do. You will hear each conversation twice.

Actividad 8

Listen as a radio program host interviews a fitness expert, doctora Benítez, about the best way to get in shape. Listen to the **entrevista** (*interview*), and choose the best answer to the questions below. You will hear this conversation twice.

1. ¿En qué es experta la doctora Benítez?

    a) deportes   b) cocinar   c) música   d) ejercicio y nutrición

2. Según la doctora, ¿cuántos minutos de ejercicio debes hacer todos los días?

    a) una hora   b) quince minutos   c) treinta minutos

3. Según Miguel, ¿por qué no puede hacer mucho ejercicio?

    a) Es demasiado perezoso.   b) Está muy ocupado.   c) Está triste.

4. ¿Qué es divertido para Miguel?

    a) jugar al tenis   b) ver la tele   c) jugar al fútbol

5. Después de jugar, ¿qué no debemos comer?

    a) cereales   b) frutas y verduras   c) pasteles

Actividad 9

Your Spanish teacher always encourages you to speak Spanish to your classmates outside of class. In order to do that, you and your friends agreed to talk on the phone and/or leave messages on each other's answering machines for at least a week. Listen to the messages your friends have left on your answering machine today. Based on the messages, decide a) where the person wants to go; b) what the person wants to do; c) what time the person wants to go. Use the chart below to record the information. You will hear each set of statements twice.

	¿Adónde quiere ir?	¿Qué quiere hacer?	¿A qué hora quiere ir?
Justo			
Eva			
José			
Margarita			
Pedro			

Realidades 1

Capítulo 4B

Nombre _____

Hora _____

Fecha _____

WRITING

Actividad 10

A. Read the following announcements of upcoming events in Madrid. Underneath each announcement, write whether or not you are going to each event and why or why not.

UNA NOCHE DE ÓPERA ITALIANA PRESENTANDO a **JOSÉ CARRERAS** en el Auditorio Nacional de Música, Madrid *el viernes a las siete de la noche*	**PARTIDO DE FÚTBOL** REAL BETIS CONTRA REAL MADRID *el domingo a las dos de la tarde en el Estadio Santiago Bernabeu*

_____   _____

_____   _____

> **Fiesta Deportiva**
>
> *¿Te gusta practicar deportes? ¿Eres atlético?*
>
> Ven a mi fiesta deportiva y puedes jugar varios deportes con muchas personas.
>
> La fiesta es desde el viernes a las cinco de la tarde hasta el lunes a las cinco de la mañana.

_____

B. Now, in the spaces below, write whether five people you know are going to any one of the events and why or why not. Follow the model.

Modelo	*Mi amiga Ana va al partido de fútbol porque le gusta mucho el fútbol.*

Mi amigo Ronaldo no va al concierto porque no le gusta la ópera.

1. _____

2. _____

3. _____

4. _____

5. _____

Actividad 11

Every time a classmate asks Eugenio if he wants to do something fun, he declines and gives a different excuse. In the spaces below, write the question that each classmate asks and Eugenio's varying answers. Follow the model.

Modelo

—¿_Vas a levantar pesas conmigo?_____

—No, _no puedo levantar pesas porque me duele la cabeza._

1. —¿_____?

—No, _____.

2. —¿_____?

—No, _____.

3. —¿_____?

—No, _____.

4. —¿_____?

—No, _____.

5. —¿_____?

—No, _____.

6. —¿_____?

—No, _____.

7. —¿_____?

—No, _____.

Realidades 1

Capítulo 4B

Nombre _____

Fecha _____

Hora _____

WRITING

Actividad 12

When put in the right order, each set of blocks below will ask a question. Unscramble the blocks by writing the contents of each block in the blank boxes. Then, answer the questions in the space provided.

1.

JUEG	DE	EPOR	OS F	UÉ	D	AS L

INES	¿A Q	TES	NA?	SEMA

2.

¿A Q	MIGO	TES	US A	JUEG	UÉ D

S?	AN T	EPOR

3.

GA?	L ES	FAVO	¿CUÁ	RITO	JUE

RTE	UIÉN	Y Q	TU	DEPO

Realidades ❶

Capítulo 4B

Nombre _____

Hora _____

Fecha _____

WRITING

Actividad 13

You are having a mid-semester party.

A. First, fill in the invitation below with the information about your party.

FIESTA DE MEDIO SEMESTRE

Lugar: _____

Hora: _____

Comida: _____

_____

RSVP: _____

B. Since you don't have everyone's mailing address, you have to e-mail some people about the party. Write your e-mail below. In addition to inviting them, tell them what activities you will have at the party, and where your house is (**está cerca de la biblioteca,** etc.).

Estimados amigos:

_____

_____

_____

_____

_____

_____

_____

_____

_____

¡Me gustaría ver a todos en la fiesta!

Un fuerte abrazo,

_____

VIDEO

Antes de ver el video

Actividad 1

Look at this family tree. Label each person with his or her relationship to Ricardo.

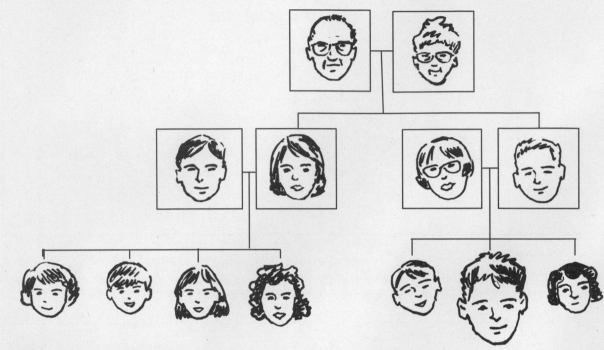

Ricardo

¿Comprendes?

Actividad 2

Cristina had a birthday party with some of her family members. How much do you remember about that party? Write **cierto** or **falso** next to each statement.

1. Angélica hace un video de la fiesta de su hermano. _____

2. El papá de Cristina saca fotos de la fiesta. _____

3. A Gabriel le gustan los deportes. _____

4. El perro de Cristina se llama Piñata. _____

5. La abuela de Cristina decora la fiesta con papel picado. _____

6. Capitán es muy sociable, le encanta estar con la familia. _____

7. Carolina es la hermana de Gabriel y Angélica. _____

8. Ricardo es el abuelo de Esteban. _____

Realidades ❶

Capítulo 5A

Nombre _____

Hora _____

Fecha _____

VIDEO

Actividad 3

Who is being described? Write his or her name next to the description.

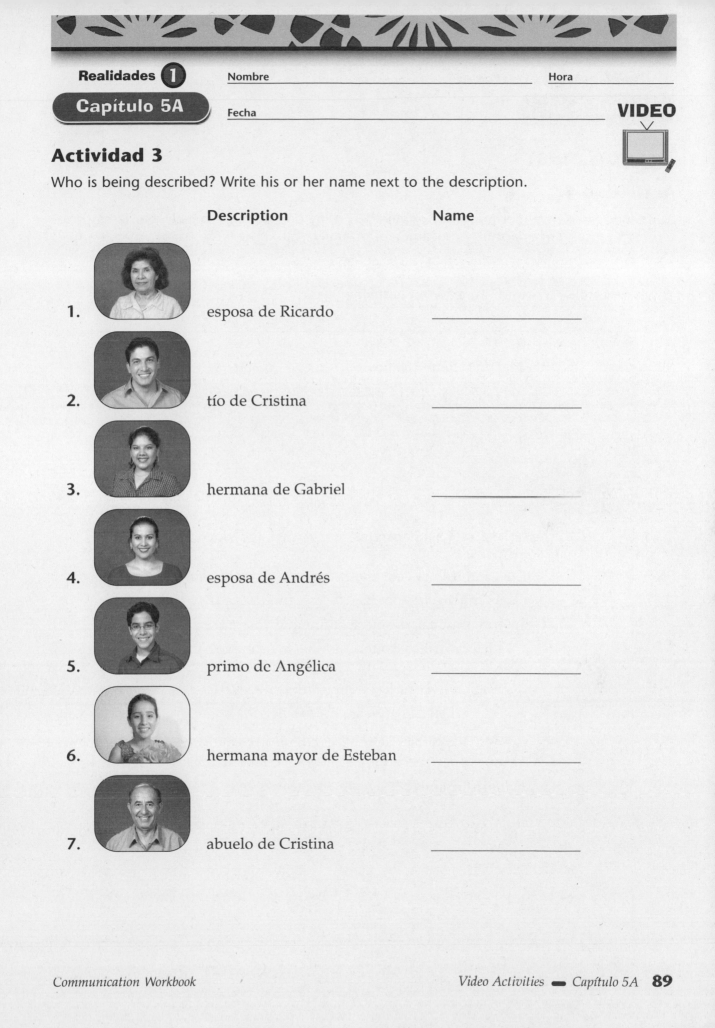

	Description	Name
1.	esposa de Ricardo	_____
2.	tío de Cristina	_____
3.	hermana de Gabriel	_____
4.	esposa de Andrés	_____
5.	primo de Angélica	_____
6.	hermana mayor de Esteban	_____
7.	abuelo de Cristina	_____

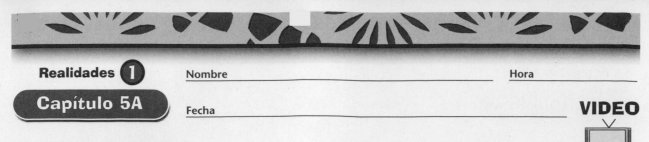

Realidades ①

Capítulo 5A

Nombre _____

Hora _____

Fecha _____

VIDEO

Y, ¿qué más?

Actividad 4

At Cristina's party we met many family members. Why don't you introduce your family, too? Write three sentences about your family or a family you know well. Follow the examples below.

Yo vivo en mi casa con mi mamá y mi hermano.

TÚ: _____

Mi hermano se llama Martín y tiene 10 años.

TÚ: _____

Yo tengo muchos primos y primas.

TÚ: _____

The lyrics for "Las mañanitas" as sung on the video are:

Éstas son las mañanitas que cantaba el rey David

a las muchachas bonitas, te las cantamos a ti.

Despierta, mi bien, despierta, mira que ya amaneció,

ya los pajarillos cantan, la luna ya se metió.

These are the early morning birthday songs

that King David used to sing

to pretty girls, and so we sing them to you.

Wake up, my dear, wake up, look, dawn has already come,

the little birds are singing, the moon is gone.

Realidades ❶

Capítulo 5A

Nombre _____

Fecha _____

Hora _____

AUDIO

Actividad 5

Beto is showing Raúl a picture of his family at a birthday party. Identify as many people as you can and write their names and relationship to Beto under the pictures. If Beto refers to a pet, simply write the pet's name under the picture. You will hear this conversation twice.

_____ _____ _____

_____ _____ _____

_____ _____ _____

_____ _____ _____

_____ _____ _____

_____ _____ _____

Realidades ❶

Capítulo 5A

Nombre _____

Hora _____

Fecha _____

AUDIO

Actividad 6

You are chosen to participate in a popular radio quiz show on a local Spanish radio station. When it is your turn, you are happy to hear that your questions are in the category of **FAMILIA**. See if you can answer all of the questions correctly on the entry card below. Each question becomes a little more difficult. You will hear each set of questions twice.

1. _____

2. _____

3. _____

4. _____

5. _____

Actividad 7

Listen as three brothers talk to their mother after school. Try to fill in all of the squares in the grid with the correct information about Julio, Mateo, and Víctor. Remember, you might not hear the information given in the same order as it appears in the grid. You will hear this conversation twice.

	¿Cuántos años tiene?	¿Qué le gusta hacer?	¿Qué tiene que hacer?	¿Qué tiene en la mochila?
Julio				
Mateo				
Víctor				

AUDIO

Actividad 8

Listen as two students tell their host families in Chile about their own families back home. As you listen to both of them, see if you can tell which family is being described. Put a check mark in the appropriate box on the grid. You will hear each set of statements twice.

La familia Gómez

La familia Sora

	1	2	3	4	5	6	7	8
La familia Gómez								
La familia Sora								

Realidades ❶

Capítulo 5A

Nombre _____

Fecha _____

Hora _____

AUDIO

Actividad 9

Listen to the following phone calls to Ana, a favorite local talk show host. Each caller has a problem with someone in his or her family. As you listen to each caller, take notes on his or her problems. After all of the callers have spoken, write a sentence of advice for each caller. You may write your advice in English. You will hear set of statements twice.

	PROBLEMA	CONSEJO
Maritza		
Armando		
Andrés		
María Luisa		

Realidades 1

Capítulo 5A

Nombre _____

Hora _____

Fecha _____

WRITING

Actividad 10

Look at the pages from the Rulfo family photo album below. Then, write one or two sentences describing the people in each photo. What is their relationship to each other? What do you think they are like, based on the pictures?

Juanito, Lolita y Pepe

Pepe, Marcos, Romana, Timoteo y Luisita

"El cumpleaños de Rafael"

1. Foto 1

_____

_____

_____

2. Foto 2

_____

_____

_____

3. Foto 3

_____

_____

_____

Nombre _____   Hora _____

Fecha _____   **WRITING**

Actividad 11

People have many obligations during the day. Using **tener que**, write what you think the following people have to do at the time of day or place given. Follow the model.

> **Modelo**   mi padre / a las 7:00 de la mañana
>
> *Mi padre tiene que desayunar a las siete de la mañana.*

1. yo / a las 7:30 de la mañana

   _____

2. tú / en la clase de español

   _____

3. los estudiantes / en la clase de inglés

   _____

4. el profesor / en la clase de matemáticas

   _____

5. las personas de la escuela / a las doce de la tarde (al mediodía)

   _____

6. Uds. / en la clase de arte

   _____

7. los estudiantes malos / en la clase de educación física

   _____

8. mi amigo / a las 3:00 de la tarde

   _____

9. mis hermanos y yo / a las 5:00 de la tarde

   _____

10. mi familia / a las 6:00 de la tarde

    _____

Actividad 12

A. Your family tree is very complex. It takes many links to connect everyone in the family. Using possessive adjectives, write 10 sentences about how people are related in your family. Use the model to help you.

Modelo   *Mi tío tiene dos hijos.*

   Mi abuelo es el padre de mi tía.

1. _____
2. _____
3. _____
4. _____
5. _____
6. _____
7. _____
8. _____
9. _____
10. _____

B. Now, draw your family tree.

Realidades 1

Capítulo 5A

Nombre _____

Hora _____

Fecha _____

WRITING

Actividad 13

Your pen pal from Argentina has asked you to tell her about a member of your family. First, tell her the person's name, age, and relationship to you. Then, describe what the person is like.

Once you finish writing, read your description and check to make sure that all the words are spelled correctly and that you have used accents where necessary. Also, check to make sure the endings of the adjectives agree with the nouns they are describing.

Hola, Ana Sofía:

_____

_____

_____

_____

_____

_____

_____

_____

_____

_____

_____

Saludos,

_____

Realidades ❶

Capítulo 5B

Nombre _____

Hora _____

Fecha _____

VIDEO

Antes de ver el video

Actividad 1

Select from the word bank the appropriate nouns to write under each heading: things needed to set the table, things to eat, and things to drink.

menú	tacos	tenedor	flan
enchiladas	limonada	servilleta	postre
café	refresco	cuchillo	jugo de naranja

Para poner la mesa

_____

_____

_____

_____

Para comer

_____

_____

_____

_____

Para beber

_____

_____

_____

_____

¿Comprendes?

Actividad 2

Angélica's family is having dinner at the restaurant **México Lindo**. Find the best choice to complete each statement by writing the letter in the space provided.

1. El camarero está nervioso; _____

    a. tiene mucho trabajo.

    b. es su primer día de trabajo.

    c. tiene sueño.

2. El papá de Angélica pide un té helado _____

    a. porque tiene calor.

    b. porque es delicioso.

    c. porque tiene frío.

3. La mamá de Angélica pide de postre _____

    a. arroz con pollo.

    b. tacos de bistec.

    c. flan.

4. La mamá de Angélica necesita _____

    a. una servilleta.

    b. el menú.

    c. un cuchillo y un tenedor.

Actividad 3

Match each person with the things he or she ordered. Write the letter of the foods and beverages in the spaces provided.

1. Mamá _____   a. jugo de naranja y fajitas de pollo

2. Angélica _____   b. enchiladas

3. Papá _____   c. café, ensalada de frutas y flan

4. Esteban _____   d. té helado, tacos de bistec y café

5. Cristina _____   e. refresco y arroz con pollo

6. Sr. del pelo castaño _____   f. hamburguesa y refresco

Y, ¿qué más?

Actividad 4

You and your friend Graciela are having dinner at a Mexican restaurant with your family. Graciela doesn't speak Spanish, so your mom orders dinner for her. Then, you give your order. Look at the menu to see your options, then write your order in the space provided in the dialogue below.

MENÚ		
BEBIDAS	**PLATO PRINCIPAL**	**POSTRES**
Refrescos	Enchiladas	Flan
Jugo de naranja	Tacos de carne/pollo	Helado
Té helado/caliente	Fajitas de carne/pollo	Frutas frescas
Café	Burritos	

CAMARERO: ¿Qué van a pedir para beber?

MAMÁ: La joven quiere un jugo de naranja, y yo quiero un refresco.

TÚ: _____

CAMARERO: ¿Qué quieren pedir para el plato principal?

MAMÁ: Para la joven enchiladas, y yo quiero arroz con pollo.

TÚ: _____

CAMARERO: ¿Quieren pedir algo de postre?

MAMÁ: Para la joven un flan. Yo no quiero nada, gracias.

TÚ: _____

Realidades 1

Capítulo 5B

Nombre _____

Fecha _____

Hora _____

AUDIO

Actividad 5

You are delighted to find out that you can understand a conversation that a family at a table near you in a restaurant is having in Spanish. The family doesn't seem very happy with the waiter. Listen to find out what each family member is upset about. By looking at the pictures in the grid below, check off the item that is causing the problem. You will hear each conversation twice.

salt & pepper						
glass						
fork						
sugar bowl						
knife						
spoon						
fish						
napkin						
menu						

Actividad 6

Five young people go to a department store to buy hats (**sombreros**) as presents for their friends. Listen as each person describes the person he or she is buying the present for. Write the name of each person described under the hat that best matches that person. You will hear each conversation twice.

Communication Workbook

Realidades ①

Capítulo 5B

Nombre _____

Fecha _____

Hora _____

AUDIO

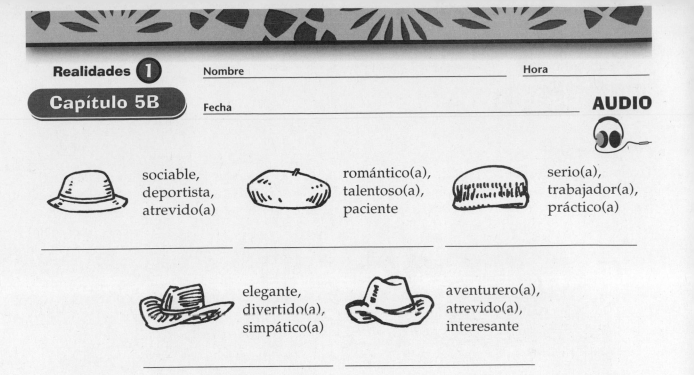

sociable, deportista, atrevido(a)

_____

romántico(a), talentoso(a), paciente

_____

serio(a), trabajador(a), práctico(a)

_____

elegante, divertido(a), simpático(a)

_____

aventurero(a), atrevido(a), interesante

_____

Actividad 7

Listen as a group of friends discuss Julia's upcoming surprise birthday party. Look at the list of party items. Write the name of each person next to the item that he or she is bringing. Circle any item that still needs to be assigned. You will hear this conversation twice.

Los platos _____	Los refrescos _____	Las servilletas _____
Los vasos _____	Los globos _____	El postre _____
Los tenedores _____	La piñata _____	Las flores _____
Las cucharas _____	Las luces _____	El helado _____

Actividad 8

Iván knows many different people from various places. Listen to him describe these people. Fill in the chart as you hear each piece of information given. You will hear each set of statements twice.

	¿De dónde es/son?	¿Dónde está(n)?	¿Está(n) contento/a/os/as?
Juanita			
Los tíos			
Iván y su familia			
Felipe			
Juanita y Julie			

AUDIO

Actividad 9

Listen as a girl describes a photo of a party to her friend who was unable to attend. Write the names of each person described on the line that corresponds to each picture. You will hear the dialogues twice.

A. _____   D. _____

B. _____   E. _____

C. _____   F. _____

Communication Workbook

Realidades ❶

Capítulo 5B

Nombre _____

Fecha _____

Hora _____

WRITING

Actividad 10

Draw a picture of yourself and three other people in your family. Then, write a description of the person below each picture. You can draw imaginary family members if you prefer.

1.

_____ Yo _____

_____
_____
_____
_____
_____
_____

2.

_____

_____
_____
_____
_____
_____
_____

3.

_____

_____
_____
_____
_____
_____
_____

4.

_____

_____
_____
_____
_____
_____
_____

Realidades 1

Capítulo 5B

Nombre

Fecha

Hora

WRITING

Actividad 11

In preparation for their upcoming party, Juan and Elisa are talking on the phone about who is coming and what each guest is bringing. Read Elisa's guest list below, then complete the friends' conversation by writing sentences that include the correct form of either **venir** or **traer**.

Nuestra fiesta

Anita - la pizza
Pablo y José - la salsa
Jorge y Marta - la limonada y los refrescos
Luisa y Marcos - las galletas de chocolate
Nosotros - la carne

JUAN: ¿Anita viene a la fiesta el sábado?

ELISA: _____.

JUAN: ¡Qué bien! ¿También van a venir Pablo y José?

ELISA: Sí. Ellos _____.

JUAN: ¿Qué traen ellos?

ELISA: _____.

JUAN: Bien. Y ¿quién trae las bebidas?

ELISA: Pues, _____.

JUAN: Sí. Ahora, ¿quiénes traen el postre?

ELISA: _____.

JUAN: ¡Perfecto! ¿Y nosotros? ¿_____?

ELISA: ¡Traemos la carne, por supuesto!

Realidades ❶

Capítulo 5B

Nombre _____

Hora _____

Fecha _____

WRITING

Actividad 12

Describe the following people. Consider their mood and location, their personality and appearance. Be creative and use the pictures and model to help you.

Modelo

Él es joven. Su pelo es corto y negro.

Es un chico estudioso.

Está en casa ahora porque está enfermo.

1. _____

_____

_____

_____

2. _____

_____

_____

_____

3. _____

_____

_____

_____

4. _____

_____

_____

_____

Realidades ①

Capítulo 5B

Nombre _____

Fecha _____

Hora _____

WRITING

Actividad 13

There is going to be a picnic at your new house, and your mother is telling you who is coming and what he or she will be bringing. Write what your mother says, using a name, a description word, and an item from the columns below. Use either **venir** or **traer** in your sentence. Use the names only once. Follow the model.

Nombre	Descripción	Va a traer
Los Sres. Vázquez	viejo	platos
	joven	tenedores
La Srta. Espinosa	contento	vasos
	simpático	pollo
Antonio Jerez	artístico	hamburguesas
	pelirrojo	pasteles
Fernando y María Sosa	enfermo	servilletas
	guapo	limonada
Catalina de la Cuesta	alto	cuchillos
	bajo	tazas

Modelo   *La señorita Espinosa viene a la fiesta. Ella es la mujer joven y simpática que vive cerca de nuestra casa. Ella siempre está contenta y trae los pasteles.*

1. _____

   _____

2. _____

   _____

3. _____

   _____

4. _____

   _____

Realidades ①

Capítulo 6A

Nombre _____

Fecha _____

Hora _____

VIDEO

Antes de ver el video

Actividad 1

Make a list of five items in your bedroom and five adjectives that describe your bedroom.

Cosas en mi dormitorio

_____

_____

_____

_____

_____

Descripción de mi dormitorio

_____

_____

_____

_____

_____

¿Comprendes?

Actividad 2

Below are some words and phrases that you have learned so far. On the lines below, write only the words that you most likely heard in the video episode about Ignacio's room.

a veces	ratón	bistec	¿A qué hora?	almuerzo
foto	desordenado	lámpara	pequeños	estante
pared	bueno	casa	mochila	peor
abuelos	bailar	cuarto	bicicleta	escritorio
calculadora	¿Adónde?	fiesta	discos compactos	color

_____ _____ _____

_____ _____ _____

_____ _____ _____

_____ _____ _____

_____ _____ _____

VIDEO

Actividad 3

Put the following scenes from the video in chronological order by numbering them from 1–7.

_____

_____

_____

_____

_____

_____

_____

Nombre _____   Hora _____

Fecha _____   **VIDEO**

Y, ¿qué más?

Actividad 4

What is your room like? Is it messy or neat? What do you have to the left and to the right of the room? What do you have on the wall, on the nightstand, or on a bookshelf? Can you compare your room to someone else's? Describe your room, using as much new vocabulary as you can. Follow the sample paragraph below.

Modelo

Mi cuarto es menos ordenado que el cuarto de mi hermana. A la izquierda tengo un estante, muy desordenado, con discos compactos. A la derecha está mi escritorio con libros y revistas. Tengo una foto de mi familia en la pared. También tengo otra foto de mi hermana en su cuarto, ¡y está ordenado!

_____

_____

_____

_____

_____

_____

Nombre _____

Hora _____

Fecha _____

AUDIO

Actividad 5

Marta and her sister Ana have very similar bedrooms. However, since they have unique personalities and tastes, there are some differences! For each statement you hear, check off in the appropriate column whose bedroom is being described. You will hear each statement twice.

El dormitorio de Marta

El dormitorio de Ana

	Marta	Ana		Marta	Ana
1.	❏	❏	6.	❏	❏
2.	❏	❏	7.	❏	❏
3.	❏	❏	8.	❏	❏
4.	❏	❏	9.	❏	❏
5.	❏	❏	10.	❏	❏

Realidades ①

Capítulo 6A

Nombre _____

Hora _____

Fecha _____

AUDIO

Actividad 6

Your Spanish teacher asks you to represent your school at a local university's **Competencia Escolar** (*Scholastic Competition*) for secondary Spanish students. She gives you a tape to practice with for the competition. As you listen to the recording, decide whether the statement is true or false and mark it in the grid. You will hear each set of statements twice.

	1	2	3	4	5	6	7	8	9	10
Cierto										
Falso										

Actividad 7

Sra. Harding's class is planning an Immersion Weekend for the school district's Spanish students. Listen as four committee members discuss the best food to have, the best activities for younger and older students, and the best colors for the t-shirt (**camiseta**) that will be given to all participants. To keep track of what everyone thinks, fill in the grid. You will hear each set of statements twice.

	La mejor comida	Las actividades para los estudiantes menores	Las actividades para los estudiantes mayores	El mejor color para la camiseta
1				
2				
3				
4				

Realidades ①

Capítulo 6A

Nombre _____

Fecha _____

Hora _____

AUDIO

Actividad 8

Your friend is babysitting for a family with an eight-year-old boy and a ten-year-old girl. Since they are a Spanish-speaking family, your friend wants you to go with her in case she doesn't understand everything that the mother tells her. Listen to the conversation to learn all the ground rules. Write either **sí** or **no** in each column that matches what the mother says that the boy or girl can do. Be sure to write **no** in both columns if neither is allowed to do it. Write **sí** in both columns if both are allowed to do it. You will hear this conversation twice.

Nombre _____

Hora _____

Fecha _____

AUDIO

Actividad 9

Look at the pictures in the chart below as you hear people describe their friends' bedrooms. Place a check in the chart that corresponds to all of the items mentioned by the friend. You will hear each set of statements twice.

	Javier	Sara	María	Marcos

Nombre _____ Hora _____

Fecha _____ **WRITING**

Actividad 10

Answer the following questions about your bedroom in complete sentences. If you prefer, you may write about your ideal bedroom.

1. ¿Cuál es tu color favorito?

_____

2. ¿De qué color es tu dormitorio?

_____

3. ¿Tienes una alfombra en tu dormitorio? ¿De qué color es?

_____

4. ¿Tienes un despertador? ¿Cuándo usas tu despertador?

_____

_____

5. ¿Qué muebles (*furniture*) tienes en tu dormitorio?

_____

_____

6. ¿Qué cosas electrónicas tienes en tu dormitorio?

_____

7. ¿Prefieres los videos o los DVDs? ¿Cuántos tienes?

_____

8. ¿Cuántos discos compactos tienes?

_____

Realidades 1

Capítulo 6A

Nombre _____

Fecha _____

Hora _____

WRITING

Actividad 11

A. Draw your bedroom or your ideal bedroom (including furniture, electronics, windows, books, decorations, and other possessions) in the space provided below.

B. Now, compare the room that you drew with Juan's room on the left. Use the correct form of some of the following adjectives, or think of others: **práctico, interesante, grande, pequeño, mejor, peor, bonito, ordenado.**

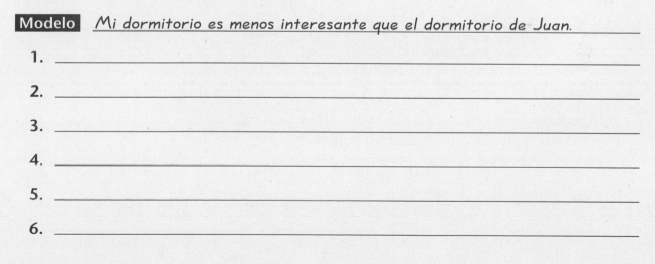

| Modelo | *Mi dormitorio es menos interesante que el dormitorio de Juan.* |

1. _____

2. _____

3. _____

4. _____

5. _____

6. _____

Realidades 1

Capítulo 6A

Nombre _____

Hora _____

Fecha _____

WRITING

Actividad 12

You and your friends are comparing your English classes to determine which teacher's class to take next year. Read the information below, then compare the classes based on the criteria indicated. Follow the model.

	Clase A	Clase B	Clase C
Hora	Primera	Tercera	Octava
Profesor(a)	Profesora Brown — interesante	Profesor Martí — aburrido	Profesor Nicólas — muy interesante
Número de estudiantes	25	20	22
Dificultad	Difícil	Muy difícil	Fácil
Libros	Muy buenos	Aburridos	Buenos
Opinión general	A	B –	A–

Modelo   Profesor   _El profesor Martí es el menos interesante de los tres_
profesores.

1. Hora (*temprano* or *tarde*)

   _____

2. Número de estudiantes (*grande* or *pequeña*)

   _____

3. Dificultad (*fácil* or *difícil*)

   _____

4. Libros (*buenos* or *malos*)

   _____

5. Opinión general (*mejor* or *peor*)

   _____

Realidades 1

Capítulo 6A

Nombre _____

Hora _____

Fecha _____

WRITING

Actividad 13

Your parents are hosting a family reunion, and nine extra people will be sleeping at your house. On the lines below, write where nine guests would sleep at your house. You may use your imagination if you prefer.

1. _____
   _____

2. _____
   _____

3. _____
   _____

4. _____
   _____

5. _____
   _____

6. _____
   _____

7. _____
   _____

8. _____
   _____

9. _____
   _____

Realidades 1

Capítulo 6B

Nombre _____

Hora _____

Fecha _____

VIDEO

Antes de ver el video

Actividad 1

Think of five chores you do at home. Then, write whether you like or don't like doing them using **me gusta** and **no me gusta nada**. Follow the model.

| Modelo | _No me gusta nada limpiar mi dormitorio._ |

1. _____

2. _____

3. _____

4. _____

5. _____

¿Comprendes?

Actividad 2

As you know from the video, Jorgito does all of the chores even though some were Elena's responsibility. Next to each chore listed below, tell whether it was Elena's responsibility or Jorgito's responsibility by writing the appropriate name in the space provided.

1. _____ quitar el polvo

2. _____ poner la mesa del comedor

3. _____ lavar los platos en la cocina

4. _____ hacer la cama en el dormitorio de Jorge

5. _____ hacer la cama en el cuarto de Elena

6. _____ arreglar el dormitorio de Jorge

7. _____ pasar la aspiradora

8. _____ dar de comer al perro

Realidades ①

Capítulo 6B

Nombre _____

Hora _____

Fecha _____

VIDEO

Actividad 3

Use the stills below from the video to help you answer the questions. Use complete sentences.

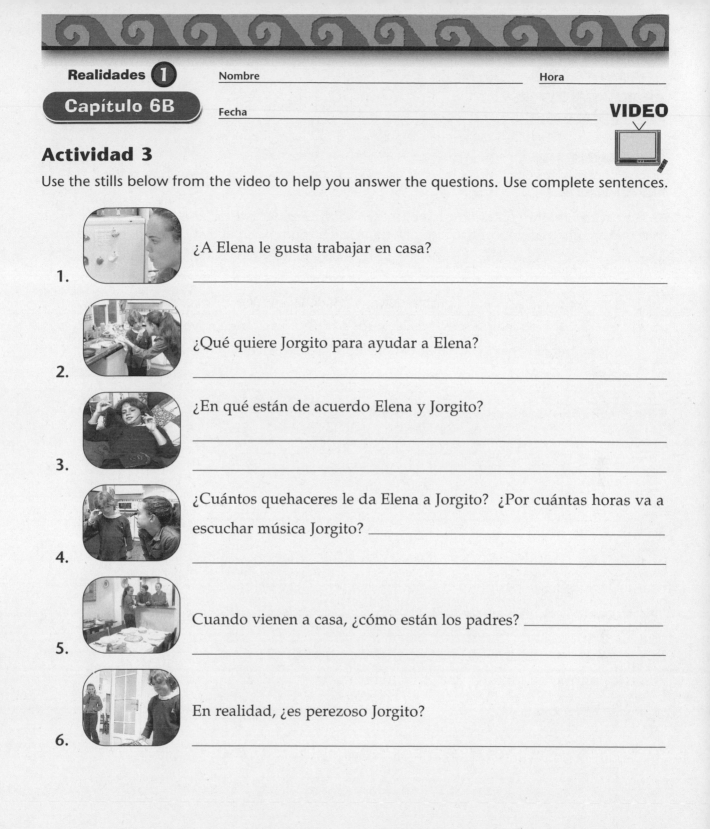

1. ¿A Elena le gusta trabajar en casa?

_____

2. ¿Qué quiere Jorgito para ayudar a Elena?

_____

3. ¿En qué están de acuerdo Elena y Jorgito?

_____

_____

4. ¿Cuántos quehaceres le da Elena a Jorgito? ¿Por cuántas horas va a

escuchar música Jorgito? _____

_____

5. Cuando vienen a casa, ¿cómo están los padres? _____

_____

6. En realidad, ¿es perezoso Jorgito?

_____

Nombre _____

Hora _____

Fecha _____

VIDEO

Y, ¿qué más?

Actividad 4

What activities might you do in each of these rooms? From the list in the box below, name at least two things that you might logically do in each room. Each activity should be used only once.

hacer la cama   pasar la aspiradora   escuchar música   cocinar la comida
poner la mesa   lavar los platos   quitar el polvo
comer la cena   arreglar el dormitorio desordenado   hacer la tarea

1. dormitorio de Elena

_____ _____

2. sala

_____ _____

3. comedor

_____ _____

4. cocina

_____ _____

5. dormitorio de Jorge

_____ _____

Realidades 1

Capítulo 6B

Nombre _____

Hora _____

Fecha _____

AUDIO

Actividad 5

Listen as people look for things they have misplaced somewhere in their house. After each conversation, complete the sentence that explains what each person is looking for (**busca**) and in which room it is found. You will hear each dialogue twice.

1. La muchacha busca _____.

    Está en _____.

2. El muchacho busca _____.

    Está en _____.

3. La mujer busca _____.

    Está en _____.

4. El muchacho busca _____.

    Está en _____.

5. La muchacha busca _____.

    Está en _____.

Actividad 6

Señor Morales's nephew, Paco, volunteers to help his uncle move into a new apartment. However, Señor Morales is very distracted as he tells Paco where to put different things. Listen as he gives his nephew instructions and record in the grid below whether you think what he tells him to do each time is **lógico** (logical) **o ilógico** (illogical). You will hear each dialogue twice.

	1	2	3	4	5	6	7	8	9	10
lógico										
ilógico										

Actividad 7

Nico's parents are shocked when they come home from a trip to find that he hasn't done any of the chores that he promised to do. As they tell Nico what he needs to do, fill in the blanks below each picture with the corresponding number. You will hear each set of statements twice.

Actividad 8

Listen as each person rings a friend's doorbell and is told by the person who answers the door what the friend is doing at the moment. Based on that information, in which room of the house would you find the friend? As you listen to the conversations, look at the drawing of the house and write the number of the room that you think each friend might be in. You will hear each dialogue twice.

1. _____
2. _____
3. _____
4. _____
5. _____
6. _____

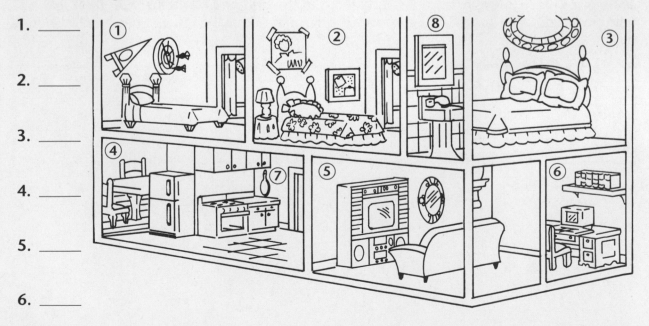

Actividad 9

Some people always seem to get out of doing their chores at home. Listen as a few teens tell their parents why they should not or cannot do what their parents have asked them to do. As you listen, write in the chart below what the parent requests, such as **lavar los platos**. Then write in the teens' excuses, such as **está lavando el coche**. You will hear each conversation twice.

	Los quehaceres	Las excusas
Marcos		
Luis		
Marisol		
Jorge		
Elisa		

Realidades 1

Capítulo 6B

Nombre _____

Fecha _____

Hora _____

WRITING

Actividad 10

The Justino family is getting ready for their houseguests to arrive. Help Sra. Justino write the family's to-do list. Follow the model.

Modelo

En el dormitorio, tenemos que quitar el polvo,
arreglar el cuarto y pasar la aspiradora.

1. _____

_____

_____

2. _____

_____

_____

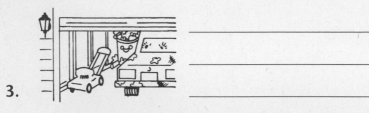

3. _____

_____

_____

4. _____

_____

_____

Realidades 1

Capítulo 6B

Nombre _____

Hora _____

Fecha _____

WRITING

Actividad 11

The Boteros's son is going to stay with his grandmother in Puerto Rico for a month. His parents want to make sure that he is well-behaved and helps out around the house. Write ten commands the Boteros might give to their son. Follow the model.

Modelo   *Ayuda en la cocina, hijo.* _____

1. _____

2. _____

3. _____

4. _____

5. _____

6. _____

7. _____

8. _____

9. _____

10. _____

Realidades 1

Capítulo 6B

Nombre _____

Fecha _____

Hora _____

WRITING

Actividad 12

The Galgo family is very busy on Sunday. Look at their schedule below and write what each family member is doing at the time given. Use your imagination, and use the model to help you.

	10:00	12:00	3:00	8:00
La Señora Galgo	hacer ejercicio	almorzar	trabajar	dormir
El Señor Galgo	trabajar	cortar el césped	preparar la cena	jugar al tenis
Rodrigo	arreglar el cuarto	comer	tocar la guitarra	estudiar
Mariana	nadar	poner la mesa	leer	ver la tele

Modelo   12:00   _A las doce, la Sra. Galgo está almorzando con sus amigos y el Sr._
Galgo está cortando el césped. Rodrigo está comiendo una manzana y
Mariana está poniendo la mesa.

1. 10:00

_____

_____

_____

_____

2. 3:00

_____

_____

_____

_____

3. 8:00

_____

_____

_____

_____

Realidades **1**

Capítulo 6B

Nombre _____

Hora _____

Fecha _____

WRITING

Actividad 13

A. Read the letter that Marta wrote to "Querida Adela," an advice column in the local paper, because she was frustrated with having to help around the house.

> *Querida Adela:*
>
> *Yo soy una hija de 16 años y no tengo tiempo para ayudar en la casa. Mis padres no comprenden que yo tengo mi propia vida y que mis amigos son más importantes que los quehaceres de la casa. ¿Qué debo hacer?*
>
> *—Hija Malcontenta*

B. Now, imagine that you are Adela and are writing a response to Marta. In the first paragraph, tell her what she must do around the house. In the second, tell her what she can do to still have fun with her friends. Use the sentences already below to help you.

Querida Hija Malcontenta:

Es verdad que tú tienes un problema. Piensas que tu vida con tus amigos es más importante que tu vida con tu familia. Pero, hija, tú tienes responsabilidades. Arregla tu cuarto. _____

_____

_____

Tienes que ser una buena hija.

Después de ayudar a tus padres, llama a tus amigos por teléfono.

_____

_____

_____. Tus padres van a estar más contentos y tú vas a tener una vida mejor.

Buena suerte

Adela

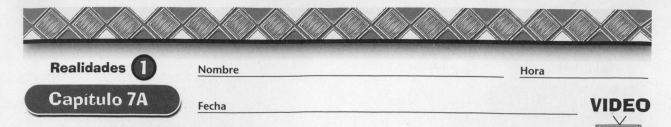

VIDEO

Antes de ver el video

Actividad 1

In the next video, Claudia and Teresa go shopping for clothes. In order to make decisions on what they want they will sometimes make comparisons. Using the following words, make a comparative statement for each set. Follow the model.

Modelo blusa roja / blusa amarilla

La blusa roja es más bonita que la blusa amarilla.

1. botas marrones / botas negras

_____

2. una falda larga / una mini falda

_____

3. un traje nuevo / un traje de moda (in fashion)

_____

4. Claudia – 16 años / Teresa – 15 años

_____

5. suéter que cuesta 40 dólares / suéter que cuesta 30 dólares

_____

¿Comprendes?

Actividad 2

Identify the speaker of the following quotes by writing the name of each person on the space provided.

1. "Tienes ropa muy bonita."   _____

2. "Quiero comprar algo nuevo."   _____

3.   "¿Qué tal esta tienda?"   _____

4.  "Pues entonces, ¿esta falda y esta blusa?" _____

5. "Busco algo bonito para una fiesta." _____

6. "Bueno, hay cosas que no cuestan tanto." _____

7. "Bueno, uhm, aquí en México no llevamos
esa ropa en las fiestas." _____

8. "¡... pero es mi gorra favorita!" _____

Actividad 3

Can you remember what happened in the video? Write the letter of the correct answer on the line.

1. A Teresa no le gusta la falda y el vestido; _____

   a. le quedan bien.

   b. le quedan más o menos.

   c. le quedan mal.

2. A Teresa no le gusta su ropa, pero sí tiene ropa _____

   a. bonita.

   b. fea.

   c. muy vieja.

3. Teresa quiere _____

   a. comprar algo extravagante.

   b. comprar algo nuevo.

   c. no ir a la fiesta.

Realidades ①

Capítulo 7A

Nombre _____

Hora _____

Fecha _____

VIDEO

4. Claudia quiere ver _____

   a. cuánto cuestan la falda y la blusa.

   b. si le quedan bien los jeans y la camiseta.

   c. otras cosas más bonitas.

5. Por fin las chicas deciden comprar _____

   a. unos jeans de cuatrocientos pesos con una camiseta de doscientos pesos.

   b. en otra tienda.

   c. una falda de trescientos pesos y un suéter de doscientos pesos.

Y, ¿qué más?

Actividad 4

Do you like the clothes that you have in your closet? Write one sentence about something in your closet that you do like, and why. Then write one sentence about something in your closet that you don't like, and why not. Follow the models.

| Modelo 1 | *Me gusta el suéter negro porque es bonito y puedo llevarlo* |

cuando hace frío.

_____

_____

| Modelo 2 | *No me gustan los pantalones rojos porque son feos y me quedan mal.* |

_____

_____

Actividad 5

Isabel is working at a laundry (**lavandería**) in Salamanca. As the customers bring in their order, write how many clothing items each person has from each category in the appropriate boxes. Then total the order and write the amount in the blanks provided in the grid for each customer. You will hear each dialogue twice.

LAVANDERÍA DOS PASOS

(Note: € is the symbol for Euros)

	Precios	Cliente 1	Cliente 2	Cliente 3	Cliente 4	Cliente 5
Blusas	3 €					
Vestidos	6 €					
Pantalones	8 €					
Faldas	5 €					
Suéteres	5 €					
Camisas	3 €					
Jeans	7 €					
Chaquetas	9 €					
Camisetas	3 €					
	TOTAL	€	€	€	€	€

Actividad 6

Listen to the following items available from one of the shopping services on TV. You might not understand all of the words, but listen for the words that you do know in order to identify which item is being discussed. Then write down the price underneath the correct picture. You will hear each set of statements twice.

_____   _____   _____   _____   _____

Realidades 1

Capítulo 7A

Nombre _____

Fecha _____

Hora _____

AUDIO

Actividad 7

Listen as friends talk about their plans for the weekend. Where are they thinking about going? What are they thinking about doing? How are they planning to dress? As you listen for these details, fill in the chart. You will hear each dialogue twice.

	¿Adónde piensa ir?	¿Qué piensa hacer?	¿Qué piensa llevar?
1. Paco			
2. Anita			
3. Ernesto			
4. Kiki			

Actividad 8

Susi is spending the summer in Ecuador, where she is living with a wonderful host family. As the summer comes to a close, she is searching for the perfect thank-you gifts for each member of the family. Listen as she talks to the sales clerk. In the chart below, write in the item that she decides to buy for each person in her new "family." You will hear this conversation twice.

Para la madre	Para el padre	Para el hijo, Luis	Para la hija, Marisol	Para el bebé

Communication Workbook

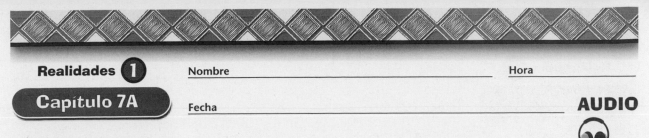

Realidades 1

Capítulo 7A

Nombre _____

Hora _____

Fecha _____

AUDIO

Actividad 9

What you wear can reveal secrets about your personality. Find out what type of message you send when you wear your favorite clothes and your favorite colors. As you listen to the descriptions, write down at least one word or phrase for each color personality and at least one article of clothing favored by that person. You will hear each set of statements twice.

EL COLOR	LA ROPA	LA PERSONALIDAD
Rojo		
Amarillo		
Morado		
Azul		
Anaranjado		
Marrón		
Gris		
Verde		
Negro		

Realidades ①

Capítulo 7A

Nombre _____

Fecha _____

Hora _____

WRITING

Actividad 10

Answer the following questions about clothing and shopping in complete sentences.

1. ¿Quién va mucho de compras en tu familia?

_____

2. ¿Piensas comprar ropa nueva esta estación? ¿Qué piensas comprar?

_____

_____

3. ¿Cuál prefieres, la ropa del verano o la ropa del invierno? ¿Por qué?

_____

_____

4. ¿Prefieres la ropa de tus amigos o la ropa de tus padres? ¿Por qué?

_____

_____

5. ¿Prefieres llevar ropa formal o informal?

_____

6. ¿Qué llevas normalmente para ir a la escuela?

_____

_____

7. ¿Cuál es tu ropa favorita? Describe.

_____

_____

_____

Realidades ①

Capítulo 7A

Nombre _____

Hora _____

Fecha _____

Actividad 11

Some students are thinking about what to wear for the next school dance. Look at the pictures, then write complete sentences telling what the students might be thinking. Use the verbs **pensar, querer,** or **preferir.** Follow the model.

Modelo

María piensa llevar un vestido negro al baile. También quiere llevar
unos zapatos negros. Quiere ser muy elegante.

1. _____

_____

_____

2. _____

_____

_____

3. _____

_____

_____

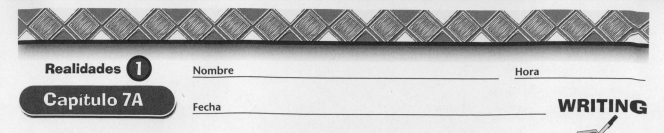

Actividad 12

Pedro works in a department store and handles customer inquiries in the clearance clothing department. The items in his department are on sale, while the items in the rest of the store are full price. Help him answer customers' questions about the merchandise by writing complete sentences that include demonstrative adjectives. Follow the model.

Modelo   ¿Cuánto cuestan los suéteres?

Estos suéteres aquí cuestan cuarenta dólares y esos allí cuestan sesenta.

1. ¿Cuánto cuesta una gorra negra?

   _____

2. ¿Cuánto cuestan los pantalones?

   _____

3. ¿Las camisas cuestan diez dólares?

   _____

4. ¿Cuánto cuesta un traje de baño?

   _____

5. ¿Los jeans cuestan mucho?

   _____

6. ¿La sudadera azul cuesta veinte dólares?

   _____

7. ¿Cuánto cuestan las botas aquí?

   _____

8. ¿Los abrigos cuestan mucho?

   _____

Realidades 1

Capítulo 7A

Nombre _____

Fecha _____

Hora _____

WRITING

Actividad 13

You get a discount at the clothing store where you work after school, so you are going to buy presents for your friends and family there. Write complete sentences telling who you will buy gifts for and why you will choose each person's gift. Use the model to help you.

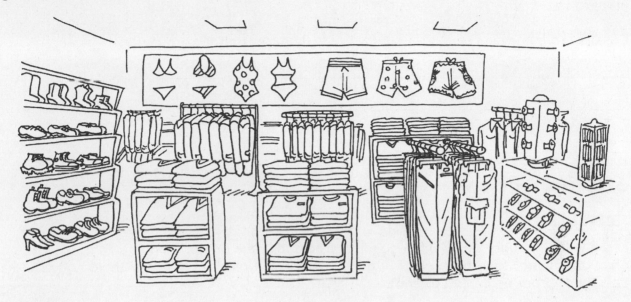

Modelo   *Pienso comprar este suéter azul para mi madre porque ella prefiere la ropa del invierno.*

1. _____

   _____

2. _____

   _____

3. _____

   _____

4. _____

   _____

5. _____

   _____

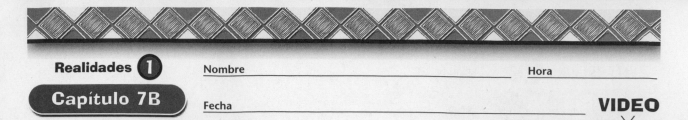

Realidades ①

Capítulo 7B

Nombre _____

Fecha _____

Hora _____

VIDEO

Antes de ver el video

Actividad 1

Where do you like to shop? With a partner, write three things you like to buy and the best place to buy them.

Cosas para comprar

_____

_____

_____

Lugares donde comprarlas

_____

_____

_____

¿Comprendes?

Actividad 2

In the video, Claudia and Manolo go many places to find a gift for Manolo's aunt. Look at the places from the video below and number them in the order in which Manolo and Claudia pass them (from beginning to end).

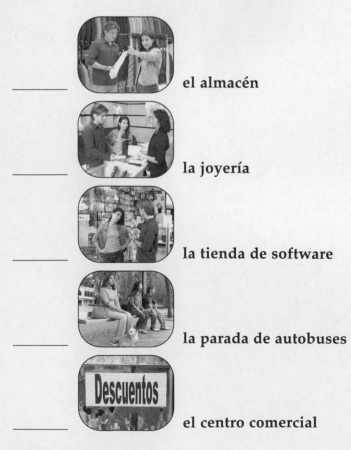

_____ el almacén

_____ la joyería

_____ la tienda de software

_____ la parada de autobuses

_____ el centro comercial

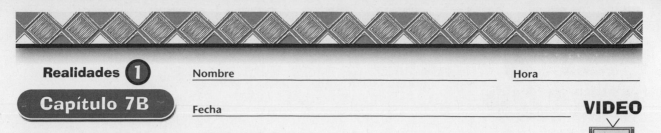

Realidades ❶

Capítulo 7B

Nombre _____ Hora _____

Fecha _____

VIDEO

Actividad 3

What happens when Claudia helps Manolo shop? Circle the letter of the correct answers.

1. Manolo necesita comprar un regalo para su tía porque
   a. mañana es su cumpleaños.
   b. mañana es su aniversario de bodas.
   c. mañana es su quinceañera.

2. El año pasado Manolo le compró a su tía
   a. unos aretes en la joyería.
   b. un libro en una librería.
   c. una corbata muy barata.

3. En el centro comercial, ellos ven
   a. vidcojucgos y software.
   b. pocas cosas en descuento.
   c. anteojos para sol, bolsos, carteras y llaveros.

4. Por fin, deciden comprar para la tía
   a. una cartera.
   b. un collar.
   c. un anillo.

5. Hay una confusión y Manolo le regala a la tía
   a. una pulsera.
   b. unos guantes.
   c. un collar de perro.

Realidades **1**

Capítulo 7B

Nombre _____

Fecha _____

Hora _____

VIDEO

Y, ¿qué más?

Actividad 4

You are shopping for a birthday gift for your mother. Fill in the dialogue below with your possible responses.

DEPENDIENTE: ¿Qué desea usted?

TÚ: _____

_____

DEPENDIENTE: ¿Prefiere ver ropa, perfumes o joyas para ella?

TÚ: _____

_____

DEPENDIENTE: Aquí hay muchos artículos, pero no cuestan tanto.

TÚ: _____

_____

Realidades ①

Capítulo 7B

Nombre _____

Fecha _____

Hora _____

AUDIO

Actividad 5

Sometimes giving gifts is even more fun than receiving them! Listen as people talk about gifts they enjoy giving to their friends and family. Match the pictures below with the corresponding description you hear. Then, in the spaces next to each gift, write where the person bought the gift and what the person paid for it. You will hear each set of statements twice.

	Descripción	Lugar de compra	Precio
1.	_____	_____	_____
2.	_____	_____	_____
3.	_____	_____	_____
4.	_____	_____	_____
5.	_____	_____	_____

Actividad 6

Listen to the following mini-conversations about different kinds of stores. Circle **lógico** if the conversation makes sense and **ilógico** if it does not. You will hear each dialogue twice.

1.	lógico	ilógico	**6.**	lógico	ilógico
2.	lógico	ilógico	**7.**	lógico	ilógico
3.	lógico	ilógico	**8.**	lógico	ilógico
4.	lógico	ilógico	**9.**	lógico	ilógico
5.	lógico	ilógico	**10.**	lógico	ilógico

Actividad 7

Listen as Lorena shows a friend her photographs. Write a sentence describing each one as you hear Lorena describe it. You will hear each conversation twice.

1. Lorena _____ hace _____.

2. Lorena _____ hace _____.

3. Lorena _____ hace _____.

4. Lorena _____ hace _____.

5. Lorena _____ hace _____.

Actividad 8

You have been waiting in line all day at the mall, so you have overheard many conversations as you waited. See if you can match each conversation with the illustrations below and write the number of each conversation under the correct illustration. You will hear each conversation twice.

_____   _____   _____   _____

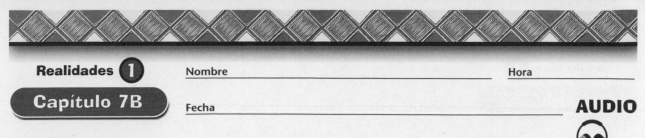

Actividad 9

As a special holiday service, **El Almacén Continental** is sponsoring a hotline that customers can call to get gift ideas. Listen as callers tell the store specialist what they have bought for a particular person in the past. Then listen to the specialist's suggestion for this year's gift. Use the chart below to take notes. You will hear each conversation twice.

	La personalidad y las actividades de la persona	El regalo del año pasado	¿Un regalo para este año?
1			
2			
3			
4			
5			

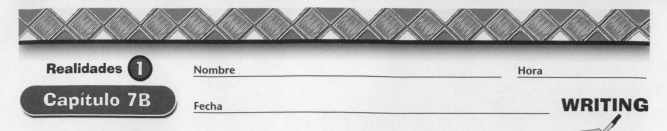

Realidades ❶

Capítulo 7B

Nombre _____

Fecha _____

Hora _____

WRITING

Actividad 10

You are talking to a friend about what you buy when you go shopping. Tell what items you usually buy in each of the specialty shops suggested by the pictures. Then, tell what other items are available at the store. Use the model to help you.

Modelo

<u>En la zapatería, compro zapatos y botas. También es posible comprar</u>
<u>guantes y carteras en una zapatería.</u>

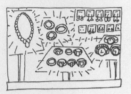

1. _____

_____

_____

_____

2. _____

_____

_____

_____

3. _____

_____

_____

_____

Realidades ①

Capítulo 7B

Nombre _____

Fecha _____

Hora _____

WRITING

Actividad 11

In your Spanish class, you are asked to learn the dates of some important events in the history and culture of Spanish-speaking countries. To help you memorize these dates, write sentences telling when each event occurred. Follow the model.

Modelo   Pablo Picasso / pintar su cuadro *Guernica* / 1937

Pablo Picasso pintó su cuadro Guernica en 1937.

1. Los Estados Unidos / declarar su independencia / el cuatro de julio, 1776

_____

2. Vicente Fox / ganar la presidencia de México / 2000

_____

3. Antonio Banderas / actuar en la película *The Mambo Kings* / 1993

_____

4. Los jugadores argentinos / ganar la Copa Mundial (*World Cup*) / 1986

_____

5. Yo / comprar mis primeros zapatos / ???

_____

6. Nosotros / entrar en la clase de español / ???

_____

7. Los Juegos Olímpicos / pasar en España / 1992

_____

8. México / declarar su independencia / el quince de septiembre, 1810

_____

9. Simón Bolívar / liberar a Venezuela / 1821

_____

Realidades 1

Capítulo 7B

Nombre _____

Fecha _____

Hora _____

WRITING

Actividad 12

The people in your neighborhood were very busy yesterday. Write at least three sentences about what they all did based on the pictures, using at least one of these verbs: **buscar, jugar, pagar, practicar, sacar, tocar.** Follow the model.

Modelo   El Sr. Rodríguez

Ayer el Sr. Rodríguez enseñó la clase de español. La clase practicó la lección. Los estudiantes usaron las computadoras para hacer las actividades.

1.   Andrés

_____

_____

_____

2.   yo

_____

_____

_____

3.   yo   mi madre

_____

_____

_____

4. tú

_____

_____

_____

5. Juana e Inés

_____

_____

_____

Actividad 13

You are writing a letter to your aunt in Mexico to tell her what you bought for your family for the holidays. In the letter, tell what you bought for each person, in what stores you found the items, and how much you paid. The letter has been started for you.

Querida Tía:

    Saludos de los Estados Unidos. Te escribo para decirte que terminé de comprar los regalos para la familia. Para _____ , compré un suéter bonito. ¡Lo encontré en el almacén por sólo veinte dólares! _____

_____

_____

_____

_____

    Bueno, nos vemos en una semana. ¡Buena suerte con las compras!

                        Un fuerte abrazo,

                        Tu sobrino(a) _____

Realidades ❶

Capítulo 8A

Nombre _____

Hora _____

Fecha _____

VIDEO

Antes de ver el video

Actividad 1

You can see and learn a lot on a day trip. Make a list of four places you would like to visit for the day, and write next to each one the main attraction that you would like to see there. Follow the model.

Lugares	Cosas que ver
Modelo *Granada, España*	*La Alhambra*
_____	_____
_____	_____
_____	_____

¿Comprendes?

Actividad 2

Raúl, Gloria, and Tomás went on a day trip to San José and Sarapiquí Park. Under each heading, write the things that they saw in San José and the things that they saw in Sarapiquí Park.

Ministerio de Cultura	mono	Parque España	Catarata La Paz
Gran Terminal del Caribe	palma	bosque lluvioso	Teatro Nacional

San José	Parque Sarapiquí
_____	_____
_____	_____
_____	_____

Communication Workbook

Actividad 3

Based on the video story that you just watched, circle the most appropriate word to complete each statement.

1. Raúl, Gloria y Tomás salieron de la casa muy (tarde / temprano) para ir al parque Sarapiquí.

2. Para ir al parque ellos tomaron el (autobús / avión).

3. El viaje dura (una hora y media / dos horas), porque el parque está a 82 (kilómetros / millas) de San José.

4. En el parque (hace mucho calor / no hace ni frío ni calor) pero llueve mucho.

5. Raúl compra los (libros / boletos) en la Estación Biológica La Selva y cuestan 3,600 (pesos / colones).

6. Tomás tiene la (mochila / cámara) y el (boleto / mapa) y está listo para explorar el parque.

7. Ellos tienen mucho cuidado cuando caminan, pues las raíces de los árboles son muy (grandes / interesantes).

8. Gloria le dice a Tomás: "Hay más de cuatrocientas especies de (monos / aves) en el parque."

9. Ellos tienen problemas al (sacar las fotos / regresar a casa). Pero Tomás (quiere / no quiere) continuar.

10. Raúl dice: "Fue un día (interesante / desastre) pero un poco (difícil / aburrido) para Tomás."

Nombre _____ Hora _____

Fecha _____

VIDEO

Y, ¿qué más?

Actividad 4

Based on what you learned in the video, imagine that you took a field trip to Costa Rica. Your best friend is curious about your trip. Answer your friend's questions below.

1. —¿Cómo es el parque Sarapiquí?

  —_____

2. —¿Sacaste fotos del parque?

  —_____

3. —¿Qué fue lo que más te gustó?

  —_____

4. —¿Qué fue lo que menos te gustó?

  —_____

5. —¿Cuál es la comida típica de Costa Rica?

  —_____

Realidades 1

Capítulo 8A

Nombre

Hora

Fecha

AUDIO

Actividad 5

You call a toll-free telephone number in order to qualify for the popular radio game show, **"Palabras Secretas"** (*Secret Words*). Your challenge is to guess each secret word within ten seconds. Listen to the clues and try to guess the word as the clock is ticking. You must write your answer down before the buzzer in order to be ready for the next one. You will hear each set of statements twice.

1. _____
2. _____
3. _____
4. _____

5. _____
6. _____
7. _____
8. _____

Actividad 6

Listen as a husband and wife talk to a travel agent about their upcoming vacation. Where would each like to go? What type of things would each like to do? Most importantly, do they agree on what is the ideal trip? As you listen, write as much information as you can in each person's travel profile in the chart below. Can you think of a place they could go where both of them would be happy? You will hear this conversation twice.

	EL SEÑOR	LA SEÑORA
¿Adónde le gustaría ir?		
¿Por qué le gustaría ir a ese lugar?		
Cuando va de vacaciones, ¿qué le gustaría hacer?	1. 2.	1. 2.
¿Qué le gustaría ver?	1. 2.	1. 2.
¿Cómo le gustaría viajar?		
¿Adónde deben ir?		

Realidades 1

Capítulo 8A

Nombre _____

Fecha _____

Hora _____

AUDIO

Actividad 7

Listen as mothers call their teenaged sons and daughters on their cell phones to see if they have done what they were asked to do. Based on what each teenager says, categorize the answers in the chart. You will hear each conversation twice.

	1	2	3	4	5	6	7	8	9	10
Teen did what the parent asked him or her to do.										
Teen is in the middle of doing what the parent asked him or her to do.										
Teen says he/she is going to do what the parent asked him/her to do.										

Actividad 8

Your Spanish teacher has asked the students in your class to survey each other about a topic of interest. In order to give you a model to follow, your teacher will play a recording of part of a student's survey from last year. Listen to the student's questions, and fill in his survey form. You will hear each conversation twice.

	¿EL LUGAR?
1. Marco	
2. Patricia	
3. Chucho	
4. Rita	
5. Margarita	

Communication Workbook

Realidades 1

Capítulo 8A

Nombre _____ Hora _____

Fecha _____

AUDIO

Actividad 9

Everyone loves a superhero, and the listeners of this Hispanic radio station are no exception. Listen to today's episode of "Super Tigre," as the hero helps his friends try to locate the evil Rona Robles! Super Tigre tracks Rona Robles down by asking people when they last saw her and where she went. Keep track of what the people said by filling in the chart. You will hear each conversation twice.

	¿Dónde la vio?	¿A qué hora la vio?	¿Qué hizo ella? (What did she do?)	¿Adónde fue ella?
1				
2				
3				
4				
5				

Where did Super Tigre finally find Rona Robles? _____

Actividad 10

Answer the following questions in complete sentences.

1. ¿Te gusta ir de viaje? ¿Te gustaría más ir de vacaciones al campo o a una ciudad?

_____

_____

2. ¿Visitaste algún parque nacional en el pasado? ¿Cuál(es)? Si no, ¿te gustaría visitar

un parque nacional? _____

_____

3. ¿Vives cerca de un lago? ¿Cómo se llama? ¿Te gusta nadar? ¿Pasear en bote?

_____

_____

4. ¿Te gusta ir al mar? ¿Qué te gusta hacer allí? Si no, ¿por qué no? _____

_____

_____

5. ¿Montaste a caballo alguna vez? ¿Te gustó o no? Si no, ¿te gustaría montar a caballo?

_____

_____

6. Describe tu lugar favorito para vivir. ¿Está cerca de un lago? ¿Cerca o lejos de
la ciudad? ¿Hay montañas / museos / parques / un mar cerca de tu casa ideal?

_____

_____

_____

_____

Actividad 11

You and your friends are talking about what you did over the weekend. Write complete sentences based on the illustrations to tell what the following people did. Follow the model.

Modelo   Pablo *vio una película* _____ .

1. Mariela y su madre _____ .

2. Nosotros _____ .

3. Yo _____ .

4. Roberto _____ .

5. Norma _____ .

6. Tú _____ .

7. Ignacio e Isabel _____ .

Realidades ①

Capítulo 8A

Nombre _____

Hora _____

Fecha _____

WRITING

Actividad 12

You and your friends were very busy yesterday. Tell all the places where each person went using the illustrations as clues. Follow the model.

Modelo

Melisa y su padre *fueron de compras.*
Después, fueron al cine.

David _____

1. _____

_____

Yo _____

2. _____

_____

Nosotros _____

3. _____

_____

Raquel y Tito _____

4. _____

_____

Realidades 1

Capítulo 8A

Nombre _____

Fecha _____

Hora _____

WRITING

Actividad 13

A. Write two sentences telling what places you visited the last time you went on vacation. You can write about your ideal vacation if you would prefer. Follow the model.

| Modelo | *Fui al parque de diversiones.* _____ |

1. _____

2. _____

B. Write two sentences telling about people you saw when you were on vacation.

| Modelo | *Vi a mi abuela.* _____ |

1. _____

2. _____

C. Now, complete the letter below to your friend. Use your sentences from Part A and Part B and additional details to tell him or her about your vacation.

Querido(a) _____ :

　　¡Hola! ¿Cómo estás? Gracias por tu carta de la semana pasada. Te voy a contar un

poco de nuestras vacaciones del mes pasado. _____

_____

_____

_____

　　Y cuando fuimos a otro lugar, vimos _____

_____

_____

_____

_____

_____

　　　　　　　　　　　　　　　　　Un abrazo,

　　　　　　　　　　　　　　　　　_____

Antes de ver el video

Actividad 1

There are lots of things you can do to make the world a better place. Under each category, write two things that you would like to do to help.

Cómo ayudar...

en mi comunidad _____

_____

con el ambiente _____

_____

¿Comprendes?

Actividad 2

In the video, the friends talk about how to help in their communities through volunteer work. Circle the letter of the appropriate answer for each question.

1. Gloria y Raúl trabajan como voluntarios en

   a. un centro de ancianos.

   b. Casa Latina.

   c. el Hospital Nacional de Niños.

2. Tomás va al hospital porque

   a. está enfermo.

   b. a él le encanta el trabajo voluntario.

   c. tiene que llevar ropa para los niños.

3. Gloria dice: "Trabajar con los niños en el hospital es

   a. muy aburrido."

   b. una experiencia inolvidable."

   c. un trabajo que no me gusta."

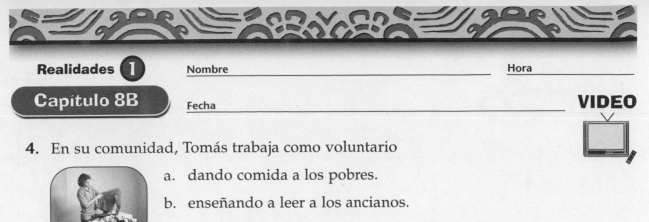

Realidades 1

Capítulo 8B

Nombre _____

Fecha _____

Hora _____

VIDEO

4. En su comunidad, Tomás trabaja como voluntario

    a. dando comida a los pobres.

    b. enseñando a leer a los ancianos.

    c. recogiendo ropa usada para los pobres.

5. Ellos también cuidan el ambiente reciclando

    a. aluminio y periódicos.

    b. papel, plástico y vidrio.

    c. papel, vidrio y aluminio.

Actividad 3

Fill in the blanks from the box below to complete the story.

reciclar	importante	libros	pasado
ancianos	comunidad	voluntarios	difícil
lava	simpáticos	trabajo	

En el Hospital Nacional de Niños, Tomás y Gloria trabajan como (1) _____ .

Allí ellos cantan, leen (2) _____ y juegan con los niños. A veces los niños

están muy enfermos y es (3) _____ , pero los niños son muy

(4) _____ . Raúl trabajó en un centro de (5) _____ el año (6)

_____ . Allí les ayudó con la comida y hablando con ellos.

    Tomás también trabaja en su (7) _____ ; él ayuda a recoger ropa usada.

Después la separa, la (8) _____ y luego la da a la gente pobre del barrio.

Es mucho (9) _____ , pero le gusta.

    Todos ellos ayudan a (10) _____ el papel y las botellas pues, piensan que

reciclar y conservar es muy (11) _____ .

Realidades 1

Capítulo 8B

Nombre _____

Hora _____

Fecha _____

VIDEO

Y, ¿qué más?

Actividad 4

Now that you have seen Tomás, Gloria, and Raúl working in various ways to help others, think about the organizations that make it possible for them to do this work. Imagine that you work with one of the organizations listed below, and write a paragraph about your experiences. Use the model to help you.

el Hospital Nacional de Niños

un centro de ancianos

el club Casa Latina

Modelo	*Me gusta trabajar en el centro de ancianos. Les ayudo con la*

comida y paso tiempo escuchando sus cuentos.

Answers will vary.

_____

_____

_____

_____

_____

_____

Realidades **1**

Capítulo 8B

Nombre _____

Fecha _____

Hora _____

AUDIO

Actividad 5

Listen as Sra. Muñoz, the Spanish Club sponsor, asks several students what they did last weekend. If a student's actions had a positive impact on their community, place a check mark in the corresponding box or boxes. If a student's actions had no positive effect on their community, place an X in the corresponding box or boxes. You will hear each conversation twice.

	Javier	Ana	José	Celi	Pablo	Laura	Sra. Muñoz
enseñar a los niños a leer							
reciclar la basura de las calles							
jugar al fútbol con amigos							
recoger y lavar la ropa usada para la gente pobre							
trabajar en un centro para ancianos							
traer juguetes a los niños que están en el hospital							
trabajar en un restaurante del centro comercial							

Actividad 6

Listen as people talk about what they did last Saturday. Did they do volunteer work in the community or did they earn spending money for themselves? Place a check mark in the correct box on the grid. You will hear each set of statements twice.

	1	2	3	4	5	6	7	8

Realidades 1

Capítulo 8B

Nombre _____

Fecha _____

Hora _____

AUDIO

Actividad 7

Listen as our leaders, friends, and family give advice to teenagers about what we must do to serve our communities. Use the grid below to take notes as you listen. Then, use your notes to complete the sentences below. For example, you might write "**El vicepresidente de los Estados Unidos** *dice que hay que reciclar la basura de las calles.*" In the last sentence, complete a statement about your personal suggestion for others. You will hear each set of statements twice.

¿Quién(es) lo dice(n)?	¿Qué dice(n)?
1. El presidente de los Estados Unidos	
2. Mis padres	
3. Los médicos del hospital	
4. Mis profesores	
5. Mis amigos y yo	

1. El presidente de los Estados Unidos _____

_____.

2. Los padres _____

_____.

3. Los médicos _____

_____.

4. Los profesores _____

_____.

5. Mis amigos _____

_____.

6. Yo

_____

_____.

Communication Workbook

Realidades ①

Capítulo 8B

Nombre _____

Fecha _____

Hora _____

AUDIO

Actividad 8

As you hear each of the following statements, imagine whom the speaker might be addressing. Choose from the list of people, and write the number of the statement on the corresponding blank. You will hear each set of statements twice.

_____ al médico   _____ a sus padres

_____ a la policía   _____ a un niño de cinco años

_____ al camarero   _____ a un voluntario del hospital

_____ a la profesora de español   _____ a una persona que trabaja en el zoológico

Actividad 9

Abuela Consuelo always has her grandchildren over for the holidays. She wants to know what they have done over the past year. They also remind her what she gave them last year as a gift. Use the grid to help keep track of each grandchild's story. You will hear each conversation twice.

	¿Qué hizo el niño el año pasado?	¿Qué le dio la abuela al niño el año pasado?
Marta		
Jorge		
Sara		
Miguel		
Angélica		

Nombre _____

Hora _____

Fecha _____

WRITING

Actividad 10

Answer the following questions in complete sentences.

1. ¿Hay lugares para hacer trabajo voluntario en tu comunidad?

   _____

   ¿Qué hacen allí? _____

   _____

2. ¿Te gustaría trabajar como voluntario en:

   un hospital? ¿Por qué? _____

   _____

   un centro para personas pobres? ¿Por qué? _____

   _____

   un centro para ancianos? ¿Por qué? _____

   _____

3. ¿Tu familia recicla? _____

   ¿Qué reciclan Uds.? _____

   _____

   ¿Por qué es importante reciclar? _____

   _____

   ¿Te gustaría ayudar con el reciclaje en tu comunidad? _____

   _____

Communication Workbook

Realidades 1

Capítulo 8B

Nombre _____

Fecha _____

Hora _____

WRITING

Actividad 11

All of the following people were asked to speak on a subject. You are reporting on what everyone says. Use each item only once. Follow the model.

yo	el trabajo voluntario
nosotros	el campamento de deportes
Sra. Ayala	el reciclaje
Dr. Riviera	el fútbol
tú	el teatro
Paco	la ropa
José y María	la salud
Alicia y yo	los quehaceres

Modelo   *La señora Ayala dice que el trabajo voluntario es una experiencia inolvidable.*

1. _____

2. _____

3. _____

4. _____

5. _____

6. _____

7. _____

Realidades 1

Capítulo 8B

Nombre _____

Fecha _____

Hora _____

WRITING

Actividad 12

You are finding out what everyone's plans are for the weekend. Choose a verb and a direct object pronoun from the banks and write a sentence about weekend plans for each subject given. Use each verb only once. Follow the model.

ayudar	dar	decir	enseñar	escribir
hacer	invitar	leer	llevar	traer

me	te	le	nos	les

Modelo _Miguel y Elena nos invitan a su fiesta._

1. Mis padres _____.

2. Yo _____.

3. Uds. _____.

4. Nuestra profesora de español _____.

5. El presidente _____.

6. Rafael y Gabriel _____.

7. Tu mejor amigo _____.

8. El Sr. Fuentes _____.

9. La Sra. Allende _____.

10. Tú _____.

Realidades 1

Capítulo 8B

Nombre _____

Hora _____

Fecha _____

WRITING

Actividad 13

Last week, your Spanish class did some volunteer work at the local nursing home. Read the thank you letter from the residents, then write a paragraph explaining at least four things that you and your classmates did for them. Remember to use the preterite tense and indirect object pronouns where necessary. Follow the model.

Queridos muchachos:

Les escribimos para decirles "gracias" por su generosa visita de la semana pasada. A la señora Blanco le gustó el libro de poesía que Uds. le regalaron. Todos lo pasamos bien. Nos gustó especialmente la canción "Feliz Navidad" que cantó Luisita. El señor Marcos todavía habla de los pasteles que las chicas le trajeron. Y nuestro jardín está más bonito que nunca, después de todo su trabajo. En fin, mil gracias de parte de todos aquí en Pinos Sombreados. Esperamos verles pronto.

Fuertes abrazos,

Los residentes

Modelo *Nosotros visitamos a los residentes de Pinos Sombreados la semana pasada.*

_____

_____

_____

_____

_____

_____

_____

Realidades ①

Capítulo 9A

Nombre _____

Hora _____

Fecha _____

VIDEO

Antes de ver el video

Actividad 1

In the second column, write the title of a movie or a television program that is associated with the category in the first column. The first one is done for you.

Programa o película	Nombre del programa o película
telenovelas	"Days of Our Lives"
noticias	
programas de entrevistas	
programas de la vida real	
películas de ciencia ficción	
programas de concurso	
programas educativos	
programas de deportes	
comedias	
dibujos animados	
películas románticas	
programas infantiles	

Realidades 1

Capítulo 9A

Nombre _____

Fecha _____

Hora _____

VIDEO

¿Comprendes?

Actividad 2

Look at the pictures and write what type of program each one is. Then, write the name of the character in the video who likes this type of program.

	CATEGORY	CHARACTER'S NAME
1.	_____	_____
2.	_____	_____
3.	_____	_____
4.	_____	_____
5.	_____	_____

Actividad 3

Using complete sentences, answer the following questions about what happens in the video.

1. ¿Quién tiene el mando a distancia primero?

_____

2. ¿Qué piensa Ana de la telenovela "El amor es loco"?

_____

Realidades 1

Capítulo 9A

Nombre _____

Fecha _____

Hora _____

VIDEO

3. ¿A quiénes les encantan las telenovelas?

_____

4. ¿Qué piensa Ignacio de los programas de la vida real?

_____

5. ¿Qué piensa Jorgito de escuchar música en el cuarto de su hermana?

_____

6. ¿Qué deciden hacer los amigos al final?

_____

7. ¿Qué quiere ver Elena en el cine? ¿Están de acuerdo Ignacio y Javier?

_____

Y, ¿qué más?

Actividad 4

What kind of TV programs do you like? What type of movies do you enjoy watching? Explain your preferences. Follow the model.

Modelo

A mí me gustan mucho los programas de concursos; son muy divertidos porque puedes jugarlos en casa con tu familia o amigos. Mi hermano prefiere los deportes; siempre quiere el mando a distancia para ver los juegos. Cuando voy al cine prefiero ver comedias, pues las películas románticas son aburridas.

_____

_____

_____

_____

Actividad 5

Your friend is reading you the television line-up for a local television station. After listening to each program description, fill in on the grid what day or days the program is shown, what time it is shown, and what type of program it is. You will hear each set of statements twice.

	Día(s)	Hora	Clase de programa
"Mi computadora"			
"La detective Morales"			
"Cine en su sofá"			
"Las aventuras del Gato Félix"			
"Cara a cara"			
"Lo mejor del béisbol"			
"Marisol"			
"Festival"			
"Treinta minutos"			
"Las Américas"			

Actividad 6

Listen as people in a video rental store talk about what kind of movie they want to rent. After listening to each conversation, put the letter of the type of film they agree on in the space provided. You will hear each conversation twice.

1. _____   A. una película policíaca

2. _____   B. una comedia

3. _____   C. un drama

4. _____   D. una película de ciencia ficción

5. _____   E. una película romántica

6. _____   F. una película de horror

7. _____   G. una película de dibujos animados

Realidades ❶

Capítulo 9A

Nombre _____

Fecha _____

Hora _____

AUDIO

Actividad 7

Listen to a film critic interviewing five people on opening night of the movie *Marruecos.* After listening to each person's interview, circle the number of stars that closely matches the person's opinion of the movie, from a low rating of one star to a high rating of four. After noting all of the opinions, give the movie an overall rating of one to four stars, and give a reason for your answer. You will hear each conversation twice.

	No le gustó nada	Le gustó más o menos	Le gustó mucho	Le encantó
1.	[★]	[★★]	[★★★]	[★★★★]
2.	[★]	[★★]	[★★★]	[★★★★]
3.	[★]	[★★]	[★★★]	[★★★★]
4.	[★]	[★★]	[★★★]	[★★★★]
5.	[★]	[★★]	[★★★]	[★★★★]

¿Cuántas estrellas para *Marruecos*? ¿Por qué? _____

_____

Actividad 8

Listen as two friends talk on the phone about what they just saw on TV. Do they seem to like the same type of programs? As you listen to their conversation, fill in the Venn diagram, indicating: 1) which programs only Alicia likes; 2) which programs both Alicia and Laura like; and 3) which programs only Laura likes. You will hear this conversation twice.

a Alicia   a ellos   a Laura

Realidades 1

Capítulo 9A

Nombre _____

Hora _____

Fecha _____

AUDIO

Actividad 9

Listen as a television critic reviews some of the new shows of the season. As you listen, determine which shows he likes and dislikes, and why. Fill in the chart. You will hear each paragraph twice.

	Le gusta...	¿Por qué le gusta?	No le gusta...	¿Por qué no le gusta?
1				
2				
3				
4				
5				

Nombre _____

Hora _____

Fecha _____

WRITING

Actividad 10

Answer the following questions about movies and television.

1. ¿Te gusta ir al cine?

_____

2. ¿Prefieres los dramas o las comedias? ¿Por qué? _____

_____

_____

3. ¿Cómo se llama tu película favorita? ¿Qué clase de película es?

_____

_____

4. ¿Te gustan las películas policíacas? ¿Por qué? _____

_____

5. ¿Te gusta más ver le tele o leer? ¿Por qué? _____

_____

_____

6. ¿Qué clase de programas prefieres? ¿Por qué? _____

_____

_____

7. ¿Cuántos canales de televisión puedes ver en casa? _____

¿Cuál es tu canal favorito? _____

¿Por qué? _____

8. ¿Tienes un programa favorito? ¿Cómo se llama? _____

_____

Realidades 1

Capítulo 9A

Nombre _____

Hora _____

Fecha _____

WRITING

Actividad 11

Your school newspaper printed a picture of the preparations for the Cinco de Mayo party at your school. Describe the photo using a form of **acabar de** + infinitive to tell what everyone just finished doing before the picture was taken.

| Modelo | *Horacio Ibáñez acaba de sacar la foto.* |

1. Isabel _____

_____

2. Julia y Ramón _____

_____

3. Yo _____

_____

4. La señora Lemaños _____

_____

5. Ana _____

_____

Realidades ①

Capítulo 9A

Nombre _____

Fecha _____

Hora _____

WRITING

Actividad 12

You and your friends are talking about movies. Tell about people's preferences by choosing a subject from the first column and matching it with words from the other two columns to make complete sentences. Use each subject only once, but words from the other columns can be used more than once. Follow the model.

nosotros	gustar	las películas románticas
mis padres	encantar	las película de horror
mí	aburrir	las películas policíacas
ti	interesar	las comedias
los profesores	disgustar	los dramas
mis amigas		
mi abuelo		

Modelo *A mí me encantan las películas románticas.* _____

1. _____

2. _____

3. _____

4. _____

5. _____

6. _____

Communication Workbook

Realidades 1

Capítulo 9A

Nombre _____

Hora _____

Fecha _____

WRITING

Actividad 13

You are writing your new Spanish-speaking pen pal an e-mail about American television. First tell him about a program that you just saw. What type of show was it? Did you like it? Was it interesting? Then, tell him about two other types of TV shows that are popular in America. Make sure to tell him your opinion of these types of shows, and what some other people you know think about them.

Fecha: 20 de abril

Tema: La televisión

Querido Pancho:

   ¡Hola! ¿Cómo estás? Acabo de terminar de ver el programa _____

_____ . A mí _____

_____

_____

_____

   En los Estados Unidos, la gente ve mucho la tele. _____

_____

_____

_____

_____

Realidades ❶

Capítulo 9B

Nombre _____

Fecha _____

Hora _____

VIDEO

Antes de ver el video

Actividad 1

How do you communicate with your friends from far away? Using the word bank below, write two sentences about how you might stay in touch with long distance friends.

cámara digital	correo electrónico
ordenador / computadora	cibercafé
navegar en la Red	página Web
información	salones de chat
dirección electrónica	foto digital

_____

_____

_____

_____

¿Comprendes?

Actividad 2

Javier is becoming accustomed to living in Spain, but he has a lot to learn about technology. What does Ana teach him? Write **cierto** (*true*) or **falso** (*false*) next to each statement.

1. Javier conoce muy bien las cámaras digitales. _____

2. Él va a enviar una tarjeta a su amigo Esteban. _____

3. Javier le saca una foto de Ana y le gusta la cámara. _____

4. Él piensa que no es muy complicada la cámara digital. _____

5. Ana lo lleva a un cibercafé, para ordenar un café. _____

6. Empiezan a navegar en la Red. _____

7. Ana busca su página Web, pero Javier no la quiere ver. _____

8. No hay mucha información en la Red. _____

Communication Workbook

9. Pueden visitar los salones de chat, pero
   prefieren escribirle un correo electrónico a Esteban. _____

10. Esteban ve la foto digital de su amigo y piensa que está triste. _____

Actividad 3

Complete the sentences below with information from the video.

1. Javier va a enviar _____ a
   su amigo Esteban.

2. Ana saca muchas fotos con su
   _____ .

3. A Javier le gusta la cámara de Ana porque no
   es muy _____ .

4. Ana y Javier van a un _____ para
   escribirle a Esteban por _____ electrónico.

5. Según Ana, el ordenador _____
   para mucho.

6. Javier quiere saber qué tal fue el _____
   de Cristina.

Nombre _____

Hora _____

Fecha _____

VIDEO

Y, ¿qué más?

Actividad 4

You heard Ana and Javier talk about the many ways they use computers. Write a paragraph describing your two favorite ways to use a computer. Use the model to give you an idea of how to start.

 *En mi casa todos usan la computadora. Para mí el uso más importante es...*

_____

_____

_____

_____

_____

_____

_____

Realidades ①

Capítulo 9B

Nombre _____

Fecha _____

Hora _____

AUDIO

Actividad 5

While navigating a new Web site, two friends click on a link to a self-quiz to find out if they are **CiberAdictos.** Based on their discussion of each question, write in the chart below whether you think they answered **sí** or **no**. According to the Web site, a score of more than six **sí** answers determines that you are a **CiberAdicto.** You will hear each set of statements twice.

	1	2	3	4	5	6	7	8	¿Es CiberAdicto?
Rafael									
Miguel									

Actividad 6

Víctor has studied for the first quiz in his beginning technology class. As the teacher reads each statement, he is to answer **falso** or **cierto**. Listen to the statements and write the answers in the boxes, and take the quiz too. Would you be able to score 100%? You will hear each statement twice.

1	2	3	4	5	6	7	8	9	10

Actividad 7

Listen to the following conversations that you overhear while sitting at a table in the Café Mariposa. After listening to what each person is saying, write what they asked for in the first column and what they were served in the second column. You will hear each statement twice.

Persona	Comida pedida	Comida servida
1. Señor Cruz		
2. Señora Vargas		
3. Señor Ávila		
4. Marcelo y Daniele		
5. Señor Urbina		
6. Señora Campos		
7. Señora Suerte		

Realidades 1

Capítulo 9B

Nombre _____

Fecha _____

Hora _____

AUDIO

Actividad 8

Listen as teenagers talk to each other about what they need to learn how to do. The second teenager is always able to suggest someone whom the first teenager should ask for help. Match the person who is suggested to the correct picture. You will hear each set of statements twice.

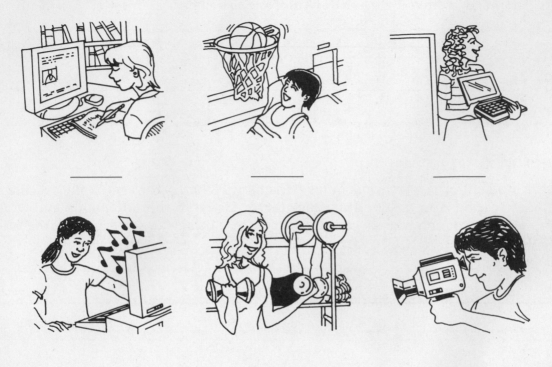

Actividad 9

Listen as two people discuss how the computer and the Internet have changed our lives. As you listen, organize their points into two columns by summarizing what they say. You will hear each set of statements twice.

Antes de la computadora y la Red	Después de la computadora y la Red
1. _____	_____
2. _____	_____
3. _____	_____
4. _____	_____

Realidades 1

Capítulo 9B

Nombre _____

Fecha _____

Hora _____

WRITING

Actividad 10

Read the following ad about a computer of the future. Then, answer the questions below.

> **CEREBRADOR: ¡El futuro ahora!**
>
> ¿Está cansado de ver las computadoras del futuro en una película o de leer sobre ellas en una novela? ¿Quiere el futuro ahora? ¡Pues **Cerebrador** lo tiene!
>
> ◆ La información, los gráficos, la música en la Red...
> *¡todo sin límite!*
>
> ◆ Grabar un disco, escribir un informe, navegar en la Red...
> *¡sólo hay que pensarlo y se logra en poco tiempo!*
>
> ◆ ¿Tiene problemas de conexión o detesta sentarse a usar la computadora?
> *Sólo necesita* **Cerebrador** *y dos metros de espacio para poder ver todo en la pantalla: documentos, correo electrónico, su página Web, etc. Conecte a su propia cabeza.*
>
> Con **Cerebrador** puede sacar fotos con una minicámara digital y crear diapositivas con ellas.
>
> Llame ahora para pedir este fenómeno.

1. ¿Cómo se llama la computadora del anuncio?

_____

2. ¿Qué dice el anuncio que Ud. puede hacer con esta computadora?

_____

_____

_____

3. ¿Qué necesita para usar una computadora? ¿Es una computadora portátil?

_____

_____

_____

4. ¿Cree Ud. que es posible comprar una computadora como ésta? ¿Por qué?

_____

_____

_____

_____

Realidades ①

Capítulo 9B

Nombre _____ Hora _____

Fecha _____

WRITING

Actividad 11

Your favorite restaurant has great food, but the wait staff is always messing up the orders. Using the pictures as clues and the correct forms of the verbs **pedir** and **servir**, write what happens when the following people order their meals. Follow the model and remember to use the proper indirect object pronouns in your sentences.

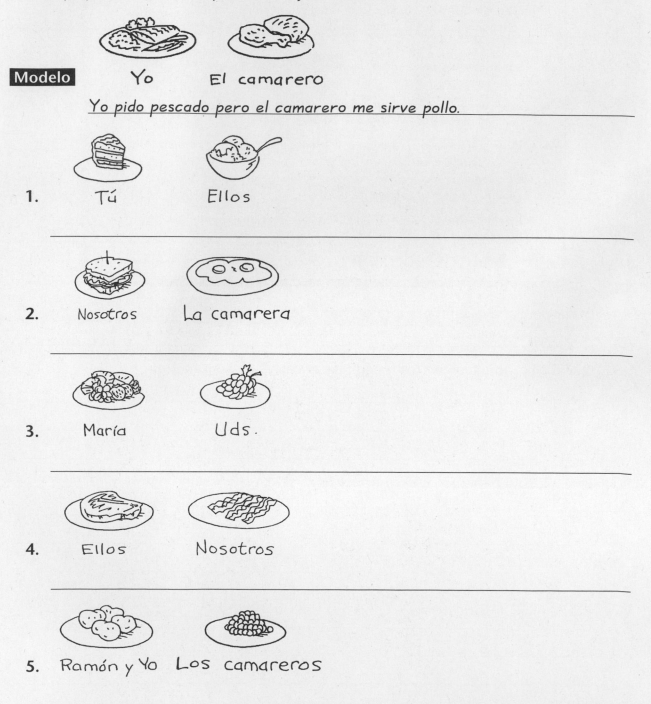

Modelo Yo   El camarero

Yo pido pescado pero el camarero me sirve pollo.

1. Tú   Ellos

_____

2. Nosotros   La camarera

_____

3. María   Uds.

_____

4. Ellos   Nosotros

_____

5. Ramón y Yo   Los camareros

_____

Realidades 1

Capítulo 9B

Nombre _____

Hora _____

Fecha _____

WRITING

Actividad 12

Answer the following questions in 2–3 complete sentences using the verbs **saber** and/or **conocer**.

1. ¿Eres talentoso(a)? ¿Qué sabes hacer? ¿Tienes unos amigos muy talentosos? ¿Qué saben hacer ellos?

_____

_____

_____

2. ¿Conoces a alguna persona famosa? ¿Quién? ¿Cómo es? ¿Alguien más en tu familia conoce a una persona famosa?

_____

_____

_____

3. ¿Qué ciudades o países conocen tú y tu familia? ¿Cuándo los visitaste? ¿Qué lugares conocen tus amigos?

_____

_____

_____

4. ¿Qué sabes de la geografía de Latinoamérica? (¿Sabes cuál es la capital de Uruguay? ¿Sabes cuántos países hay en Sudamérica?)

_____

_____

_____

Realidades ❶

Capítulo 9B

Nombre _____

Fecha _____

Hora _____

WRITING

Actividad 13

Describe the **cibercafé** below. First, tell three things that you can do there. Next, tell three items that they serve at the café, using the verb **servir** and the food items in the picture. Finally, tell what you can do if you need assistance at the **cibercafé.** Use the verb **pedir**, and the verbs **saber** and **conocer** to discuss how knowledgeable the staff is (**Ellos saben ayudar.../ Ellos conocen bien la Red...**).

Ud. puede _____

_____

_____

_____

Allí ellos _____

_____

_____

_____

_____

_____

_____

_____

_____

Song Lyrics

Track 01

ALEGRE VENGO

Alegre vengo de la montaña
De mi cabaña que alegre está
A mis amigos les traigo flores
De las mejores de mi rosal
A mis amigos les traigo flores
De las mejores de mi rosal

Ábreme la puerta
Ábreme la puerta
Que estoy en la calle
Y dirá la gente
Que esto es un desaire
Y dirá la gente
Que esto es un desaire

A la sarandela, a la sarandela
A la sarandela, de mi corazón
A la sarandela, a la sarandela
A la sarandela, de mi corazón

Allá dentro veo, allá dentro veo
Un bulto tapado
No sé si será un lechón asado
No sé si será un lechón asado
A la sarandela…

Track 02

LA MARIPOSA

La la la la laila laila laila
Bum bum bum bum bum

La la la la laila laila laila
Bum bum pata pata bum

Vamos todos a cantar,
vamos todos a bailar
la morenada.

Vamos todos a cantar,
vamos todos a bailar
la morenada.

Con los tacos,
con las manos.
¡Viva la fiesta!

Con los tacos,
con las manos.
¡Viva la fiesta!

Track 03

ERES TÚ

Como una promesa eres tú, eres tú
como una mañana de verano;
como una sonrisa eres tú, eres tú;
así, así eres tú.

Toda mi esperanza eres tú, eres tú,
como lluvia fresca en mis manos;
como fuerte brisa eres tú, eres tú;
así, así eres tú.

[estribillo]
Eres tú como el agua de mi fuente;
eres tú el fuego de mi hogar.
Eres tú como el fuego de mi hoguera;
eres tú el trigo de mi pan.

Como mi poema eres tú, eres tú;
como una guitarra en la noche.
Todo mi horizonte eres tú, eres tú;
así, así eres tú.

Eres tú como el agua de mi fuente,
eres tú el fuego de mi hogar.
Algo así eres tú;
algo así como el fuego de mi
hoguera.
Algo así eres tú;
En mi vida algo así eres tú.

Eres tú como el fuego de mi hoguera;
eres tú el trigo de mi pan.
Algo así eres tú;
algo así como el fuego de mi
hoguera.
Algo así eres tú…

Track 04

LA CUCARACHA

[estribillo]
La cucaracha, la cucaracha,
ya no quiere caminar,
porque no tiene, porque le falta
dinero para gastar.

La cucaracha, la cucaracha,
ya no quiere caminar,
porque no tiene, porque le falta
dinero para gastar.

Una cucaracha pinta
le dijo a una colorada:
Vámonos para mi tierra
a pasar la temporada.

Una cucaracha pinta
le dijo a una colorada:
Vámonos para mi tierra
a pasar la temporada.

La cucaracha, la cucaracha,
ya no quiere caminar,
porque no tiene, porque le falta
dinero para gastar.

Todas las muchachas tienen
en los ojos dos estrellas,
pero las mexicanitas
de seguro son más bellas.

Todas las muchachas tienen
en los ojos dos estrellas,
pero las mexicanitas
de seguro son más bellas.

La cucaracha, la cucaracha,
ya no quiere caminar,
porque no tiene, porque le falta
dinero para gastar.

Una cosa me da risa,
Pancho Villa sin camisa,
ya se van los carrancistas,
porque vienen los villistas.

Una cosa me da risa,
Pancho Villa sin camisa,
ya se van los carrancistas,
porque vienen los villistas.

La cucaracha, la cucaracha,
ya no quiere caminar,
porque no tiene, porque le falta
dinero para gastar.

Track 05

EL CÓNDOR PASA

Al cóndor de los Andes despertó
una luz,
una luz,
de un bello amanecer, amanecer.

Sus alas en lo alto extendió
y bajó,
y bajó,
al dulce manantial, para beber.

La nieve de las cumbres brilla ya
bajo el sol, el día y la luz.
La nieve de las cumbres brilla ya
bajo el sol, el día y la luz,
del bello amanecer, amanecer.

Al cóndor de los Andes despertó
una luz,
una luz,
de un bello amanecer, amanecer.

Sus alas en lo alto extendió
y bajó,
y bajó,
al dulce manantial, para beber.

La nieve de las cumbres brilla ya
bajo el sol, el día y la luz.
La nieve de las cumbres brilla ya
bajo el sol, el día y la luz,
del bello amanecer, amanecer.

Track 06

ASÓMATE AL BALCÓN

Asómate al balcón para que veas
mi parranda
Asómate al balcón para que veas quien
te canta
Asómate al balcón para que veas tus amigos
Asómate al balcón
Formemos un vacilón

Asómate, asómate, asómate, asómate

Yo sé que quieres dormir
Pero así es la Navidad
Y si tú no te levantas
Te sacamos de la cama
Aunque tengas que pelear

Asómate al balcón para (se repite)

¡Asómate, asómate, asómate, asómate!

Track 07

LA BAMBA

Para bailar la bamba, para bailar la
bamba
se necesita una poca de gracia,
una poca de gracia y otra cosita
y arriba y arriba,
y arriba y arriba y arriba iré,
yo no soy marinero, yo no soy
marinero,
por ti seré, por ti seré, por ti seré.

Bamba, bamba...

Una vez que te dije, una vez que te
dije
que eras bonita, se te puso la cara,
se te puso la cara coloradita
y arriba y arriba,
y arriba y arriba y arriba iré,
yo no soy marinero, yo no soy
marinero,
soy capitán, soy capitán, soy
capitán.

Bamba, bamba...

Para subir al cielo, para subir al
cielo
se necesita una escalera grande,
una escalera grande y otra chiquita
y arriba y arriba,
y arriba y arriba y arriba iré,
yo no soy marinero, yo no soy
marinero,
por ti seré, por ti seré, por ti seré.

Bamba, bamba...

Nombre _____ Hora _____

Fecha _____

Track 08

HIMNO DEL ATHLETIC DE BILBAO

Tiene Bilbao un gran tesoro
que adora y mima con gran pasión.
Su club de fútbol
de bella historia,
lleno de gloria,
mil veces campeón.

Athletic, Athletic club
de limpia tradición,
ninguno más que tú
lleva mejor blasón.

Del fútbol eres rey,
te llaman el león
y la afición el rey
del fútbol español.

Cantemos pues los bilbainitos,
a nuestro club con gran amor,
para animarle con nuestro himno,
el canto digno del Alirón.

¡Alirón! ¡Alirón!
el Athletic es campeón.

Track 9

PARA ROMPER LA PIÑATA

Echen confites y canelones
pa' los muchachos
que son comilones.
Castaña asada, piña cubierta,
pa' los muchachos que van a la puerta.

Ándale, Lola,
no te dilates
con la canasta
de los cacahuates.

En esta posada
nos hemos chasqueado,
porque la dueña
nada nos ha dado.

Track 10

PIÑATA

Dale, dale, dale,
no pierdas el tino,
porque si lo pierdes
pierdes el camino.

Track 11

LAS MAÑANITAS

Éstas son las mañanitas
que cantaba el Rey David,
pero no eran tan bonitas
como las cantan aquí.

[estribillo]
Despierta, mi bien, despierta,
mira que ya amaneció,
ya los pajarillos cantan,
la Luna ya se metió.

Despierta, mi bien, despierta,
mira que ya amaneció,
ya los pajarillos cantan,
la Luna ya se metió.

Si el sereno de la esquina
me quisiera hacer favor,
de apagar su linternita
mientras que pasa mi amor.

[estribillo]
Despierta, mi bien, despierta,
mira que ya amaneció,
ya los pajarillos cantan,
la Luna ya se metió.

Despierta, mi bien, despierta,
mira que ya amaneció,
ya los pajarillos cantan,
la Luna ya se metió.

Track 12

DE COLORES

De colores, de colores se visten los campos en la primavera.
De colores, de colores son los pajaritos que vienen de afuera.
De colores, de colores es el arco iris que vemos salir.
Y por eso los grandes amores de muchos colores me gustan a mí.
Y por eso los grandes amores de muchos colores me gustan a mí.

De colores, de colores brillantes y finos se viste la aurora.
De colores, de colores son los mil reflejos que el sol atesora.
De colores, de colores se viste el diamante que vemos lucir.
Y por eso los grandes amores de muchos colores me gustan a mí.
Y por eso los grandes amores de muchos colores me gustan a mí.

Track 13

MÉXICO LINDO Y QUERIDO

Voz de la guitarra mía,
al despertar la mañana,
quiere cantar su alegría
a mi tierra mexicana.

Yo le canto a tus volcanes,
a tus praderas y flores
que son como talismanes
del amor de mis amores.

México lindo y querido
si muero lejos de ti
que digan que estoy dormido
y que me traigan aquí.

México lindo y querido
si muero lejos de ti
que digan que estoy dormido
y que me traigan aquí.

Voz de la guitarra mía,
al despertar la mañana,
quiere cantar su alegría
a mi tierra mexicana.

Yo le canto a tus volcanes,
a tus praderas y flores
que son como talismanes
del amor de mis amores.

México lindo y querido
si muero lejos de ti
que digan que estoy dormido
y que me traigan aquí.

México lindo y querido
si muero lejos de ti
que digan que estoy dormido
y que me traigan aquí.

Track 14

MI CAFETAL

Porque la gente vive criticándome
paso la vida sin pensar en ná.

Porque la gente vive criticándome
paso la vida sin pensar en ná.

Pero no sabiendo que yo soy el hombre
que tengo un hermoso y lindo cafetal.

Pero no sabiendo que yo soy el hombre
que tengo un hermoso y lindo cafetal.

Yo tengo mi cafetal
y tú ya no tienes ná...

Yo tengo mi cafetal
y tú ya no tienes ná...

Colombia mi tierra bonita

Nada me importa que la gente diga
que no tengo plata que no tengo ná.

Nada me importa que la gente diga
que no tengo plata que no tengo ná.

Pero no sabiendo que yo soy el hombre
que tengo un hermoso y lindo cafetal.

Pero no sabiendo que yo soy el hombre
que tengo un hermoso y lindo cafetal.

Yo tengo mi cafetal
y tú ya no tienes ná...

Yo tengo mi cafetal
y tú ya no tienes ná...

Track 15

MARÍA ISABEL

La playa estaba desierta,
el mar bañaba tu piel,
cantando con mi guitarra
para ti, María Isabel.

La playa estaba desierta,
el mar bañaba tu piel,
cantando con mi guitarra
para ti, María Isabel.

[estribillo]
Toma tu sombrero y póntelo,
vamos a la playa, calienta el sol.

Toma tu sombrero y póntelo,
vamos a la playa, calienta el sol.

Chiri biri bi, poro, pom, pom.
Chiri biri bi, poro, pom, pom.
Chiri biri bi, poro, pom, pom.
Chiri biri bi, poro, pom, pom.

En la arena escribí tu nombre
y luego yo lo borré
para que nadie pisara
tu nombre: María Isabel.

En la arena escribí tu nombre
y luego yo lo borré
para que nadie pisara
tu nombre: María Isabel.

[estribillo]
Toma tu sombrero y póntelo,
vamos a la playa, calienta el sol.

Toma tu sombrero y póntelo,
vamos a la playa, calienta el sol.

Chiri biri bi, poro, pom, pom.
Chiri biri bi, poro, pom, pom.
Chiri biri bi, poro, pom, pom.
Chiri biri bi, poro, pom, pom.

La Luna fue caminando,
bajo las olas del mar;
tenía celos de tus ojos
y tu forma de mirar.

La Luna fue caminando,
bajo las olas del mar;
tenía celos de tus ojos
y tu forma de mirar.

[estribillo]
Toma tu sombrero y póntelo,
vamos a la playa, calienta el sol.

Toma tu sombrero y póntelo,
vamos a la playa, calienta el sol.

Chiri biri bi, poro, pom, pom.
Chiri biri bi, poro, pom, pom.
Chiri biri bi, poro, pom, pom.
Chiri biri bi, poro, pom, pom.

Track 16

LA GOLONDRINA

¿Adónde irá veloz y fatigada,
la golondrina que de aquí se irá?
Allí en el cielo se mirará angustiada,
sin paz ni abrigo que dio mi amor.

Junto a mi pecho allí hará su nido,
en donde pueda la estación pasar.
También yo estoy en la región perdida
haciendo salto y sin poder volar.

También yo estoy en la región perdida
haciendo salto y sin poder volar.

Junto a mi pecho allí hará su nido,
en donde pueda la estación pasar.
También yo estoy en la región perdida
haciendo salto y sin poder volar.

Track 17

¡VIVA JUJUY!

Vamos con ese bailecito

Adentrito cholo

¡Viva Jujuy!
¡Viva la Puna!
¡Viva mi amada!
¡Vivan los cerros
pintarrajeados
de mi quebrada...!

¡Viva Jujuy!
¡Viva la Puna!
¡Viva mi amada!
¡Vivan los cerros
pintarrajeados
de mi quebrada...!

De mi quebrada
humahuaqueña...

No te separes
de mis amores,
¡tú eres mi dueña!

La, lara, rara, rara

No te separes
de mis amores,
¡tú eres mi dueña!

Dos, dos y se va la otrita

Adentro

Viva Jujuy
y la hermosura
de las jujeñas!
Vivan las trenzas
bien renegridas
de mi morena!

Viva Jujuy
y la hermosura
de las jujeñas!
Vivan las trenzas
bien renegridas
de mi morena!

De mi morena
mal pagadora

No te separes
de mis amores
¡tú eres mi dueña!

La, lara, rara, rara

No te separes
de mis amores
¡tú eres mi dueña!

Track 18

ADIÓS MUCHACHOS

Adiós muchachos, compañeros de mi vida,
barra querida de aquellos tiempos.
Me toca a mí hoy emprender la retirada,
debo alejarme de mi buena muchachada.

Adiós, muchachos,
ya me voy y me resigno,
contra el destino nadie la talla.
Se terminaron para mí todas las farras.
Mi cuerpo enfermo no resiste más.

Dos lágrimas sinceras
derramo en mi partida
por la barra querida
que nunca me olvidó.
Y al darle a mis amigos
mi adiós postrero
les doy con toda el alma
mi bendición.

Adiós muchachos, compañeros de mi vida,
barra querida de aquellos tiempos.
Me toca a mí hoy emprender la retirada,
debo alejarme de mi buena muchachada.

Adiós, muchachos,
ya me voy y me resigno,
contra el destino nadie la talla.
Se terminaron para mí todas las farras.
Mi cuerpo enfermo no resiste más.

Notes

Notes

Notes

Notes

Notes

Notes

Test Preparation

Table of Contents

Tema 5: Fiesta en familia

Tema 6: La casa

Tema 7: De compras

Tema 8: Experiencias

Tema 9: Medios de comunicación

Communication Workbook

To the Student

Did you know that becoming a better reader in Spanish can improve your scores on standardized reading tests in English? Research has shown that the skills you develop by reading in a second language are transferred to reading in your first language. Research also shows that the more you practice for standardized tests and work on test-taking strategies, the more your scores will improve. The goal of this book is to help you improve your test-taking strategies and to provide extra practice with readings in both Spanish and English.

Getting to Know the Test

The practice tests in this book offer a variety of readings to reflect the types of passages you might expect to find on a standardized test. They also provide practice for three different types of questions you are apt to encounter on such a test: multiple choice, Short Response, and Extended Response.

Multiple Choice Multiple choice questions always have four answer choices. Pick the one that is the best answer. A correct answer is worth 1 point.

Short Response This symbol appears next to questions requiring short written answers:

This symbol appears next to questions requiring short written answers that are a creative extension based on the reading:

Take approximately 3 to 5 minutes to answer a Short Response question. Read all parts of the question carefully, plan your answer, then write the answer in your own words. A complete answer to a Short Response question is worth 2 points. A partial answer is worth 1 or 0 points.

NOTE: If a Short Response question is written in English, write your answer in English, unless the instructions tell you to do otherwise. If it is written in Spanish, write your answer in Spanish.

Extended Response This symbol appears next to questions requiring longer written answers based on information that can be inferred from the reading:

This symbol appears next to questions requiring longer written answers that are a creative extension based on the reading:

```
READ
THINK
CREATE
```

Take approximately 5 to 15 minutes to answer an Extended Response question. A complete answer is worth 4 points. A partial answer is worth 3, 2, 1, or 0 points.

NOTE: If an Extended Response question is written in English, write your answer in English. If it is written in Spanish, write your answer in Spanish.

Taking These Practice Tests

Your teacher will assign a test for classwork or homework, or you might be taking these tests on your own. Each reading is followed by questions, and the Practice Test Answer Sheet immediately follows the questions. For multiple choice questions, you should bubble-in the response. For Short and Extended Response questions, write your answers on the lines provided.

Tips for Improving Your Score

Know the Rules

Learn the rules for any test you take. For example, depending on how a test is scored, it may or may not be advisable to guess if you are not sure of the correct answer. Find that out before you begin the exam. Be sure you understand:

- how much time is allowed for the test
- the types of questions that will be asked
- how the questions should be answered
- how they will be scored

Know Yourself and Make a Plan

Ask yourself: "How will I prepare for the test?" First, ask your teacher to help you list your strengths and weaknesses on tests. Then make a detailed plan for practicing or reviewing. Give yourself plenty of time to prepare. Don't leave everything until the night before. Set aside blocks of uninterrupted time for studying, with short breaks at regular intervals.

Before the Test

Do something relaxing the night before. Then get a good night's sleep, and be sure to eat a nutritious meal before the test. Wear comfortable clothing. If possible, wear a watch or sit where you can see a clock. Make sure you have all the materials you will need. Find out in advance if you will need a certain type of pencil, for example, and bring several with you—already sharpened. Be sure you know where the test is being given and at what time. Plan to arrive early.

Know What You Are Being Asked

There are two basic types of test questions: objective, one-right-answer questions and essay questions. It is essential that you read <u>all</u> questions carefully. Ask yourself, "What are they asking me?" The purpose of a standardized reading test is to determine:
*   how well you understand what you read
*   how well you are able to use the critical thinking and problem-solving skills that are so critical for success in today's world

Here is a list of basic reading skills:
*   Understanding major ideas, details, and organization
*   Drawing conclusions
*   Understanding cause and effect
*   Comparing and contrasting
*   Finding, interpreting, and organizing information
*   Understanding author's purpose and/or viewpoint
*   Understanding character and plot development

Always read the questions <u>before</u> you read the passage. This will help you focus on the task. If it is allowed, ask your teacher to explain any directions you do not understand.

Watch Your Time

Allot a specific amount of time per question—approximately 1 minute for multiple choice, 3 to 5 minutes for Short Response, and 5 to 15 minutes for Extended Response. Do not spend too much time on any one question, and monitor your time so that you will be able to complete the test.

Show What You Know, Relax, and Think Positively

Answer those questions that you are sure about first. If a question seems too difficult, skip it and return to it later. Remember that while some questions may seem hard, others will be easy. You may never learn to love taking tests, but you can control the situation and make sure that you reach your full potential for success.

Above all, relax. It's natural to be nervous, but think positively. Just do your best.

Multiple Choice Questions: Helpful Hints

Multiple choice questions have only one right answer. There is no "creative" response, only a correct one. This book provides extensive practice for the types of multiple choice items that you might find on a standardized reading test. There are four answer choices (A, B, C, D or F, G, H, J) per question. Allot approximately 1 minute to answer a multiple choice question. Answers are worth 1 point each.

- Read the question carefully.
- Try to identify the answer <u>before</u> you examine the choices.
- Eliminate obviously incorrect choices by lightly crossing them out.
- Try to narrow the choices down to two.
- Depending on how a test is to be scored, you may or may not want to guess (for these practice tests, check that you will **not** be penalized for guessing wrong).

Short and Extended Response: Helpful Hints

The dreaded essay question will probably not be as difficult as expected if you follow these strategies:

- Read the question <u>before</u> reading the passage.
- Re-read the question as you prepare to respond: Are you being asked to list, describe, explain, discuss, persuade, or compare and contrast? These are very different things.
- Look back at the passage as often as necessary to answer the question correctly. Underline any key sections that you think might be important to your response.
- Use the margins next to the passage to jot down thoughts and ideas and to prepare a brief outline of what you will include in your answer. Use a clear, direct introduction that answers the specific question being asked. As a start, try turning the question into a statement. Include both general ideas and specific details from the reading in your answer.

- Review your response to make sure you have expressed your thoughts well. Is your introduction clear? Have you stated the general idea(s)? Have you included supporting details?
- If your response is in Spanish, check for grammar errors (subject-verb agreement, adjective agreement, correct verb endings and tenses). In either language, proofread your answer for correct spelling.

How the Test Will Be Scored

It is important to know in advance how responses will be scored. This will lower your anxiety level and help you focus. For the purpose of these practice tests, you can assume the following:

Multiple Choice Questions
Multiple choice answers are either right or wrong. You will receive credit and 1 point if you select the correct answer.

Performance-Based Questions (Short and Extended Response)
Short and Extended Response questions are called "performance tasks." They are often scored with rubrics, which describe a range of performance. You will receive credit for how close your answers come to the desired response. The performance tasks on these practice tests will require thoughtful answers. You must:
- <u>Read</u> the passage
- <u>Think</u> about the question as it relates to the passage, and
- <u>Explain</u> your answer by citing general ideas and specific details from the passage

or:
- <u>Create</u> a written document (a letter, for example) that clearly uses or models information provided in the reading passage

Rubric for Short Response Questions

2 points   The response indicates that the student has a complete understanding of the reading concept embodied in the task. The student has provided a response that is accurate, complete, and fulfills all the requirements of the task. Necessary support and/or examples are included, and the information given is clearly text-based. Any extensions beyond the text are relevant to the task.

1 point   The response indicates that the student has a partial understanding of the reading concept embodied in the task. The student has provided a response that may include information that is essentially correct and text-based, but the information is too general or too simplistic. Some of the support and/or examples may be incomplete or omitted.

0 points   The response is inaccurate, confused, and/or irrelevant, or the student has failed to respond to the task.

Rubric for Extended Response Questions

4 points   The response indicates that the student has a thorough understanding of the reading concept embodied in the task. The student has provided a response that is accurate, complete, and fulfills all the requirements of the task. Necessary support and/or examples are included, and the information given is clearly text-based. Any extensions beyond the text are relevant to the task.

3 points   The response indicates that the student has an understanding of the reading concept embodied in the task. The student has provided a response that is accurate and fulfills all the requirements of the task, but the required support and/or details are not complete or clearly text-based.

2 points   The response indicates that the student has a partial understanding of the reading concept embodied in the task. The student has provided a response that may include information that is essentially correct and text-based, but the information is too general or too simplistic. Some of the support and/or examples and requirements of the task may be incomplete or omitted.

1 point   The response indicates that the student has very limited understanding of the reading concept embodied in the task. The response is incomplete, may exhibit many flaws, and may not address all requirements of the task.

0 points   The response is inaccurate, confused, and/or irrelevant, or the student has failed to respond to the task.

Getting Started

So let's get started. If there was anything in this Introduction that you did not understand, ask your teacher about it. Glance once again at the Helpful Hints before taking the first test. In fact, it will be helpful if you review those hints each time you take one of these tests. And remember: The more you practice, the higher your scores will be.

¡Buena suerte!

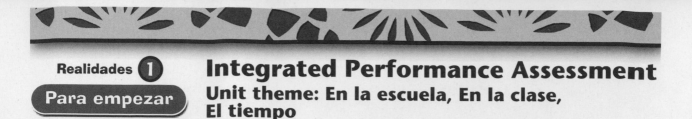

Integrated Performance Assessment
Unit theme: En la escuela, En la clase, El tiempo

Context for the Integrated Performance Assessment: Your Spanish teacher wants you to know why Spanish is an important and useful language to learn.

Interpretive Task: Watch the video "Why Study Spanish?" found on *Realidades 1, DVD 1, Capítulo 1A.* Make a list of professions where knowing Spanish has been an asset.

Interpersonal Task: Discuss the professions you learned about on the video with two other students. Brainstorm other careers or situations in which Spanish could also be an asset.

Presentational Task: Present your ideas to the class as a whole. Have a fellow student or the teacher note all the possible uses on the board so that the students can copy the complete list and keep it in their notebooks for future reference.

Interpersonal Task Rubric

	Score: 1 Does not meet expectations	Score: 3 Meets expectations	Score: 5 Exceeds expectations
Content Comprehension	Student includes few of the professions mentioned in the video and brainstorms no additional careers and situations.	Student includes some of the professions mentioned in the video and brainstorms some additional careers and situations.	Student includes all of the professions mentioned in the video and brainstorms many additional careers and situations.
Group Participation	Student participates poorly with the group.	Student participates well with the group.	Student participates very well with the group.

Presentational Task Rubric

	Score: 1 Does not meet expectations	Score: 3 Meets expectations	Score: 5 Exceeds expectations
Amount of Communication	Student gives limited or no details or examples.	Student gives adequate details or examples.	Student gives consistent details or examples.
Comprehensibility	Student's ideas lack clarity and are difficult to understand.	Student's ideas are adequately clear and fairly well understood.	Student's ideas are precise and easily understood.

Capítulo 1A   **Reading Skills: Conexiones, p. 35**

Determining the Main Idea

To determine the main idea of a reading passage, you must be able to describe what the passage is mainly about and summarize it in one sentence. A common problem for students when working with this skill is confusing an important detail in the reading passage with the main idea. Just because something is mentioned in the reading passage does not mean it is the main idea of the passage. In fact, many times the main idea is not even stated in the reading passage. This is called an implied main idea. Regardless of whether the main idea is stated or implied, the basic question remains the same: "What is this reading passage about?"

Tip

Readers are more likely to understand a reading passage when it deals with a topic with which you are already familiar. This familiarity with a topic is known as the reader's prior knowledge. Activating your prior knowledge before reading is one way to improve your understanding of a reading passage. One popular method of activating your prior knowledge is completing a K-W-L chart.

1. Before reading the **Conexiones**, *"El baile y la música del mundo hispano"* on page 35 in your textbook, complete the K and W portions of the chart. After you have written your responses, share them with a classmate. Then read *"El baile y la música del mundo hispano."* After reading, complete the L portion of the chart.

K What I Already **K**now	**W** What I **W**ant to Know	**L** What I **L**earned from Reading
List 3 things you already know about the topic "El baile y la música del mundo hispano."	*List 3 things that you would like to know about the topic "El baile y la música del mundo hispano."*	*List 2 important details that you learned from your reading. State in 1 sentence what the reading passage "El baile y la música del mundo hispano" is about.*
1. _____ 2. _____ 3. _____	1. _____ 2. _____ 3. _____	1. _____ 2. _____ 3. This passage was mostly about _____

Sample question:

2. What is the main idea of the passage *"El baile y la música del mundo hispano"*?
   A Salsa is the most popular dance in Puerto Rico.
   B Percussion is very important in the music and dance of the Spanish-speaking world.
   C The countries of the Spanish-speaking world have distinct musical styles and traditions.
   D The dances and rhythms of the Spanish-speaking world are not well known in the USA.

Strategies to Analyze Words: Context and Word Structure Clues

It is impossible to know the meaning of every word in a language. Good readers develop strategies to determine the meanings of unknown words as they read without having to look them up in the dictionary. Good readers also know that their guesses may be wrong. They then use more traditional methods of finding the word's meaning: looking it up in the dictionary or asking for assistance.

Both Spanish and English inherited many words from Latin. If you have knowledge of Latin root words, prefixes, and suffixes, you can often make educated guesses about the meaning of words that contain them. Let's take a look at the Latin root words *manus* and *ped* and how they still have meaning for speakers of English and Spanish.

Latin root	English meaning	Spanish meaning	Related words in English and Spanish
manus	hand	*mano*	manual labor/*trabajo manual* = work done by hand
ped	foot	*pie*	pedestrian/*peatón* = someone who travels on foot

Words such as "manual" that look alike and have similar meanings are called cognates.

Tip

Just because a word in Spanish looks like a word in English, the two words are not always cognates. One famous mistake for beginning Spanish students is to try to communicate "I am embarrassed" by saying, *"Yo estoy embarazada,"* which means, "I am pregnant" in Spanish! Similarly, an English speaker who assumes that every word in English that contains *ped* relates in some way to feet would be mistaken. A pediatrician is not a foot doctor, but a doctor for children.

When making an educated guess about an unusual word, good readers will always test their guess in context. In other words, you will insert your guessed meaning into the actual sentence where you found the unusual word.

1. On page 41 of your textbook, re-read the note written by Pablo. He says, *"No me gusta ni jugar videojuegos ni ver la tele."* If you know that the word *ver* means "to see" or "to watch" in English, what is the most likely meaning of *"la tele"*?
   a. the telephone   **b.** the telegraph   **c.** the television   **d.** the teller

Sample question:

2. The Latin prefix *bi-* relates to the number "two" in English. In which of the following sentences does the word containing the letters *b-i-* actually have a meaning relating to the number "two"? (Remember to use context clues.)
   A I was tired of living in a small apartment so I decided to move into something <u>bigger</u>.
   B The <u>bison</u> was one of the largest mammals to live on the North American continent.
   C Now that I can speak Spanish and English, I am <u>bilingual</u>.
   D <u>Biology</u> was my favorite subject in school.

Integrated Performance Assessment
Unit theme: ¿Qué te gusta hacer?

Context for the Integrated Performance Assessment: Since it is early in the school year, you want to learn a little about your classmates.

Interpretive Task: Watch the *Videohistoria: ¿Qué te gusta hacer?* from *Realidades 1, DVD 1, Capítulo 1A.* As you watch, write down 2 activities from the video that you like to do.

Interpersonal Task: Work with a partner and tell him/her the 2 activities you like to do. Ask your partner if he/she likes to do other activities until each of you has 5 different activities on your list.

Presentational Task: Introduce yourself to your classmates and tell them 5 activities you like to do.

Interpersonal Task Rubric

	Score: 1 Does not meet expectations	Score: 3 Meets expectations	Score: 5 Exceeds expectations
Language Use	Student uses little or no target language and relies heavily on native language word order.	Student uses the target language consistently, but may mix native and target language word order.	Student uses the target language exclusively and integrates target language word order into conversation.
Vocabulary Use	Student uses limited and repetitive language.	Student uses only recently acquired vocabulary.	Student uses both recently and previously acquired vocabulary.

Presentational Task Rubric

	Score: 1 Does not meet expectations	Score: 3 Meets expectations	Score: 5 Exceeds expectations
Amount of Communication	Student names fewer than five activities that he/she likes to do.	Student names five activities that he/she likes to do.	Student names more than than five activities that he/she likes to do.
Accuracy	Student's accuracy with vocabulary and structures is limited.	Student's accuracy with vocabulary and structures is adequate.	Student's accuracy with vocabulary and structures is exemplary.
Comprehensibility	Student's ideas lack clarity and are difficult to understand.	Student's ideas are adequately clear and fairly well understood.	Student's ideas are precise and easily understood.
Vocabulary Use	Student uses limited and repetitive vocabulary.	Student uses only recently acquired vocabulary.	Student uses both recently and previously acquired vocabulary.

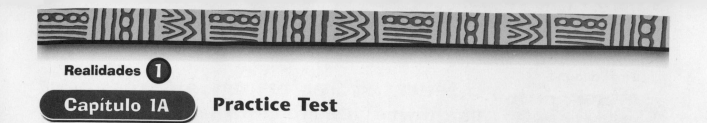

Friendship Among Latin Americans

1 Adriana and Ricardo are teenagers who immigrated to Florida from the Dominican Republic and Mexico. Adriana comes from Santo Domingo, the capital of the Dominican Republic, and Ricardo from Saltillo, Mexico. They have become friends in part because they share a sense of humor and a great love of soccer, a sport they both played in their home countries.

2 For most young Latin Americans, two very strong influences in their lives are family and a close-knit group of friends. Adriana and Ricardo have friends from a number of Spanish-speaking countries, including Guatemala, Colombia, and El Salvador. In the group are several sets of brothers and sisters, and, as is common in Latin America, they all do things together. For example, Adriana (age 14) and her sister Elena (age 12) are very close and share their social lives as well as their family life.

3 Close friendships are sometimes marked by *apodos*, or nicknames, that imply a special relationship. In Mexico, for example, *primo* and *prima* ("cousin") or *hermano* and *hermana* ("brother," "sister") are commonly used. At school, Ricardo often greets Adriana in the halls with "*¡Oye, prima!*"

4 These friends spend free time at each other's homes and they all know each other's families. Close friends are often included in family events and celebrations. Parties that Adriana, Ricardo, and their friends attend may include several generations, from babies to grandparents.

5 Young people, however, must show respect to adults and are taught to treat their parents' friends courteously. They must address them with *usted*. In certain regions of some countries, such as Mexico, Nicaragua, and Colombia, small children may even address their parents with *usted*. In these cases, a young child is also addressed with *usted* as he or she is learning to speak. The difference between *usted* and *tú* is learned later, as the children interact with playmates.

6 In Latin America, many children attend private schools from kindergarten through high school. Because of this, and because a family most likely will not move but will remain in the same home for many years, children who begin kindergarten together often remain classmates throughout their school years. As a result, lifelong friendships can begin at an early age.

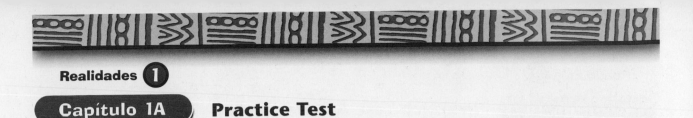

Realidades **1**

Capítulo 1A | **Practice Test**

Answer questions 1–5. Base your answers on the reading *"Friendship Among Latin Americans."*

1 Where are Adriana and Ricardo currently living?

    A   the United States

    B   the Dominican Republic

    C   Mexico

    D   Adriana in Santo Domingo and Ricardo in Saltillo

2 In the reading, which of these words is a synonym for *¡Oye!* in paragraph 3?

    F   *Buenos días*

    G   *Buenas noches*

    H   *Hola*

    J   *Mucho gusto*

3 Based on the reading, which one of the following statements is true?

    A   When they come to the United States, Spanish speakers are friendly mostly with people who came from the same country they did.

    B   To a Latin American, a friend is almost like a member of the family.

    C   Latin Americans do not address each other as *tú* until they are adults.

    D   There are no public schools in Latin America.

4 According to the reading, which of the following is a reason why lifelong friendships can be very common in Latin America?

    F   Most of your friends would be family members.

    G   Most Latin Americans have a sense of humor and share an interest in soccer.

    H   You would probably go to school together from kindergarten through high school.

    J   You would always treat each other courteously.

5 From an early age, Latin Americans tend to socialize with people older and younger than they are, as well as with people their own age. Describe what you think might be some advantages of this. If you think there are disadvantages, describe those as well. Use details and information from the reading to support your answer.

Communication Workbook

Test Preparation ▬ *Capítulo 1A*   **231**

1 Ⓐ Ⓑ Ⓒ Ⓓ   **2** Ⓕ Ⓖ Ⓗ Ⓙ   **3** Ⓐ Ⓑ Ⓒ Ⓓ

4 Ⓕ Ⓖ Ⓗ Ⓙ

5

READ
THINK
EXPLAIN

_____

_____

_____

_____

_____

_____

_____

_____

Drawing Conclusions

To draw a conclusion is to form an opinion based on evidence. If you watch television crime shows, you have seen detectives analyze a crime scene to form an opinion or draw a conclusion. Readers are often asked to draw conclusions about what they have read. This task requires readers to determine if there is enough evidence present in the text to support a certain conclusion.

Conclusion statements are rarely right or wrong; they are often presented as believable or not and are only as strong as the evidence upon which they are based. If you are successful at drawing conclusions from your reading, you are likely skilled at finding evidence that supports your conclusions.

Tip

One strategy that helps you as you draw conclusions is a two-column note activity known as Opinion-Proof. As you read, you formulate opinions about what you have read. You jot these down on the Opinion side of your notes. If your opinions are believable, then you should be able to write down on the Proof side all the evidence you find in the reading passage that lends support to your opinion.

1. On page 59 of your textbook, re-read the *diamante* poem titled *"Soy Elena."* Based on what you have read, fill in the Opinion-Proof chart below.

Opinion	Proof
Elena probably doesn't like talking out loud in class.	_____
Elena _____ _____.	*No soy ni deportista ni artística.*
Don't be surprised if Elena takes you up on a dare.	_____

Sample question:

2. Read the *diamante* poem titled "I am James" and answer the question that follows.

I am James,
no job, but busy.
On the beach, if it's sunny.
No worry, I have money.
They say I'm funny.
I'm James.

Based on the evidence presented in the poem "I am James," which conclusion below is the most believable?

A James earns most of his money from selling beach equipment.
B James is bored with his life.
C If it is raining, James will not be at the beach.
D In school, James was known as the class clown.

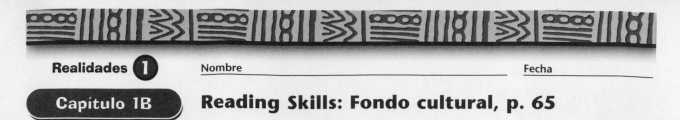

Determining the Author's Point of View

To determine the author's point of view in a reading selection, the reader must figure out how the author feels about a subject in the reading selection. To begin with, readers should be able to identify when an author feels positively, negatively, or neutral toward a subject. As you gain more practice with this skill, you should then be able to identify a wide range of emotions or attitudes shown by authors. Some of these emotions or attitudes might include: admiration, nostalgia, sarcasm, surprise, and sympathy.

Tip

To figure out the author's point of view toward his or her subject, try to locate words, phrases, or sentences in the text that have positive or negative associations or connotations. For example, consider the words listed below in columns A, B, and C. Which one of the words sounds more positive? Which sounds more negative? Which sounds more neutral?

Column A	Column B	Column C
1. denim pants	1. faded jeans	1. hand-me-downs
2. cafeteria food	2. lunch time	2. five-star meal
3. classic car	3. used car	3. mid-size car

1. On page 65 of your textbook, reread the **Fondo cultural** about *huipiles*. Look at the words below from the passage and place a + sign next to any word that has positive connotations, a – sign next to any word with negative connotations, and a **0** next to any word where the connotations seem to be neutral.

    _____ colorful

    _____ hand-woven

    _____ weaving

    _____ unique

Sample question:

2. In the **Fondo cultural**, which word best describes the author's point of view about the *huipiles* worn by the female descendants of the Maya?

    A   amazed
    B   sarcastic
    C   indifferent
    D   appreciative

Integrated Performance Assessment
Unit theme: Y tú, ¿cómo eres?

Context for the Integrated Performance Assessment: You are going on an exchange program in Mexico for a week. Your host family is looking forward to meeting you and would like to know a little about you.

Interpretive Task: Watch the *Videohistoria: Amigos por Internet* from *Realidades 1, DVD 1, Capítulo 1B*. Notice how the students introduce and describe themselves. Write a brief introduction and description of yourself.

Interpersonal Task: Read your introduction and description to a friend in Spanish class. Ask each other about activities that you do and do not like to do.

Presentational Task: Write an e-mail to your host sister or brother introducing and describing yourself. Include at least 2 activities that you like to do and 2 that you do not like to do.

Interpersonal Task Rubric

	Score: 1 Does not meet expectations	Score: 3 Meets expectations	Score: 5 Exceeds expectations
Language Use	Student uses little or no target language and relies heavily on native language word order.	Student uses the target language consistently, but may mix native and target language word order.	Student uses the target language exclusively and integrates target language word order into conversation.
Vocabulary Use	Student uses limited and repetitive language.	Student uses only recently acquired vocabulary.	Student uses both recently and previously acquired vocabulary.

Presentational Task Rubric

	Score: 1 Does not meet expectations	Score: 3 Meets expectations	Score: 5 Exceeds expectations
Amount of Communication	Student gives limited or no details or examples.	Student gives adequate details or examples.	Student gives consistent details or examples.
Accuracy	Student's accuracy with vocabulary and structures is limited.	Student's accuracy with vocabulary and structures is adequate.	Student's accuracy with vocabulary and structures is exemplary.
Comprehensibility	Student's ideas lack clarity and are difficult to understand.	Student's ideas are adequately clear and fairly well understood.	Student's ideas are precise and easily understood.
Vocabulary Use	Student uses limited and repetitive vocabulary.	Student uses only recently acquired vocabulary.	Student uses both recently and previously acquired vocabulary.

¡Hola! Me llamo Pedro

30 de septiembre

Srta. María Luisa Pardo Barros
Calle San Antonio 16
Valparaíso
Chile

Querida María Luisa:

Me llamo Peter (Pedro en español) y soy de los Estados Unidos.
Soy estudiante en Orlando, en el estado de la Florida. Hay muchas
atracciones en Orlando: Por ejemplo, el famoso parque de diver-
siones Disney World —y Sea World también.

Soy muy deportista y me encanta nadar y patinar. Mi mamá dice
que soy desordenado y que no soy nada serio. Pero sí me
gusta ir a la escuela y me gusta mucho leer
buenos libros. ¿Mi actividad
favorita? Estar con mis amigos
o hablar con ellos por teléfono.

¿Cómo eres, María Luisa?

Tu amigo,

Peter (o Pedro, si el nombre español te gusta más)

Realidades ①

Capítulo 1B   **Practice Test**

Answer questions 1–5. Base your answers on the reading *"¡Hola! Me llamo Pedro."*

1 In what city does María Luisa live?

    A   San Antonio

    B   Valparaíso

    C   Orlando

    D   The reading does not say.

2 What is the English equivalent of *Querida?*

    F   Miss

    G   Hello

    H   Dear

    J   It is María Luisa's first name and has no real English equivalent.

3 According to the reading, which one of the following statements might Peter make about himself?

    A   *Me gusta cocinar.*

    B   *Me gusta mucho practicar deportes.*

    C   *No me gusta nada estudiar.*

    D   *No soy ni serio ni trabajador.*

4 According to the reading, which one of the following words would Peter use to describe himself?

    F   *reservado*

    G   *perezoso*

    H   *sociable*

    J   *atrevido*

5   Write a brief letter in Spanish to a pen pal describing yourself and what you like and don't like to do. Use the reading as a model for your letter.

Capítulo 1B   **Practice Test Answer Sheet**

1 Ⓐ Ⓑ Ⓒ Ⓓ   **2** Ⓕ Ⓖ Ⓗ Ⓙ   **3** Ⓐ Ⓑ Ⓒ Ⓓ

4 Ⓕ Ⓖ Ⓗ Ⓙ

5

READ
THINK
EXPLAIN

_____
_____
_____
_____
_____
_____
_____
_____
_____
_____

Capítulo 2A **Reading Skills: Exploración del lenguaje, Fondo cultural, p. 81**

Recognizing Cause-Effect Relationships

To recognize cause-effect relationships in fiction, nonfiction, drama, or poetry, readers should be aware of why things happen (causes) as well as the consequences or results of actions (effects) in a reading passage.

Tip

To become familiar with this skill, readers should be able to identify certain words or phrases that are often used to show cause-effect relationships. You should also be able to use these words or phrases to describe what you have read in a reading passage.

Here are some common cause-effect words or phrases grouped by similarity in meaning:

because	hence	since
due to	therefore	so that
as a result	thus	consequently

1. On page 81 of your textbook, re-read the two sections, **Exploración del lenguaje** and the **Fondo cultural.** After you have finished reading, complete the sentences below.

   Because Spain was once part of the Roman Empire, _____
   _____.
   _____
   _____; **consequently,**
   September and *septiembre* actually mean "the seventh month."

   _____
   _____. **As a result,**
   one can find a Roman aqueduct towering over the modern Spanish city of Segovia.

Sample question:

2. Why do December and *diciembre* contain the Latin root word meaning "ten"?
   A Because Spain was once part of the Roman Empire.
   B Because in the Roman calendar there were only ten days in December.
   C Because in the Roman calendar, December was actually the tenth month.
   D Because the number ten was used to indicate the coldest month.

Analyzing the Validity and Reliability of Information

When good readers analyze information for validity and reliability, one of the most important questions that they ask themselves is: "How do I know that I can trust that this information is true or accurate?" After answering this question, readers need to determine how such information can be used.

Tip

One way to check a reading passage for validity and reliability is to distinguish between the statements in the passage that are facts and those that are opinions. Readers generally trust factual information more than they trust opinions. A factual statement generally can be put to a test to prove whether the statement is true or false. Statements that involve numbers and/or measurements are more likely to be facts than opinions. Opinions are generally statements that could be interpreted differently by different people.

Let's look at two examples concerning the weather:

   A It is 80 degrees Fahrenheit today in San José, Costa Rica.
   B It is very hot out today in San José.

With a thermometer, one could easily prove if the temperature in San José is 80 degrees Fahrenheit today. However, the word "hot" in statement B could be interpreted differently by different people. For example, some people might say that 80 degrees is too hot while others might say that 80 degrees is warm. Hence, statement A sounds more factual while statement B sounds more like an opinion.

1. On pages 90–91 of your textbook, re-read the **Lectura**, *La Escuela Español Vivo*. After you have finished reading, read the statements below and identify them as facts or as opinions.

   _____ Hay clases de música y baile.
   _____ Los sábados y los domingos hay actividades muy interesantes.
   _____ El horario del almuerzo es de 13:00 a 14:00.
   _____ Es una experiencia fabulosa en Costa Rica.

Sample question:

2. Imagine you are interested in improving your Spanish-speaking ability by studying at the **Escuela Español Vivo** in Santa Ana, Costa Rica. Which statement from the brochure would be of most interest to you?
   A Visitar un volcán.
   B Mucha práctica y conversación en español.
   C Una experiencia fabulosa en Costa Rica.
   D Amigos de muchos países.

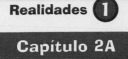

Realidades 1

Capítulo 2A

Integrated Performance Assessment
Unit theme: Tu día en la escuela

Context for the Integrated Performance Assessment: A group of students from Mexico, including Teresa, is coming to visit your school and attend classes next month. She would like some information about your schedule this year.

Interpretive Task: Watch the *Videohistoria: El primer día de clases* from *Realidades 1, DVD 1, Capítulo 2A*. Write down Teresa's classes by period as she describes her schedule. What time does she have lunch? After the video, write down your classes by period and when you have lunch.

Interpersonal Task: Discuss your schedule with a friend in Spanish class. Ask each other questions to find out what classes you and your friend like and don't like, and explain why.

Presentational Task: Send an e-mail to Teresa. Tell her what class you have each period and when you have lunch. Tell her the classes you like and don't like, and explain why.

Interpersonal Task Rubric

	Score: 1 Does not meet expectations	Score: 3 Meets expectations	Score: 5 Exceeds expectations
Language Use	Student uses little or no target language and relies heavily on native language word order.	Student uses the target language consistently, but may mix native and target language word order.	Student uses the target language exclusively and integrates target language word order into conversation.
Vocabulary Use	Student uses limited and repetitive language.	Student uses only recently acquired vocabulary.	Student uses both recently and previously acquired vocabulary.

Presentational Task Rubric

	Score: 1 Does not meet expectations	Score: 3 Meets expectations	Score: 5 Exceeds expectations
Amount of Communication	Student gives limited or no details or examples.	Student gives adequate details or examples.	Student gives consistent details or examples.
Accuracy	Student's accuracy with vocabulary and structures is limited.	Student's accuracy with vocabulary and structures is adequate.	Student's accuracy with vocabulary and structures is exemplary.
Comprehensibility	Student's ideas lack clarity and are difficult to understand.	Student's ideas are adequately clear and fairly well understood.	Student's ideas are precise and easily understood.
Vocabulary Use	Student uses limited and repetitive vocabulary.	Student uses only recently acquired vocabulary.	Student uses both recently and previously acquired vocabulary.

The High-School Experience in Latin America

1 How does the high-school experience in Latin America compare with that in the United States? There are many similarities, but there are also some noticeable differences.

2 A normal course load for a United States high-school student is usually between five and eight subjects a year, but in Latin America students are more likely to take between ten and twelve. These classes do not, however, meet every day. A class might meet only two or three times a week, which is more similar to schedules in U.S. colleges and universities. As a result, there is more variation in students' day-to-day schedules. In addition, although physical education is taught, team sports are not part of the curriculum. On the other hand, English is mandatory in many schools. Foreign language study is much more common in Latin American schools, and many students speak one or two languages besides Spanish by the time they graduate from high school.

3 Classes in Latin American schools are also structured very differently than those in the United States. Lecturing is the preferred format and there tends to be less student participation. Although extracurricular activities are offered, they are far less common than they are in U.S. schools.

4 It is unusual for Latin American schools to have the amenities, such as lockers, that students in the United States take for granted. As a result, students must carry

> **Classes in Latin American schools are also structured very differently than those in the United States. Lecturing is the preferred format and there tends to be less student participation.**

their backpacks and book bags with them throughout the school day. Latin American students also tend to have much more homework than their U.S. counterparts, so they need these accessories in order to take their books home.

5 While letter grades are routinely used in the United States, they are rarely used in Latin America. Although the grading scale varies from country to country, numerical grades, such as 1–10 or 1–20, are the norm.

6 Private schools are common in Latin America and a large number of these are operated by the Roman Catholic Church. Although parochial schools are not usually coeducational, there are many coed private schools that are not affiliated with any church. Because many of these schools are associated with certain ethnic or cultural traditions, students must study the appropriate foreign language, usually American English, German, British English, Italian, or French.

7 One of the most noticeable differences between the U.S. school system and the Latin American one is that students in Latin America are frequently required to wear uniforms. While the uniform is sometimes the same throughout the country, it is more likely identified with a certain school. The girls' uniform is usually a jumper, a blouse, and a tie, or a pleated skirt, a blouse, and a vest or blazer. Boys wear slacks, a shirt and tie, and sometimes a sweater or blazer as well.

Answer questions 1–5. Base your answers on the reading *"The High-School Experience in Latin America."*

1 How does the average number of classes per year compare for U.S. and Latin American students?

    A   Latin American students take more classes than U.S. students.

    B   Latin American students take fewer classes than U.S. students.

    C   Latin American and U.S. students take the same number of classes.

    D   Latin American and U.S. students take the same number of classes, but in Latin America classes only meet three days a week.

2 Based on the reading, why are backpacks and book bags so important for Latin American students?

    F   They are expensive and would cost a lot to replace.

    G   They are a status symbol.

    H   Latin American students don't have lockers for their books.

    J   Latin American students don't have shelves for their books.

3 How do church-affiliated schools in Latin America differ from private schools?

    A   They are usually coeducational.

    B   They are <u>not</u> usually coeducational.

    C   They require that students study another language.

    D   They are not common in Latin America.

4 How does the grading system in Latin America differ from that used in the United States?

    F   Numerical grades are rarely used.

    G   Numerical grades are regularly used.

    H   Letter grades are usually used.

    J   Letter grades are never used.

5 Why do you think English is mandatory in Latin American schools? Use details and information from the reading to support your answer.

Capítulo 2A **Practice Test Answer Sheet**

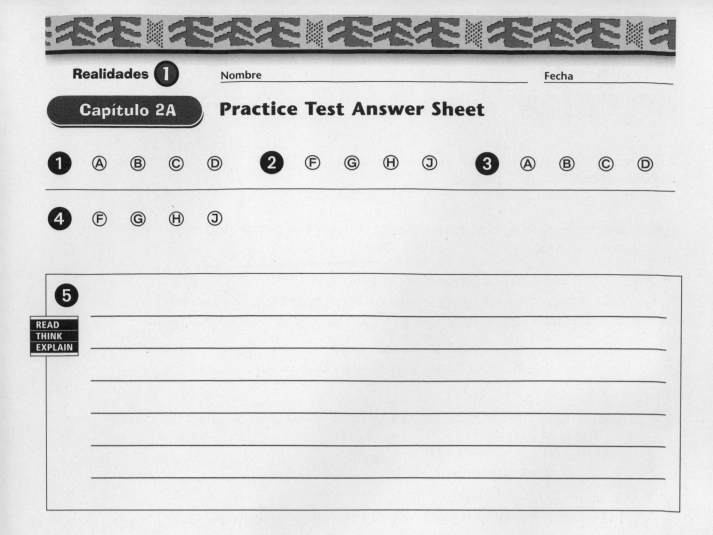

1 Ⓐ Ⓑ Ⓒ Ⓓ   **2** Ⓕ Ⓖ Ⓗ Ⓙ   **3** Ⓐ Ⓑ Ⓒ Ⓓ

4 Ⓕ Ⓖ Ⓗ Ⓙ

5

READ
THINK
EXPLAIN

_____

_____

_____

_____

_____

_____

Locates, Gathers, Analyzes, and Evaluates Written Information

By showing that they can locate, gather, analyze, and evaluate information from one or more reading passages, good readers demonstrate that they know how to conduct research. On a test, readers are often asked to locate, gather, analyze, and evaluate information from a reading passage and then show how to put that information to good use.

Tip

Readers who conduct research often read with a purpose. That means that they are thinking about a research question or problem while they read. If you encounter information in a reading passage that relates to your research question or problem, you should underline or selectively highlight that information. Later, you will come back to the sections that you selectively highlighted to analyze and evaluate the information to determine if it will be useful for your research.

1. On page 114 of your textbook, re-read the **Lectura**, *El UNICEF y una convención para los niños*. After you have finished reading, consider the following scenario:

   Imagine that you and some classmates are working on a community service project in which you encourage local students to better appreciate their schools. Now with a pencil, pen, or highlighter, underline the information below from the **Lectura** that might be useful for your project.

   ¿Sabes que es un privilegio estar en una escuela, tener una mochila con libros, unos lá pices, una calculadora, unas hojas de papel y un profesor bueno? En ciertas naciones ir a la escuela es difícil o no es possible.

   El UNICEF es la organización internacional de las Naciones Unidas que trabaja para los niños. UNICEF es una sigla inglesa que significa "Fondo Internacional de Emergencia de las Naciones Unidas para los Niños".

   Explain how the information underlined could help you with your community service project.

   _____

   _____

Sample question:

2. The information in the white sidebar box on page 114 that begins with **"Esta convención dice..."** could best be used

   A to write a report that illustrates the life of underprivileged children.

   B to make a speech demanding that children of any age be given the right to vote.

   C to lead a campaign demanding better treatment for children in a community.

   D to produce a television commercial about the history of UNICEF.

Recognizing the Use of Comparison and Contrast

To recognize comparison and contrast in a reading passage, good readers can point out how items or ideas in the reading passage are similar to or different from each other. Sometimes writers will directly state that they are comparing or contrasting items in a reading passage. Other times readers might recognize items in a reading passage that could be compared or contrasted even though the writer might not have presented the information for that purpose.

Tip

With comparison and contrast, one of the biggest challenges for students is to recognize the need to narrow the focus of their comparisons and contrasts. When producing a comparison-contrast chart, you will state things that are obvious. For example, you might choose to compare and contrast apples and oranges and then focus only on the color and shape of the fruits. You then state the obvious: *One is red while the other is orange; both are sort of round in shape.* Professional writers, on the other hand, are less likely to state the obvious. Instead, they aim to teach readers something that readers likely do not already know.

1. On page 116 of your textbook, re-read the **Perspectivas del mundo hispano, ¿Cómo es la escuela?** After you have finished reading, identify the six features of schools in Spanish-speaking countries that the writer has decided to focus on for comparison and contrast.
   - ways that students _____ teachers
   - ways that teachers _____ students
   - _____
   - use of _____ time
   - use of _____
   - number of _____

Sample question:

2. Based on the information presented in *¿Cómo es la escuela?*, which statement below is most likely to be true?
   A Students in Spanish-speaking countries are probably more comfortable in class discussions than students in the United States.
   B Students in the United States attend school more days than students in Mexico.
   C Students in the United States and in Spanish-speaking countries are very similar in the ways that they greet and address their teachers.
   D Students in Spanish-speaking countries are accustomed to listening to class lectures.

 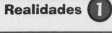
Integrated Performance Assessment
Unit theme: Tu sala de clases

Context for the Integrated Performance Assessment: Your class has decided to assemble packages of school supplies to send to UNICEF so that they can be distributed to a needy school in Latin America. You and your partner have been asked to prepare one package.

Interpretive Task: Read the article on UNICEF on page 114 of *Realidades 1* and study the photos. Make a list of 10 items that you think should be included in your package.

Interpersonal Task: Discuss the 10 items that your and your partner listed. From the items that you and your partner listed, select 8 to include in the package.

Presentational Task: Write a note to your teacher telling him/her the 8 supplies you want to include in your package and why.

Interpersonal Task Rubric

	Score: 1 Does not meet expectations	Score: 3 Meets expectations	Score: 5 Exceeds expectations
Language Use	Student uses little or no target language and relies heavily on native language word order.	Student uses the target language consistently, but may mix native and target language word order.	Student uses the target language exclusively and integrates target language word order into conversation.
Vocabulary Use	Student uses limited and repetitive language.	Student uses only recently acquired vocabulary.	Student uses both recently and previously acquired vocabulary.

Presentational Task Rubric

	Score: 1 Does not meet expectations	Score: 3 Meets expectations	Score: 5 Exceeds expectations
Amount of Communication	He/she mentions fewer than 8 items and gives few reasons.	He/she mentions 8 items and gives some reasons.	He/she mentions more than 8 items and gives many reasons.
Accuracy	Student's accuracy with vocabulary and structures is limited.	Student's accuracy with vocabulary and structures is adequate.	Student's accuracy with vocabulary and structures is exemplary.
Comprehensibility	Student's ideas lack clarity and are difficult to understand.	Student's ideas are adequately clear and fairly well understood.	Student's ideas are precise and easily understood.
Vocabulary Use	Student uses limited and repetitive vocabulary.	Student uses only recently acquired vocabulary.	Student uses both recently and previously acquired vocabulary.

A popular bilingual teen magazine is including a feature in the next issue on what the school day is like for high-school students throughout the United States. Read what this student has to say about a typical day at her school.

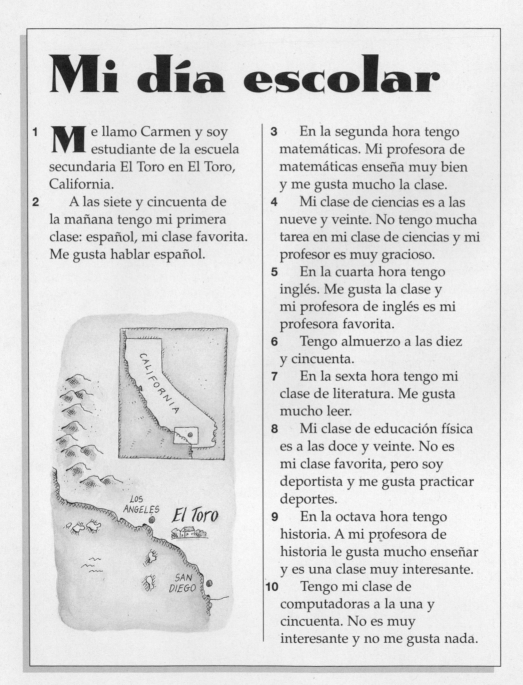

Mi día escolar

1 **M**e llamo Carmen y soy estudiante de la escuela secundaria El Toro en El Toro, California.

2 A las siete y cincuenta de la mañana tengo mi primera clase: español, mi clase favorita. Me gusta hablar español.

3 En la segunda hora tengo matemáticas. Mi profesora de matemáticas enseña muy bien y me gusta mucho la clase.

4 Mi clase de ciencias es a las nueve y veinte. No tengo mucha tarea en mi clase de ciencias y mi profesor es muy gracioso.

5 En la cuarta hora tengo inglés. Me gusta la clase y mi profesora de inglés es mi profesora favorita.

6 Tengo almuerzo a las diez y cincuenta.

7 En la sexta hora tengo mi clase de literatura. Me gusta mucho leer.

8 Mi clase de educación física es a las doce y veinte. No es mi clase favorita, pero soy deportista y me gusta practicar deportes.

9 En la octava hora tengo historia. A mi profesora de historia le gusta mucho enseñar y es una clase muy interesante.

10 Tengo mi clase de computadoras a la una y cincuenta. No es muy interesante y no me gusta nada.

CALIFORNIA

LOS ANGELES *El Toro*

SAN DIEGO

Answer questions 1–5. Base your answers on the reading *"Mi día escolar."*

❶ What time does Carmen's first class begin?

    A   7:50 A.M.

    B   9:20 A.M.

    C   10:20 A.M.

    D   2:30 P.M.

❷ According to the reading, why does Carmen like her math class so much?

    F   Her teacher doesn't give much homework.

    G   It's right before lunch.

    H   She has a very good teacher.

    J   It isn't difficult for her.

❸ Who is Carmen's favorite teacher?

    A   her Spanish teacher

    B   her science teacher

    C   her math teacher

    D   her English teacher

❹ Which class is Carmen's least favorite?

    F   her computer class

    G   her science class

    H   her physical education class

    J   her history class

❺ Based on what you know about Carmen, what kinds of factors influence whether she likes a class or not?

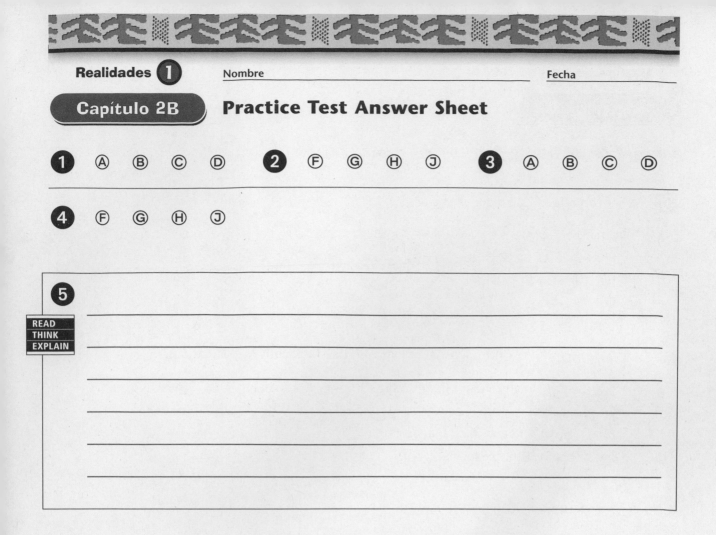

1 Ⓐ Ⓑ Ⓒ Ⓓ   **2** Ⓕ Ⓖ Ⓗ Ⓙ   **3** Ⓐ Ⓑ Ⓒ Ⓓ

4 Ⓕ Ⓖ Ⓗ Ⓙ

5

READ
THINK
EXPLAIN

_____

_____

_____

_____

_____

_____

Recognizing the Use of Comparison and Contrast

To recognize comparison and contrast in a reading passage, good readers can point out how items or ideas in the reading passage are similar to or different from each other. Sometimes writers will directly state that they are comparing or contrasting items in a reading passage. Other times readers might recognize items in a reading passage that could be compared or contrasted even though the writer might not have presented the information for that purpose.

Tip

The Venn diagram is an excellent visual tool to help you see differences and similarities when comparing and contrasting. The area where two circles overlap is the place to list the similarities between items. In the areas that do not overlap, the differences between items are listed.

1. On page 137 of your textbook, re-read **Actividad 20 "¿Qué comida hay en el Ciberc@fé @rrob@?"** After you have finished reading, use the Venn diagram below to list the similarities and differences between different menu items.

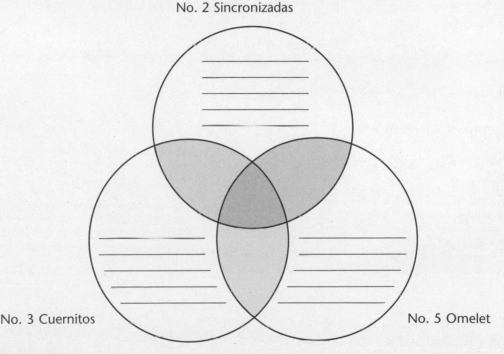

No. 2 Sincronizadas

No. 3 Cuernitos   No. 5 Omelet

Sample question:

2. Menu item No. 4 **Chilaquiles** is different from all the other menu choices because
   A it is the only menu item that costs less than $15.00.
   B it is the only menu item that is offered with *cóctel de fruta*.
   C it is the only menu item that does not contain *jamón*.
   D it is the only menu item that comes with *tortilla de harina*.

Determining the Main Idea

To determine the main idea of a reading passage, the reader must be able to describe what a reading passage is about. He or she should be able to summarize the main idea of a reading passage in one sentence. A common problem for students when working with this skill is confusing an important detail in the reading passage with the main idea. Just because something is mentioned in the reading passage does not mean it is the main idea of the passage. Many times the main idea is not even stated in the reading passage. This is often called an implied main idea. No matter if the main idea is stated or implied, the basic question remains the same: "What is this reading passage about?"

Tip

One way to determine the main idea of a reading passage is to locate the important details in a passage and then ask yourself, "What do these details have in common?" For some readers, this is like a game of addition: each time a new detail is added, the overall main idea, like the total, must change.

1. On page 138 of your textbook, re-read the **Lectura,** *Frutas y verduras de las Américas.* After you have finished reading, try to "add" the details below to determine a possible main idea for the reading passage.

   A La pulpa del aguacate es una fuente de energía, proteínas, vitaminas, y minerales.
   +
   B El mango tiene calcio y vitaminas A y C como la naranja.
   +
   C La papaya tiene más vitamina C que la naranja.
   +
   D El licuado de plátano es delicioso y muy nutritivo.

   Details A + B + C + D = Main Idea _____

   _____

Sample question:

2. Based on the details presented above, another good title for the reading passage would be
   A "Promoting Good Health with Latin American Fruits."
   B "Eat More Fruits and Vegetables."
   C "Menu Ideas from Latin America."
   D "Diet and Exercise with Latino Flavor."

Integrated Performance Assessment
Unit theme: ¿Desayuno o almuerzo?

Context for the Integrated Performance Assessment: A group of students from San José, Costa Rica is coming to spend two weeks with your Spanish class. You are on the committee that is planning a welcome breakfast for the students.

Interpretive Task: Watch the *Videohistoria: El desayuno from Realidades 1, DVD 2, Capítulo 3A* without the vocabulary words displayed. Decide if the breakfast should be a typical Costa Rican breakfast, an American breakfast, or a combination of both. Make a list of foods that you think the breakfast should include.

Interpersonal Task: Discuss the kind of breakfast and the foods with two or three other members of the breakfast committee. Share your opinion with them and listen to their opinions. Working with the committee, decide on the kind of meal and the food you will have for the welcome breakfast.

Presentational Task: Make an oral presentation to the class explaining the committee's decisions about the welcome breakfast. Include the type of meal and the food you have chosen.

Interpersonal Task Rubric

	Score: 1 Does not meet expectations	Score: 3 Meets expectations	Score: 5 Exceeds expectations
Language Use	Student uses little or no target language and relies heavily on native language word order.	Student uses the target language consistently, but may mix native and target language word order.	Student uses the target language exclusively and integrates target language word order into conversation.
Vocabulary Use	Student uses limited and repetitive language.	Student uses only recently acquired vocabulary.	Student uses both recently and previously acquired vocabulary.

Presentational Task Rubric

	Score: 1 Does not meet expectations	Score: 3 Meets expectations	Score: 5 Exceeds expectations
Amount of Communication	Student gives limited or no details about the type of breakfast and the chosen food.	Student gives adequate details about the type of breakfast and the chosen food.	Student gives consistent details about the type of breakfast and the chosen food.
Accuracy	Student's accuracy with vocabulary and structures is limited.	Student's accuracy with vocabulary and structures is adequate.	Student's accuracy with vocabulary and structures is exemplary.
Comprehensibility	Student's ideas lack clarity and are difficult to understand.	Student's ideas are adequately clear and fairly well understood.	Student's ideas are precise and easily understood.
Vocabulary Use	Student uses limited and repetitive vocabulary.	Student uses only recently acquired vocabulary.	Student uses both recently and previously acquired vocabulary.

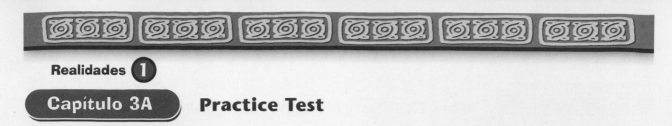

The Hidden Corn: A Mayan Legend

1 Long ago, corn was hidden inside a large rock and no one knew that it was there. One day, a group of black ants saw a tiny crack in the rock and crawled inside, where they found the corn and tasted it. It was so good that they carried out some kernels to eat later. However, a few of the kernels were too heavy to carry far, so the ants left them behind.

2 Fox came by and found the kernels. He quickly ate them and exclaimed, "How delicious! Now if I could only find some more!" All day long, Fox stayed near the place where he'd found the kernels, looking for more. Finally, when the sun was almost gone and there was just a thin glow of gold left on the horizon, Fox saw the ants making their way to the rock. They entered the tiny crack and later came out loaded down with kernels of corn. After they had left, Fox pried at the crack, but he couldn't get inside the rock. Again he had to be content with eating the kernels the ants could not carry away.

3 When Fox returned home, all the other animals saw how happy and well fed he was. They asked him why, but Fox would not say. So the animals made a plan to find out. That night, they followed Fox to the rock. They saw him eating the corn and they tried it too. "How delicious!" they exclaimed. When they found out that the black ants were bringing the corn out from the rock, they asked them if

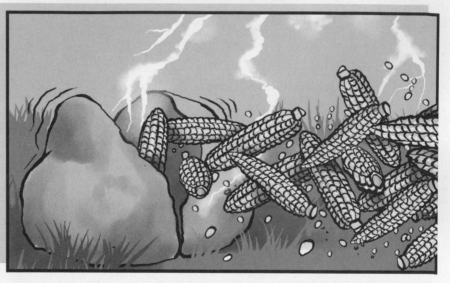

they would bring out more. The ants agreed but found that they could not bring out nearly enough for all the animals.

4 So the animals asked the red ants and the rat to help, but neither could fit through the crack. Finally, they went to Man and said, "If you will help us, we will give you the secret of this delicious food." Man asked the thunder gods for help, and they sent for Yaluk, the most powerful.

5 Yaluk asked the woodpecker to tap on the thinnest part of the rock and then hide his head. In an instant, Yaluk tossed down a great lightning bolt at the spot where the woodpecker had tapped. The rock burst open, and thousands of golden ears of corn poured out.

6 And so it was that Man and all the animals received the gift of corn. The only unfortunate thing was that when Yaluk threw down his lightning bolt, the woodpecker forgot to hide his head. A piece of rock hit him and his head began to bleed. That is why to this day the woodpecker has a red head.

Capítulo 3A **Practice Test**

Answer questions 1–5. Base your answers on the reading *"The Hidden Corn: A Mayan Legend."*

❶ How did Fox first find the corn?

    A   He saw the black ants carrying the kernels.

    B   He found some kernels lying on the ground.

    C   He saw it through a tiny crack in the rock where it was hidden.

    D   He stepped on the rock where it was hidden.

❷ At the beginning of the story, Fox and the black ants are the only ones enjoying the gift of corn. Who is enjoying it at the end?

    F   the red ants and the rat

    G   Yaluk and the other thunder gods

    H   Man and all the animals

    J   the woodpecker

❸ A "just so" story is one in which the events of the story explain a fact of nature, as in "How the Leopard Got His Spots." Which of the following lines from this legend sounds like part of a "just so" story?

    A   "Fox pried at the crack, but he couldn't get inside the rock."

    B   "Man asked the thunder gods for help."

    C   "Yaluk tossed down a great lightning bolt."

    D   "The woodpecker has a red head."

❹ Why does the writer of this legend call corn a "gift"?

    F   Corn was a very important food for the Mayas.

    G   Corn is the color of gold.

    H   Corn is very rare and needs special conditions to grow.

    J   Gift-giving is very important in the Mayan culture.

❺ Choose a passage in this story in which the visual imagery is especially vivid. Explain how the words used in this passage helped to create a clear picture in your mind.

Nombre ______________________ Fecha ______________

Capítulo 3A

Practice Test Answer Sheet

1 Ⓐ Ⓑ Ⓒ Ⓓ   2 Ⓕ Ⓖ Ⓗ Ⓙ   3 Ⓐ Ⓑ Ⓒ Ⓓ

4 Ⓕ Ⓖ Ⓗ Ⓙ

5

READ
THINK
EXPLAIN

Capítulo 3B   **Reading Skills: Conexiones, p. 157**

Interpreting Diagrams, Graphs, and Statistical Illustrations

When good readers encounter a diagram or graph, they are able to make meaning from what they see. In essence, they are able to translate the information that is presented visually in the diagram or graph into useful information. To demonstrate understanding of the information in the diagrams or graphs, readers are often asked to make comparisons involving the information in the diagrams or graphs.

Tip

One strategy that will help you discover the meaning from diagrams or graphs is to practice translating pieces of information from the diagram or graph into sentences. In describing what you see in graphs, you should become familiar making statements with the following words or expressions of comparison:

> more than → most → greater than
> larger → largest
> bigger → biggest
> less than → least → fewer than
> smaller → smallest
> equal → same → different

1. On page 157 of your textbook, review the graph presented in the **Conexiones "Las matemáticas."** Based on what you see in the graph, complete the sentences below.

   Three students report that their most preferred fruit is _____.
   The largest number of students report that _____
   _____.
   The food that _____ is *bistec*.
   Both *manzanas* and *refrescos* _____.

Sample question:

2. Based on the information presented in the graph on page 157 of your textbook, which statement below is true?
   A More students prefer *manzanas* to *papas*.
   B The same number of students prefer *refrescos* as *manzanas*.
   C *Refrescos* are more popular than *manzanas*.
   D The most preferred food is *bistec*.

Determining the Main Idea and Identifying Relevant Details

To know the relevant details in a reading passage is to know which ones are most important. The first step in identifying the relevant details is to identify the main idea of the passage. The relevant details are the ones that help support the main idea. After reading a passage, good readers ask themselves, "What is this passage mostly about?" and "Which details in the passage help support, explain, or prove the main idea?"

Tip

Some readers are better able to identify the main idea and the relevant details when they have a graphic organizer. The graphic organizer below presents the main idea as if it were the roof of a house and the relevant details as the columns supporting the roof or main idea.

MAIN IDEA

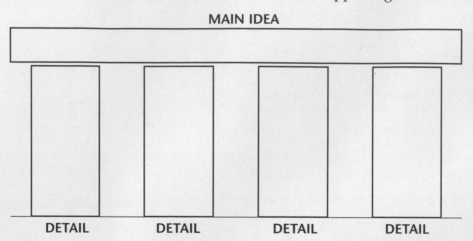

DETAIL   DETAIL   DETAIL   DETAIL

1. On page 162 of your textbook, re-read the **Lectura,** *La comida de los atletas.* After reading, write the statements below in their appropriate place in the above graphic organizer. One statement is irrelevant; it is neither the main idea nor a supporting detail.
   - Para la cena el atleta come papas, carne sin grasa y más verduras y frutas.
   - Los jugadores de fútbol comen comidas equilibradas con muchos carbohidratos, minerales y vitaminas.
   - Carlos Tévez es jugador del equipo Manchester United, un equipo de fútbol profesional en Inglaterra.
   - La noche antes del partido, el jugador bebe un litro de jugo de naranja.
   - Un jugador típico come mucho pan con mantequilla y jalea, yogur y té.
   - Para el almuerzo antes del partido, come pan, pasta, pollo sin grasa, verduras, frutas y una ensalada.

Sample question:

2. Which statement below does NOT help support the main idea of the **Lectura,** *La comida de los atletas*?
   - **A** Carlos Tévez plays soccer for Manchester United, a professional team in England.
   - **B** The night before a game, a player drinks a liter of orange juice.
   - **C** For dinner, the athlete eats potatoes, lean meat, and more vegetables and fruits.
   - **D** A typical player eats a lot of bread with butter and jelly; yogurt; and tea.

Realidades 1
Capítulo 3B

Integrated Performance Assessment
Unit theme: Para mantener la salud

Context for the Integrated Performance Assessment: You are concerned that you are not taking good care of your health. You have decided to make some changes, but you do not know where to start.

Interpretive Task: Listen to a radio announcer as he interviews people about their lifestyles on *Realidades 1, Audio CD 7, Track 6.* (Don't worry about the directions given on the CD itself. Use these directions instead.) As you hear what the people do and eat, decide whether you should or should not do and eat what they do. Make a list of at least 4 ideas you hear under the headings "Debo..." and "No debo..."

Interpersonal Task: You still need some suggestions. Discuss your list of what you should or should not do and eat with your partner. Listen to his/her suggestions. If you hear more good ideas, add them to your list.

Presentational Task: Write a summary of what you should and should not do and eat. There should be at least 5 items in each category.

Interpersonal Task Rubric

	Score: 1 Does not meet expectations	Score: 3 Meets expectations	Score: 5 Exceeds expectations
Language Use	Student uses little or no target language and relies heavily on native language word order.	Student uses the target language consistently, but may mix native and target language word order.	Student uses the target language exclusively and integrates target language word order into conversation.
Vocabulary Use	Student uses limited and repetitive language.	Student uses only recently acquired vocabulary.	Student uses both recently and previously acquired vocabulary.

Presentational Task Rubric

	Score: 1 Does not meet expectations	Score: 3 Meets expectations	Score: 5 Exceeds expectations
Amount of Communication	Student mentions fewer than five things he/she should do and eat and fewer than five things he/she should not do or eat.	Student mentions five things he/she should do and eat and five things he/she should not do or eat.	Student mentions more than five things he/she should do and eat and more than five things he/she should not do or eat.
Accuracy	Student's accuracy with vocabulary and structures is limited.	Student's accuracy with vocabulary and structures is adequate.	Student's accuracy with vocabulary and structures is exemplary.
Comprehensibility	Student's ideas lack clarity and are difficult to understand.	Student's ideas are adequately clear and fairly well understood.	Student's ideas are precise and easily understood.
Vocabulary Use	Student uses limited and repetitive vocabulary.	Student uses only recently acquired vocabulary.	Student uses both recently and previously acquired vocabulary.

Communication Workbook

Test Preparation ━ *Capítulo 3B* **259**

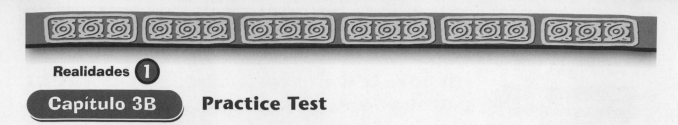

Pizza, ensaladas y ... helado de fresas

1 Juanito es un chico muy gracioso, inteligente y simpático. Le gusta practicar deportes, jugar videojuegos y montar en bicicleta, pero no le gusta mucho ni ir a la escuela ni estudiar. Y tampoco le gusta comer muchas cosas. Sus comidas favoritas son la pizza, las ensaladas y ... el helado de fresas. Nunca come otras cosas; siempre come pizza, ensaladas y ... helado de fresas. No necesita otras comidas.

2 En el desayuno generalmente come una ensalada de frutas, pero unos días toma una ensalada de papas. En el almuerzo de la escuela come pizza con queso y jamón. Si tiene mucha hambre también toma una ensalada de lechuga y tomates o una ensalada de verduras. Sus amigos quieren compartir sus comidas con él, pero Juanito nunca <u>prueba</u> nuevas comidas. Le encantan las de siempre: la pizza, las ensaladas y ... el helado de fresas.

3 En casa por la noche siempre come lo mismo: pizza (los sábados la come con queso, jamón, judías verdes y cebolla), una ensalada de verduras o frutas y ... un helado de fresas.

4 Todos los días, sin variar: pizza, ensalada y ... helado de fresas. Pero un día ¡no hay ni pizza, ni ensalada ni helado en casa! La mamá de Juanito prepara algo diferente: un sándwich de jamón y queso. Como Juanito tiene MUCHA hambre, prueba un poquito ... ¿Crees que le gusta?

5 Como le gustan las pizzas con jamón y queso ... ¡Le encanta el sándwich de jamón y queso! Ahora Juanito come pizza, ensaladas, helado de fresas y ... sándwiches de jamón y queso.

Communication Workbook

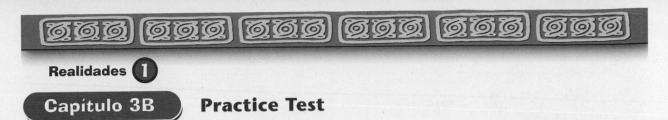

Answer questions 1–5. Base your answers on the reading *"Pizza, ensaladas y . . . helado de fresas."*

1 How would you describe Juanito?

    A He likes to play videogames and study.

    B He's a nice kid who likes to read about different foods.

    C He's fun to be with, but he spends too much time making pizzas.

    D He's a nice kid who doesn't have much variety in his diet.

2 Based on the context, what do you think the word *prueba* means in paragraph 2?

    F shares

    G proves

    H tries

    J prepares

3 Which statement is <u>not</u> true?

    A Juanito's friends never want to share their food with him.

    B Juanito eats pizza every day.

    C Juanito's diet doesn't have much variety.

    D Sometimes Juanito has potato salad for breakfast.

4 Juanito never varies the way he has his

    F breakfast.

    G ice cream.

    H pizza.

    J salads.

5 Escribe una lista de otros ingredientes para las pizzas de Juanito.

6 Plan a weekly menu for Juanito—in Spanish—with the foods you think he should be eating. Remember to label the days of the week, the meals of the day, and any snack (*la merienda*) you think Juanito should have.

Capítulo 3B   **Practice Test Answer Sheet**

1 Ⓐ Ⓑ Ⓒ Ⓓ   **2** Ⓕ Ⓖ Ⓗ Ⓙ   **3** Ⓐ Ⓑ Ⓒ Ⓓ

4 Ⓕ Ⓖ Ⓗ Ⓙ

5

READ
THINK
EXPLAIN

_____
_____
_____
_____
_____
_____

6

READ
THINK
EXPLAIN

_____
_____
_____
_____
_____
_____
_____
_____

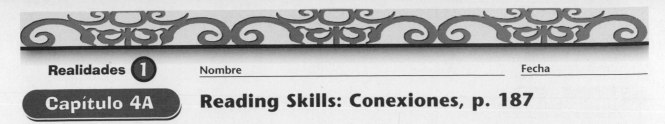

Locates, Gathers, Analyzes, and Evaluates Written Information

By showing that they can locate, gather, analyze, and evaluate information from one or more reading passages, good readers demonstrate that they know how to conduct research. On a test, readers are often asked to locate, gather, analyze, and evaluate information from a reading passage and then show how to put that information to good use.

Tip

Readers who conduct research are skilled at organizing information that they find useful. This means that the readers have a way of putting the information that they find into different categories. Your ability to categorize depends on your ability to see similarities between different pieces of information. Look at these different features of a typical high school below. Which ones would you group together? If you put them into a category, how would you label that category?

A Algebra
B Baseball team
C Community service club
D Debate team

E Earth and space science
F Football team
G Geography
H History

1. On page 187 in your textbook, re-read the **Conexiones** *"La historia"* about Old San Juan. Organize the pieces of information from the reading into two categories. Then, give each category a title.

   A Cristóbal Colón llega a San Juan durante la segunda visita a las Américas en 1493.
   B Los jóvenes pasan el tiempo con sus amigos en los parques, cafés y plazas del Viejo San Juan.
   C En la Catedral de San Juan descansan los restos de Juan Ponce de Léon, famoso explorador de la Florida.
   D El Morro fue construido en el siglo XVI para combatir los ataques de los piratas ingleses y franceses.
   E Mucha gente canta, baila y come en los restaurantes típicos del Viejo San Juan.

   Category 1:
   Title _____ includes letters _____
   Category 2:
   Title _____ includes letters _____

Sample question:

2. If writing a research paper about the history of San Juan, which information below would NOT be helpful?
   A Cristóbal Colón llega a San Juan durante la segunda visita a las Américas en 1493.
   B Los jóvenes pasan el tiempo con sus amigos en los parques, cafes y plazas del Viejo San Juan.
   C En la Catedral de San Juan descansan los restos de Juan Ponce de Léon, famoso explorador de la Florida.
   D San Juan llega a ser la capital de Puerto Rico en 1521.

Determining the Author's Purpose

To determine the author's purpose for writing a book, a story, an article, or any other text, the reader must figure out why the author wrote that particular book, story, article, or text. Some common purposes for writing are to inform, to entertain, to persuade, or to describe. Readers should also be able to explain why the author uses different techniques or includes different features within a text.

Tip

To figure out the author's purpose, ask yourself these questions:
- Where was this text first published or posted?
- What kinds of people would read this kind of newsletter, advertisement, pamphlet, book, magazine, Web site, or text?
- Why would someone want to read this newsletter, advertisement, pamphlet, book, magazine, Web site, or text?

1. On page 188 and 189 in your textbook, re-read the **Lectura,** *Al centro comercial* and answer the following questions about the brochure *¡Vamos a la Plaza del Sol!*

    Where was this text first published or posted?
    _____

    What kinds of people do you think would read this kind of text?
    _____
    _____

    Why would someone want to read this text?
    _____
    _____

Sample question:

2. What was the author's purpose for publishing the brochure "*¡Vamos a la Plaza del Sol!*"?
    A to inform readers about the different events taking place at the Plaza del Sol shopping center
    B to entertain readers by presenting interesting stories about the Plaza del Sol shopping center
    C to convince readers to buy more products at the Plaza del Sol shopping center
    D to describe how to play Andean music, how to do yoga, how to dance flamenco, and how to make pastries

Integrated Performance Assessment
Unit theme: ¿Adónde vas?

Context for the Integrated Performance Assessment: Your school's Spanish Club is going to Mexico City for a week in January. Among the many activities planned is a visit to the *Plaza del Sol.* In fact, your sponsor has told you that you can all go to the mall on either Saturday or Sunday and on one evening during the week. He/she has formed a committee to select the evening and the weekend day; you are a member of the committee.

Interpretive Task: Read the mall advertisement on pages 188–189 of *Realidades 1.* Select the evening and the weekend day you would like to go to the mall. Write your decision on a piece of paper along with why you want to go on those days.

Interpersonal Task: Discuss your opinion and your reasons with the other 2 or 3 members of the committee. Listen to their opinions and reasons. As a group, select the evening and the weekend day for the visits to the mall.

Presentational Task: Make an oral presentation to the members of the Spanish Club announcing when the club will go to the mall and explaining the reasons for the committee's decision.

Interpersonal Task Rubric

	Score: 1 Does not meet expectations	Score: 3 Meets expectations	Score: 5 Exceeds expectations
Language Use	Student uses little or no target language and relies heavily on native language word order.	Student uses the target language consistently, but may mix native and target language word order.	Student uses the target language exclusively and integrates target language word order into conversation.
Vocabulary Use	Student uses limited and repetitive language.	Student uses only recently acquired vocabulary.	Student uses both recently and previously acquired vocabulary.

Presentational Task Rubric

	Score: 1 Does not meet expectations	Score: 3 Meets expectations	Score: 5 Exceeds expectations
Amount of Communication	Student gives limited or no details or reasons.	Student gives adequate details or reasons.	Student gives consistent details or reasons.
Accuracy	Student's accuracy with vocabulary and structures is limited.	Student's accuracy with vocabulary and structures is adequate.	Student's accuracy with vocabulary and structures is exemplary.
Comprehensibility	Student's ideas lack clarity and are difficult to understand.	Student's ideas are adequately clear and fairly well understood.	Student's ideas are precise and easily understood.
Vocabulary Use	Student uses limited and repetitive vocabulary.	Student uses only recently acquired vocabulary.	Student uses both recently and previously acquired vocabulary.

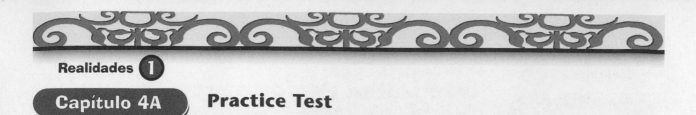
Aztec Games and Rituals

1   A god of games?! The ancient Aztecs of Mexico had just such a god: Macuilxóchitl (ma-quill-SO-chi-tul), which tells us something about the importance of games in the Aztec culture. And their games were not simply pastimes; they had religious significance as well.

2   *Pelota* was the forerunner of all present-day games that are played with a rubber ball. It was played on a large, H-shaped court. The ball was extremely hard, so hard that the players had to wear padded clothing for protection. They were allowed to hit the ball only with their elbows, hips, and knees. The object of the game was to knock the ball through a stone ring at either end of the court. The team of the first person to succeed in doing this won the game. And it was very important to win, for the team that lost was sacrificed!

3   *Patolli* was a very different type of game, much more enjoyable for all concerned and very popular. It was a board game similar to parcheesi played on a cross-shaped board. Specially marked beans were used as dice. Twelve differently colored counters were divided among the players, who moved them around the board depending upon the throw of the dice.

4   One of the most dramatic of the Aztec rituals was also a ritual for many other indigenous groups. It is still performed by the Totonac of Papantla, a village near Veracruz, Mexico. It is the ancient ritual of the *voladores*, or fliers. It survives to this day because the Spanish missionaries did not forbid it. They did not realize that it was a religious ritual and not just a dangerous sport.

5   Picture a pole a hundred feet high. At its top is a platform on which five men stand in costumes decorated with brightly colored feathers. One man is playing a flute. The other four suddenly leap into the air. You gasp, then realize that each of them is attached to the top of the pole by a rope tied around the ankles. As they fall, the ropes unravel, causing them to circle the pole. The length of the ropes is such that each *volador* flies around the pole thirteen times before landing on the ground.

6   The calendar was at the center of Aztec life. Perhaps the four *voladores* originally represented the four seasons, each with thirteen weeks (the thirteen circuits of the pole). Or the total number of circuits (13) that the *voladores* (4) make may have represented the 52 years that made up a cycle in the ancient sacred calendar. Today, however, it is not the religious aspect of the event, but its spectacular grace and daring that attract spectators.

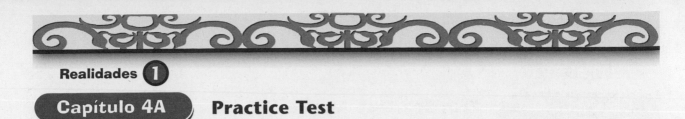

Answer questions 1–5. Base your answers on the reading
"Aztec Games and Rituals."

❶ The Aztec game of *pelota* has elements of two modern games in it. Which ones?

    A   soccer and baseball

    B   basketball and baseball

    C   volleyball and soccer

    D   soccer and basketball

❷ The Aztec game of *pelota* could still be played today exactly as it was originally, but one element of the game would have to be changed. What is that element?

    F   The players would have to wear unpadded clothing.

    G   Both men and women would have to be allowed to play.

    H   The losing team would have to be allowed to go home after the game.

    J   The court would have to be shaped like the letter *E*.

❸ What present-day sport is most comparable to the ritual of the *voladores?*

    A   high diving

    B   bungee jumping

    C   skateboarding

    D   rappeling

❹ Why can people still see the *voladores* perform today?

    F   It was not just an Aztec ritual.

    G   The Spanish missionaries enjoyed the grace and daring of the dangerous sport.

    H   The missionaries didn't understand what was happening.

    J   The missionaries encouraged religious rituals.

❺ Imagine that you were alive during the Aztec empire and you observed one of the games or rituals described in this text. Write about your experience attending the event. Include details about the setting, other people who were there, the event itself, and its outcome.

Nombre ______________________ Fecha ______________

Capítulo 4A

Practice Test Answer Sheet

1 Ⓐ Ⓑ Ⓒ Ⓓ 2 Ⓕ Ⓖ Ⓗ Ⓙ 3 Ⓐ Ⓑ Ⓒ Ⓓ

4 Ⓕ Ⓖ Ⓗ Ⓙ

5

READ
THINK
EXPLAIN

Identifying Methods of Development and Patterns of Organization

Good readers understand the tools and techniques of authors. To identify the methods of development used by an author in a text, good readers must first determine the author's purpose by asking, "Why was this text written?" After determining the author's purpose, readers next ask, "What techniques did the author use to achieve his or her purpose?" These techniques are known as methods of development and could include, among other things, the organization pattern, the word choice, or the sentence structure used in the text.

Tip

To understand the methods of development used by authors, it helps to start thinking like a writer. Imagine how your writing would change depending on the different purposes you have as a writer. For example, think about cars and all the reasons you might have to write about them. How would you write an advertisement to sell a used car? Would your writing techniques change or stay the same if you were helping complete a police report about a car accident that you witnessed? What would happen to those writing techniques if your purpose for writing was to request information from a manufacturer about electric cars? Would those same techniques work in a speech to convince your parents to lend you their car for the entire weekend?

1. On page 209 in your textbook, re-read **Actividad 20** *"La ciudad deportiva"* and answer the following questions about the advertisement *"Mi sueño."*

   What do you think was the author's purpose for writing this text?

   _____

   _____

   What techniques does the author use to achieve his purpose? Think about the way that the text is organized, the types of sentences used and the words chosen.

   _____

   _____

   _____

   _____

Sample question:

2. Which technique below is NOT used by the author in composing *"Mi sueño"*?
   A He lists all his accomplishments as a professional athlete to impress his customers.
   B He portrays himself as someone willing to share his good fortune with others.
   C He describes his facilities and staff as being of the highest quality.
   D He shows himself to be dedicated to his primary customers: families and children.

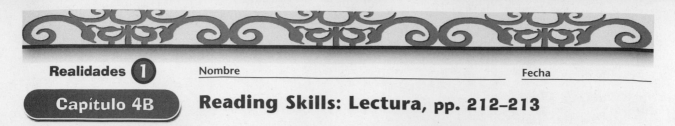

Capítulo 4B   **Reading Skills: Lectura, pp. 212–213**

Recognizing the Use of Comparison and Contrast

To recognize comparison and contrast in a reading passage, good readers can point out how items or ideas in the reading passage are similar to or different from each other. Sometimes writers will directly state that they are comparing or contrasting items in a reading passage. Other times readers might recognize items in a reading passage that could be compared or contrasted even though the writer might not have presented the information for that purpose.

Tip

After reading a text in which the author uses comparison and contrast, it is helpful for the reader to restate what he or she read using some of these common expressions:

_____, but _____.

_____; however, _____.

_____. On the other hand, _____.

Although _____, _____.

While _____, _____.

Both _____ and _____.

_____. Similarly, _____.

_____. Likewise, _____.

1. On pages 212–213 in your textbook, re-read the **Lectura,** *Sergio y Lorena: El futuro del golf.* Then, fill in the blanks of the sentences below with information that shows how Sergio and Lorena are both similar and different.

   With regard to interests, both Sergio and Lorena _____

   _____.

   Sergio won his first professional tournament when he was 17 years old. Similarly, Lorena _____.

   Regarding their goals, _____.

   Lorena became the top female golfer in the world. Sergio, however, _____

   _____.

Sample question:

2. Which statement below is true about Sergio and Lorena?
   A Both of them won their first professional tournaments before they were eighteen years old.
   B Both of them attend universities in their home countries.
   C While Lorena enjoys mountain biking, Sergio enjoys camping.
   D In 2008, Lorena became the #1 ranked female golfer in the world, while Sergio was ranked #4 among the top male golfers.

Integrated Performance Assessment
Unit theme: ¿Quieres ir conmigo?

Context for the Integrated Performance Assessment: A group of students from Madrid is coming to spend two weeks in your school. They would like to know if American students do the same activities on Saturdays that Spanish students do.

Interpretive Task: Watch the *Videohistoria: ¡A jugar!* from *Realidades 1, DVD 2, Capítulo 4B* (without the vocabulary words displayed) in which several students from Madrid talk about their Saturday activities. Make a list of these activities.

Interpersonal Task: Compare your list with your partner's list to make sure that you both know what the Spanish students do on Saturdays. Work with your partner to add a list of activities that American students often do on Saturdays.

Presentational Task: Write an e-mail to one of the students from Madrid comparing the activities students in Spain and the U.S. do on Saturdays. Be sure to include similarities and differences.

Interpersonal Task Rubric

	Score: 1 Does not meet expectations	Score: 3 Meets expectations	Score: 5 Exceeds expectations
Language Use	Student uses little or no target language and relies heavily on native language word order.	Student uses the target language consistently, but may mix native and target language word order.	Student uses the target language exclusively and integrates target language word order into conversation.
Vocabulary Use	Student uses limited and repetitive language.	Student uses only recently acquired vocabulary.	Student uses both recently and previously acquired vocabulary.

Presentational Task Rubric

	Score: 1 Does not meet expectations	Score: 3 Meets expectations	Score: 5 Exceeds expectations
Amount of Communication	Student gives little information about the similarities and differences between the activities of students in Spain and the U.S.	Student gives some information about the similarities and differences between the activities of students in Spain and the U.S.	Student gives much information about the similarities and differences between the activities of students in Spain and the U.S.
Accuracy	Student's accuracy with vocabulary and structures is limited.	Student's accuracy with vocabulary and structures is adequate.	Student's accuracy with vocabulary and structures is exemplary.
Comprehensibility	Student's ideas lack clarity and are difficult to understand.	Student's ideas are adequately clear and fairly well understood.	Student's ideas are precise and easily understood.
Vocabulary Use	Student uses limited and repetitive vocabulary.	Student uses only recently acquired vocabulary.	Student uses both recently and previously acquired vocabulary.

Una conversación difícil

1 Es viernes y son las siete de la noche. Generalmente me gusta estar con mis amigos los fines de semana. ¿Adónde vamos mis amigos y yo? Al centro comercial. Al cine. Al parque, donde jugamos al fútbol americano o, en el invierno, al gimnasio, donde jugamos al básquetbol o al vóleibol.

2 Pero mañana, no. Mañana me gustaría ir de pesca con papá. Es un día muy especial: es su <u>cumpleaños</u>.

—¿Papá?

—¿Sí, Roberto?

—Papá, me gustaría...

—Sí, Roberto. Te gustaría ir al parque. Lo siento, pero estoy cansado.

—No, papá. Quiero ir al campo con...

—A ver... Quieres ir al campo con Ramón y su familia mañana. Estoy ocupado, Roberto. Puedes hablar con tu mamá...

—¡No, no, papá! Quiero ir de pesca...

—¿De pesca? ¿Cómo vas a ir de pesca? No puedes ir solo. ¿Con quién vas a ir de pesca?

—Contigo, papá. Quiero pasar el día de tu cumpleaños contigo.

—¿Conmigo? ¿Mi cumpleaños? ¡No me digas!

—¿No vas a estar ni cansado ni ocupado, papá?

—No, no, Roberto. ¿Quién puede estar cansado en su cumpleaños? Pero sí voy a estar ocupado. Voy a ir de pesca contigo.

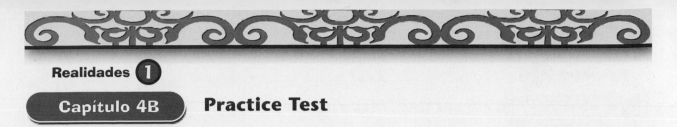

Capítulo 4B **Practice Test**

Answer questions 1–6. Base your answers on the reading *"Una conversación difícil."*

1 What does <u>cumpleaños</u> mean in paragraph 2?

    A   vacation

    B   birthday

    C   free time

    D   a kind of park

2 What is different about this weekend?

    F   Roberto is going to the mall with his friends.

    G   Roberto is going either to the park or to the gym with his friends.

    H   It is Roberto's birthday.

    J   It is Roberto's father's birthday.

3 Why doesn't Roberto's father want to go to the park?

    A   He's tired.

    B   He's sick.

    C   He's busy.

    D   It's Friday evening.

4 Why does Roberto want to go to the country?

    F   He wants to be with Ramón and his family.

    G   He wants to go fishing with his father.

    H   He can talk to his mother there.

    J   It's his birthday.

5 Which of the following is the best reason why Roberto's father is so happy at the end of the story?

    A   He loves to go fishing.

    B   He isn't tired or busy anymore.

    C   Roberto wants to spend the day with him.

    D   Tomorrow is his birthday.

6 This year Roberto may not have bought his father a birthday present. As far as his father is concerned, however, Roberto is giving him the best gift possible. There is a common English expression that says, "It's the thought that counts." Briefly explain this expression in relation to the story and give an example from your own experience.

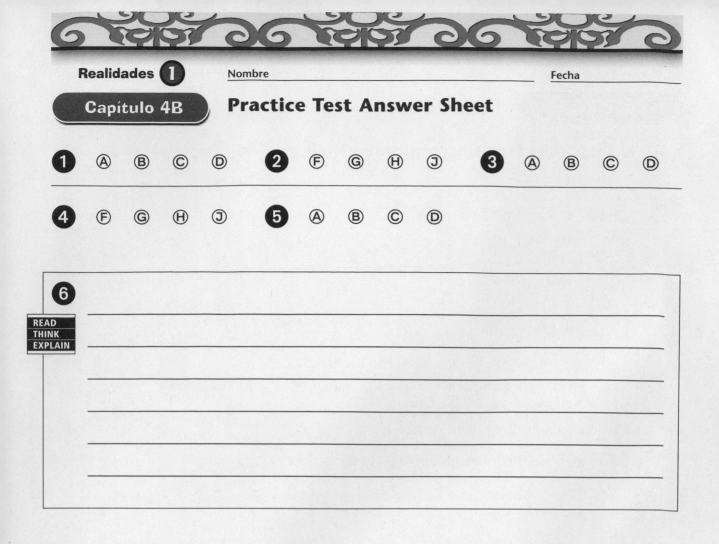

1 Ⓐ Ⓑ Ⓒ Ⓓ   2 Ⓕ Ⓖ Ⓗ Ⓙ   3 Ⓐ Ⓑ Ⓒ Ⓓ

4 Ⓕ Ⓖ Ⓗ Ⓙ   5 Ⓐ Ⓑ Ⓒ Ⓓ

6
READ
THINK
EXPLAIN

_____

_____

_____

_____

_____

_____

Strategies to Analyze Words: Context and Word Structure Clues

It is impossible to know the meaning of every word in a language. Good readers develop strategies to determine the meanings of unknown words in their reading without having to look them up in the dictionary. Good readers also know that their guesses may be wrong, so they develop strategies to check their guesses. Then, they use more traditional methods of finding the word's meaning: looking it up in the dictionary or asking for assistance.

Tip

Knowing the English equivalent of common Spanish suffixes can help you build your vocabulary both in English and Spanish. For example, page 235 of your textbook, the section **Exploración del lenguaje** is about Spanish diminutives. The suffix *-ito* or *-ita* in a Spanish word can be used to show affection for that particular person or thing, or it can be used to indicate that the person or thing is little or small in size. Likewise, in English, the suffix *-ette* can indicate that a person or thing is little or small in size; the suffixes *-y* or *-ie* can be used to show affection for a person or thing.

You must be aware that just because an English word ends with *-ette*, *-y*, or *-ie*, does not mean that the suffixes can always translate to a term of affection or to something small. When making an educated guess about an unusual word, you should always test your guess in context. In other words, insert your guessed meaning into the actual sentence where you found the unusual word.

1. Read the following sentence: "When I am with my <u>sweetie</u>, the days always seem <u>rosy</u>." Only one of the underlined words uses the *-ie* or *-y* suffix as a term of affection. Which one is it? Now read this sentence: "The artist hardly needed any paint from his <u>palette</u> to paint the <u>statuette</u>." Only one of the underlined words uses the *-ette* suffix to indicate something small in size. Which one is it?

Sample question:

2. Read the passage below and answer the question that follows.

Fred's mom is blond, and his aunt is <u>brunette</u>. Fred loves his aunt, and she is crazy about him. "Come visit me, <u>Freddy</u>!" she'll often say over the telephone. Whenever Fred visits her in her small apartment, she always has a special <u>chocolatey</u> treat waiting for him in her <u>kitchenette</u>.

Based on your understanding of the underlined words in the passage, which statement below is TRUE?
A Fred's aunt is short with brown hair.
B Freddy is small in size.
C "Chocolatey" is a term of affection.
D The aunt's kitchen is small in size.

Realidades **1**   Nombre _____   Fecha _____

Capítulo 5A   **Reading Skills: Lectura, p. 238**

Determining the Main Idea and Identifying Relevant Details

To know the relevant details in a reading passage is to know which ones are most important. The first step in identifying the relevant details is to identify the main idea of the passage. The relevant details are the ones that help support the main idea. After reading a passage, good readers ask themselves, "What is this passage mostly about?" and "Which details in the passage help support, explain, or prove the main idea?"

Tip

Some readers are better able to identify the main idea and the relevant details when they have a graphic organizer. Below is a cluster or a web where the main idea is the central circle and the relevant details sprout out from the center like spokes on a wheel.

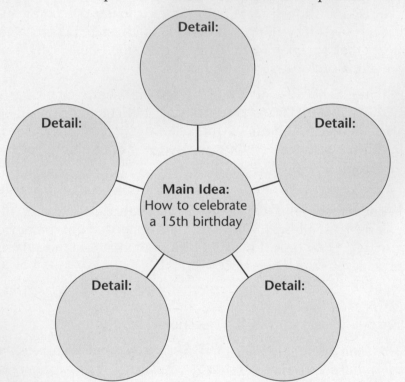

1. On page 238 in your textbook, re-read the **Lectura,** *Mis padres te invitan a mi fiesta de quince años.* The main idea of this passage is about how to celebrate a fifteenth birthday. Use the cluster graphic organizer above to list any relevant details in the passage that show the features of a fifteenth birthday celebration.

Sample question:

2. Which is NOT one of the relevant details featured in the **Lectura** about celebrating a fifteenth birthday party?
   A The fifteen-year-old girl and her parents and friends go to church in the afternoon.
   B A reception is held at an elegant restaurant.
   C The fifteen-year-old girl's first dance is with her boyfriend.
   D There are decorations, music, and dancing at the reception.

Integrated Performance Assessment
Unit theme: Una fiesta de cumpleaños

Context for the Integrated Performance Assessment: An exchange student from Mexico is spending a semester at your school. The Spanish Club is in charge of planning several special activities for her. Her birthday is next month and you are on the committee in charge of planning the celebration.

Interpretive Task: Watch the *Videohistoria: ¡Feliz cumpleaños!* from *Realidades 1, DVD 3, Capítulo 5A* (without the words displayed) to see how Cristina celebrates her birthday. Make a list of what the club needs to plan the party as well as the activities that are going to take place during the party. You should have at least 8 items on your list.

Interpersonal Task: Discuss your list with the 2 or 3 other members of the committee. Listen to the committee's suggestions and add a few new ideas to your list.

Presentational Task: Make an oral presentation to the members of the Spanish Club describing what the members need to get for the party and what they are going to do during the party.

Interpersonal Task Rubric

	Score: 1 Does not meet expectations	Score: 3 Meets expectations	Score: 5 Exceeds expectations
Language Use	Student uses little or no target language and relies heavily on native language word order.	Student uses the target language consistently, but may mix native and target language word order.	Student uses the target language exclusively and integrates target language word order into conversation.
Vocabulary Use	Student uses limited and repetitive language.	Student uses only recently acquired vocabulary.	Student uses both recently and previously acquired vocabulary.

Presentational Task Rubric

	Score: 1 Does not meet expectations	Score: 3 Meets expectations	Score: 5 Exceeds expectations
Amount of Communication	Student gives limited or no details about what students will need for the party and what they will do at the party.	Student gives adequate details about what students will need for the party and what they will do at the party.	Student gives consistent details about what students will need for the party and what they will do at the party.
Accuracy	Student's accuracy with vocabulary and structures is limited.	Student's accuracy with vocabulary and structures is adequate.	Student's accuracy with vocabulary and structures is exemplary.
Comprehensibility	Student's ideas lack clarity and are difficult to understand.	Student's ideas are adequately clear and fairly well understood.	Student's ideas are precise and easily understood.
Vocabulary Use	Student uses limited and repetitive vocabulary.	Student uses only recently acquired vocabulary.	Student uses both recently and previously acquired vocabulary.

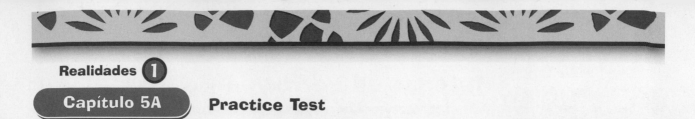

Holidays in the Hispanic World

1   Some holidays are celebrated differently in Latin America and Spain than in the United States. *La Nochebuena*, or Christmas Eve, for example, is when most of the Spanish-speaking world celebrates Christmas. A nativity scene (*un nacimiento* or *un pesebre*) is a common decoration in homes. It may be small—the Dominican Republic is known for its truly miniature figures—or large enough to fill an entire room or patio. But large or small, it is often very elaborate, with hills, trees, roads, little houses, and small mirrors to represent ponds. *El nacimiento* is usually the focal point of the festivities, with family gathered around to sing carols to the accompaniment of a guitar or a bamboo pipe or maracas. Colored paper lanterns, balloons, piñatas, and dancing are often part of the evening celebration.

2   Epiphany (*el Día de los Reyes*), on January 6, marks the formal end of the Christmas holidays. Traditionally, it was the day on which children in Spanish-speaking countries received their gifts, because it commemorates the arrival of the Three Kings into Bethlehem with their gifts of gold, frankincense, and myrrh. Today, however, in more and more homes, gifts are opened on Christmas Day or on Christmas Eve.

3   In much of Latin America, the weather is warm during the end-of-year holidays (below the equator it is the beginning of summer) and *el Año Nuevo* may be celebrated with fireworks and even barbecues. In Spain, it is the custom to eat twelve grapes at the stroke of midnight, one grape each time the clock chimes.

4   *El Día de la Raza*, October 12, celebrates the blending of the Spanish and indigenous cultures that resulted from Columbus's landing in the Americas. It is sometimes called *el Día de la Hispanidad*. In recent years, however, it has become of less importance than specific national holidays. *El Día de la Independencia* is, of course, celebrated on different days in different countries. For example, September 15 is the national holiday of four Central American nations: Guatemala, Honduras, El Salvador, and Nicaragua. Paraguay celebrates its independence from Spain on May 14; Argentina, May 25; Venezuela, July 5; Colombia, July 20; Peru, July 28; Bolivia, August 6; Ecuador, August 10; Mexico, September 16; and Chile and Costa Rica, September 18. The Dominican Republic celebrates its independence from Haiti on February 27; Uruguay, its independence from Brazil on August 25; Panama, its independence from Colombia on November 3. And Spain's national holiday? *El Día de la Hispanidad*—October 12.

Holidays in the Hispanic World (*continued*)

5   Another major fall holiday is *el Día de los Muertos* (All Souls' Day) on November 2. This holiday is a day of remembrance for all those who have died. It is a very special celebration in Mexico. There are, of course, prayers, religious services, and visits to the cemetery. Families build special altars, called *ofrendas*, in their homes. These *ofrendas* are decorated with flowers and candles, but they are not at all solemn. Photographs of loved ones who have died are displayed among objects that they cherished or used most—a rocking chair, for example, or reading glasses, gardening tools, or cooking utensils. *El Día de los Muertos* is also celebrated by eating a sweetened

bread—*el pan de muerto*—which is either shaped like skulls and crosses, or decorated with white sugar candies in the shape of skulls, crosses, coffins, and tombs. For children, there are white masks, tin or wire skeletons attached to strings, and even toy coffins that contain a skeleton that jumps out when a string is pulled.

6   In the calendar of the Catholic Church, almost every day is dedicated to one or more saints. A person's "saint's day," or *santo*, is the day dedicated to the saint who has that person's name (or one derived from it). For example, *el santo* for every José, Josefina, or Josefa is St. Joseph's Day (March 19), and *el santo* for every Pablo, Paulo, Paulina, and Paula is St. Paul's Day (June 29). Traditionally, part of a person's name was determined by the saint's day on which he or she was born. For example, if a girl whose family planned to name her María Luisa happened to be born on May 30—St. Ferdinand's Day—she would likely be named María Luisa Fernanda to honor that saint. In fact, the traditional Mexican "Happy Birthday" song, *Las mañunitas*, is actually a song for a saint's day.

   This custom is disappearing, however, and a person's birthday and saint's day are often not the same. In many countries, a person's saint's day is considered more important than a birthday. Even non-Catholics may celebrate their *santo*, for no one wants to miss out on his or her special day for a party and a few gifts. So truly every day is *un día de fiesta en el mundo hispano!*

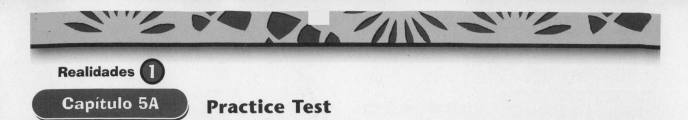

Answer questions 1–6. Base your answers on the reading *"Holidays in the Hispanic World."*

1 In a traditional Latin American home, which of the following most closely compares with the Christmas tree in a traditional U.S. home?

    A *la Nochebuena*

    B *el nacimiento*

    C *la piñata*

    D *el Día de los Reyes*

2 Which one of the following statements is true?

    F All of the nations of Central America have the same Independence Day.

    G In the United States, the best-known national holiday among the Latin American nations is *el Día de los Reyes*.

    H Of the nations of Latin America, all but two celebrate their national holiday within the five-month period from May to September.

    J All of the Spanish-speaking countries of Latin America got their independence from Spain.

3 What holiday in the United States has the same underlying purpose as *el Día de los Muertos*?

    A the Fourth of July

    B Memorial Day

    C Labor Day

    D Veterans' Day

4 Complete this statement: Today a person's *santo* is most often

    F a saint's birthday.

    G his or her own birthday.

    H the day dedicated to the saint who has the same or a similar name.

    J either March 19, May 30, or June 29.

5 READ THINK EXPLAIN October 12 was once a fairly major holiday throughout the Americas. Why do you suppose that in most countries the national holiday has become of greater importance than Columbus Day? Do you think this is a good thing or a bad thing? Why?

6 READ THINK EXPLAIN If you live far to the north or to the south of the equator, there are considerable differences in the way in which you might celebrate the end-of-year holidays. Explain why and describe at least three of those differences.

Nombre ______________________ Fecha ____________

Capítulo 5A

Practice Test Answer Sheet

1 Ⓐ Ⓑ Ⓒ Ⓓ 2 Ⓕ Ⓖ Ⓗ Ⓙ 3 Ⓐ Ⓑ Ⓒ Ⓓ

4 Ⓕ Ⓖ Ⓗ Ⓙ

5 READ THINK EXPLAIN

6 READ THINK EXPLAIN

Identifying Methods of Development and Patterns of Organization

Good readers understand the tools and techniques of authors. To identify the methods of development used by an author in a text, good readers must first determine the author's purpose by asking, "Why was this text written?" After determining the author's purpose, readers next ask, "What techniques did the author use to achieve his or her purpose?" These techniques are known as methods of development and could include, among other things, the organization pattern, the word choice, or the sentence structure used in the text.

Tip

One common pattern of organization for writers is the process paper. The process paper could be a set of instructions, a recipe, a "how-to" guide, or even the summary of a story. In a process paper, you explain the steps in a process. A graphic organizer known as a flow chart helps you keep track of all those steps. The flow chart also helps you see which steps come first in the process and which ones follow.

1. After re-reading the recipe for *Arroz con leche* in **Actividad 17 *"Un postre delicioso"*** on page 259 in your textbook, fill in the recipe steps in the flow chart below.

Six steps for making *Arroz con leche*

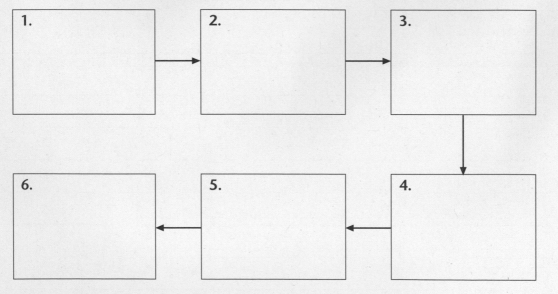

Sample question:

2. According to the recipe for *Arroz con leche*, when should the cook add the sugar and vanilla to the rice?
   A Before cooking it slowly for one hour.
   B After putting it in the refrigerator.
   C After cooking it slowly for one hour.
   D While soaking the rice for one hour and a half.

Making and Confirming Inferences

One indication of good readers is their ability to read between the lines of a text. Not only do they literally read and comprehend what a text says, but they also make inferences from what they read. An inference is an educated guess about something written in the text. An inference, because it is a guess, can never be absolutely right or wrong. However, an inference, like a conclusion, can be believable based upon the evidence that is present in the text. Confirming an inference means locating the evidence in the text that lends support to the inference.

Tip

One strategy that helps students as they make and confirm inferences is a two-column note activity known as opinion-proof. As you read, you formulate educated guesses or opinions about what you have read. You jot these down on the Opinion side of your notes. If your opinions are believable, then you should be able to write down on the Proof side all the evidence you find in the reading passage that lends support to your opinion or inference.

1. On page 262 in your textbook, read the **Lectura, *Una visita a Santa Fe.*** Based on what you have read, fill in the missing blanks of the Opinion-Proof chart below.

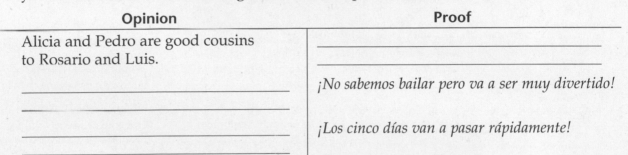

Opinion	Proof
Alicia and Pedro are good cousins to Rosario and Luis.	_____
	_____
_____	*¡No sabemos bailar pero va a ser muy divertido!*
_____	
_____	*¡Los cinco días van a pasar rápidamente!*

Sample question:

2. Based on the information presented in the letter from Alicia and Pedro to Rosario and Luis, the reader can infer that
   A   Santa Fe is a city with over 400 years of history and culture.
   B   Rosario and Luis will likely be bored during their visit to Santa Fe.
   C   Alicia and Pedro are not easily embarrassed.
   D   the *fandango* is a dance better known for its excitement than for its history.

Integrated Performance Assessment
Unit theme: ¡Vamos a un restaurante!

Context for the Integrated Performance Assessment: Angélica is a Spanish-speaking student from San Antonio, Texas. She and her family love to go to their favorite restaurant, *Casa Río.* She wants to know if your favorite restaurant is similar to her favorite restaurant.

Interpretive Task: Watch the *Videohistoria: En el Restaurante Casa Río* (without the words displayed) from *Realidades 1, DVD 3, Capítulo 5B.* You will see Angélica and her family dining at *Casa Río.* Look carefully for similarities and differences between *Casa Río* and your favorite restaurant. Make a list of the similarities and differences you see and hear.

Interpersonal Task: Tell your partner the name of your favorite restaurant. Describe the similarities and differences between *Casa Río* and your favorite restaurant. Listen to your partner's description. Ask each other questions in order to find more similarities and differences.

Presentational Task: Write an e-mail to Angélica telling her about your favorite restaurant and how it is similar to and different from *Casa Río.*

Interpersonal Task Rubric

	Score: 1 Does not meet expectations	Score: 3 Meets expectations	Score: 5 Exceeds expectations
Language Use	Student uses little or no target language and relies heavily on native language word order.	Student uses the target language consistently, but may mix native and target language word order.	Student uses the target language exclusively and integrates target language word order into conversation.
Vocabulary Use	Student uses limited and repetitive language.	Student uses only recently acquired vocabulary.	Student uses both recently and previously acquired vocabulary.

Presentational Task Rubric

	Score: 1 Does not meet expectations	Score: 3 Meets expectations	Score: 5 Exceeds expectations
Amount of Communication	Student gives limited or no details about how different or similar his/her favorite restaurant is to Casa Río.	Student gives adequate details about how different or similar his/her favorite restaurant is to Casa Río.	Student gives consistent details about how different or similar his/her favorite restaurant is to Casa Río.
Accuracy	Student's accuracy with vocabulary and structures is limited.	Student's accuracy with vocabulary and structures is adequate.	Student's accuracy with vocabulary and structures is exemplary.
Comprehensibility	Student's ideas lack clarity and are difficult to understand.	Student's ideas are adequately clear and fairly well understood.	Student's ideas are precise and easily understood.
Vocabulary Use	Student uses limited and repetitive vocabulary.	Student uses only recently acquired vocabulary.	Student uses both recently and previously acquired vocabulary.

Communication Workbook

EL SOL, viernes 18 de julio

NOTICIAS DE CELEBRACIONES

Esta semana en San Antonio muchas familias celebran ocasiones muy especiales.

Quinceañera

Mirella Lugo Armas, hija de Humberto Lugo Díaz y Carmen Armas Garza de Lugo, celebra sus quince años el domingo 20 de julio a las 6:00 P.M. en el restaurante Casa Estrella. Hay una gran fiesta con una banda de música tejana después de la cena.

Boda

Dolores Lara Villarreal y Roberto Pastor Peña celebran su boda en la iglesia de San Antonio, el sábado 19 de julio a las 8:00 P.M. Después de la ceremonia hay una fiesta con música y una cena en casa de la familia Lara.

Día del santo

Santiago Paredes Sánchez celebra el día de su santo el viernes 25 de julio. Hay una comida en su honor en casa de sus abuelos a las 2:00 P.M.

Graduación

Ana Luisa Martínez Puente celebra su graduación de la Memorial High School el día 22 de julio. Después de la graduación hay una barbacoa para la familia y los amigos en el parque Fiesta Texas a las 4:00 P.M.

Cincuenta años

Roberto González Juárez y María Luisa Gallardo Correa de González celebran su aniversario de bodas el 25 de julio en el salón de fiestas La Suerte. Van a celebrar la ocasión con una comida deliciosa para la familia y los amigos.

Answer questions 1–6. Base your answers on the reading *"Noticias de celebraciones."*

1   Which of the celebrations has a party outside?

    A   *cincuenta años*

    B   *graduación*

    C   *día del santo*

    D   *quinceañera*

2   What do all of the notices of celebrations have in common?

    F   They all mention a meal.

    G   They all mention music.

    H   They all take place in the evening.

    J   They all mention a ceremony.

3   Which of these occasions is celebrated only in the Hispanic culture?

    A   *boda*

    B   *cincuenta años*

    C   *quinceañera*

    D   *graduación*

4   Which of the celebrations mentions the names of the parents of the honored person or people?

    F   *graduación*

    G   *quinceañera*

    H   *día del santo*

    J   *boda*

5   READ THINK EXPLAIN   Which of these celebrations do you think might have more guests that are family members than friends? Why do you think these celebrations might be more for family members?

6   READ THINK EXPLAIN   Clasifica las fiestas de 5 a 1. El 5 es para la fiesta más formal, y el 1 es para la fiesta menos formal. Explica tus clasificaciones "5" y "1".

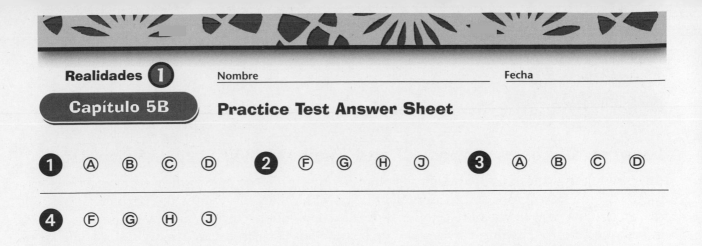

❶ Ⓐ   Ⓑ   Ⓒ   Ⓓ   **❷** Ⓕ   Ⓖ   Ⓗ   Ⓙ   **❸** Ⓐ   Ⓑ   Ⓒ   Ⓓ

❹ Ⓕ   Ⓖ   Ⓗ   Ⓙ

❺

READ
THINK
EXPLAIN

_____

_____

_____

_____

_____

_____

❻

READ
THINK
EXPLAIN

_____

_____

_____

_____

_____

_____

_____

_____

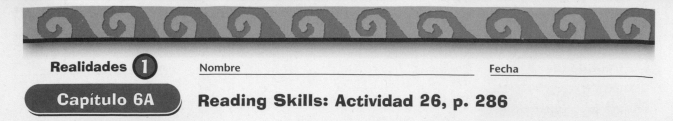

Locates, Gathers, Analyzes, and Evaluates Written Information

By showing that they can locate, gather, analyze, and evaluate information from one or more reading passages, good readers demonstrate that they know how to conduct research. On a test, readers are often asked to locate, gather, analyze, and evaluate information from a reading passage and then show how to put that information to good use.

Tip

Readers who conduct research are skilled at translating information from their reading into their own words. If they encounter information in one format, such as a chart, they are able to restate that information in a different format, such as in sentences or as bullets. This is how they demonstrate their comprehension of what they have read.

1. Review **Actividad 26** *"¿Duermes bien?"* on page 286, and then complete the two exercises below.

   Use four sentences to restate some of the information presented in the two pie graphs.

   _____

   _____

   _____

   _____

   Use one paragraph with a topic sentence and supporting sentences to restate the information presented as bullets.

   _____

   _____

   _____

   _____

   _____

   _____

   _____

   _____

Sample question:

2. Imagine that a friend was sleeping only 5–6 hours on school nights. Which information from the graphs and bullets in **Actividad 26** would be LEAST likely to make your friend start sleeping more?

   A Las personas que duermen menos de seis horas por noche sufren más lesiones.

   B 52% de las personas duermen ocho horas o más en los fines de la semana.

   C Las personas que duermen menos de seis horas por noche tienen más problemas de relaciones interpersonales.

   D Solamente 15% de las personas duermen menos de seis horas durante la semana.

Communication Workbook

Understanding Tone

To understand an author's tone in a reading passage, good readers focus not just on what is said, but also on how it is said. Like identifying an author's point of view, identifying an author's tone requires readers to ask, "What is the author's attitude or feelings about the subject of the reading passage?" First, readers should be able to identify when an author feels positive, negative, or neutral toward a subject. As readers gain more practice with this skill, they should be able to identify a wide range of tones used by authors. Some of these might include: admiration, nostalgia, objectivity, sarcasm, surprise, and sympathy.

Tip

One way to begin to understand an author's tone is to separate the statements of fact from the statements of opinion. While statements of fact make an author seem more objective, statements of opinion often express the author's feelings about a subject.

1. After reviewing the **Lectura,** *El desastre en mi dormitorio* on pages 288 and 289 in your textbook, identify the statements from the reading passage as facts or opinions. Then, for each opinion, identify the feelings that it reveals about the author.

	Fact or Opinion	Feelings Expressed by Opinions
Rosario: *"Estoy desesperada."*	_____	_____
Rosario: *"Hay pizza debajo de la cama."*	_____	_____
Rosario: *"[Negro] es el peor color y es feísimo."*	_____	_____
Magdalena: *"Uds. son muy diferentes."*	_____	_____
Magdalena: *"Ella cree que el color negro es el más bonito."*	_____	_____

Sample question:

2. How does the tone expressed in Rosario's letter compare to the tone expressed in Magdalena's letter?
   A Rosario seems more helpful than Magdalena.
   B Magdalena seems more exaggerated than Rosario.
   C Both Rosario and Magdalena have an angry tone in their letters.
   D Magdalena seems more objective than Rosario.

Integrated Performance Assessment
Unit theme: En mi dormitorio

Context for the Integrated Performance Assessment: Your Spanish class is going to have a debate. The topic of the debate is the following statement: It is important to clean your bedroom every day.

Interpretive Task: Watch the *Videohistoria: El cuarto de Ignacio* from *Realidades 1, DVD 3, Capítulo 6A* (without the words displayed) and listen to the opinions of Ignacio and his mother. As you listen, think about the debate statement and write down a few ideas that support your opinion.

Interpersonal Task: Explain your opinion to a group of 2 or 3 other students. Listen to the opinions of the other students in your group. Ask questions in order to get more information to help you take a stand in the debate.

Presentational Task: Make an oral presentation to the class in which you take a side on the debate statement and give reasons for your opinion.

Interpersonal Task Rubric

	Score: 1 Does not meet expectations	Score: 3 Meets expectations	Score: 5 Exceeds expectations
Language Use	Student uses little or no target language and relies heavily on native language word order.	Student uses the target language consistently, but may mix native and target language word order.	Student uses the target language exclusively and integrates target language word order into conversation.
Vocabulary Use	Student uses limited and repetitive language.	Student uses only recently acquired vocabulary.	Student uses both recently and previously acquired vocabulary.

Presentational Task Rubric

	Score: 1 Does not meet expectations	Score: 3 Meets expectations	Score: 5 Exceeds expectations
Amount of Communication	Student gives limited arguments to support his/her side.	Student gives adequate arguments to support his/her side.	Student gives consistent arguments to support his/her side.
Accuracy	Student's accuracy with vocabulary and structures is limited.	Student's accuracy with vocabulary and structures is adequate.	Student's accuracy with vocabulary and structures is exemplary.
Comprehensibility	Student's ideas lack clarity and are difficult to understand.	Student's ideas are adequately clear and fairly well understood.	Student's ideas are precise and easily understood.
Vocabulary Use	Student uses limited and repetitive vocabulary.	Student uses only recently acquired vocabulary.	Student uses both recently and previously acquired vocabulary.

Communication Workbook

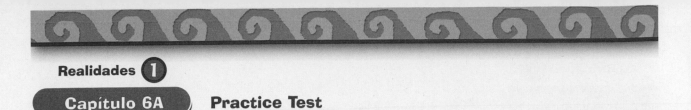
How "Spanish" Is Spanish Architecture?

1 If you were to travel from the southwestern United States to the southern tip of South America, many buildings would look fairly familiar in almost every place you visited. Although regional differences would be obvious, you would still be aware of a certain look shared by many communities in the southwestern United States and Latin America. In large part, that look can be traced to the architecture of Moorish Spain.

2 The Moors were North African Arabs who ruled most of the Iberian Peninsula (Spain and Portugal) for nearly 800 years—from the early eighth century until the late fifteenth century. Many elements of Latin American architecture were first introduced to Spain by the Moors during that period.

3 Patios, for example, became common in cities such as Córdoba and Sevilla beginning in the early eleventh century.

Because of widespread political and social unrest during that time, houses were built with heavy doors and thick, fortress-like walls. These walls also helped shield the rooms inside from the sun's heat. The patios, placed in the center of the house and accessible from all first-floor rooms, often had tiled floors. In the center, surrounded by lemon trees and flowers, there was often a pool or a large clay pot filled with cool water. Patios were thus probably the first naturally "air-conditioned" rooms. Throughout Latin America today, as well as in Spain, central patios are still a popular feature of many commercial buildings as well as homes.

4 Another common element of Latin American architecture is the *balcón*, or *mirador*. In Moorish Spain, homes typically had balconies off the second-floor sleeping areas. These balconies, which often included intricately designed wrought iron railings and grates, overlooked the patio. During the period when Latin America was being

colonized by Spain, balconies became common in Latin America as well. There was, however, a major difference: most Latin American balconies do not overlook the patio. Instead, they face outward so that people can view the street life of the town.

5 Buildings in Moorish Spain usually differed from those in northern Europe in another way as well. Although wood was used as a building material, it was not nearly as common as stone, brick, and adobe (heavy clay bricks made of sun-dried earth and straw). Today, builders in Latin America and the southwestern United States continue to use many of these same materials and techniques first introduced by the Moors.

Realidades 1

Capítulo 6A   **Practice Test**

Answer questions 1–5. Base your answers on the reading *"How "Spanish" is Spanish Architecture?"*

1 When did the Moors conquer Spain?

    A   in the early 500s

    B   in the early 700s

    C   in the early 800s

    D   in the early 1200s

2 According to the article, what was the main reason why the doors and walls of Spanish homes were so thick during the time of Moorish rule?

    F   They kept the house warm.

    G   They were used for defense and protection.

    H   They enclosed the patio.

    J   The Moors were used to living in homes with thick walls.

3 Which of the following is the best English equivalent of *mirador* in paragraph 4?

    A   a door with a mirror in it

    B   a heavy mirror

    C   a door onto a patio

    D   an overlook

4 Why do architectural features that date to the period of Moorish influence in Spain exist in the southwestern United States and Latin America today?

    F   It gets very hot in those regions.

    G   Those regions were conquered by the Moors.

    H   Those regions were colonized by the Spanish.

    J   There is much political and social unrest in those regions.

5   Based on what you have read, compare and contrast typical modern homes in Spain and in the United States. What cultural influences might be responsible for these similarities and differences?

1. Ⓐ Ⓑ Ⓒ Ⓓ   2. Ⓕ Ⓖ Ⓗ Ⓙ   3. Ⓐ Ⓑ Ⓒ Ⓓ

4. Ⓕ Ⓖ Ⓗ Ⓙ

5.

READ
THINK
EXPLAIN

_____
_____
_____
_____
_____
_____
_____
_____
_____
_____

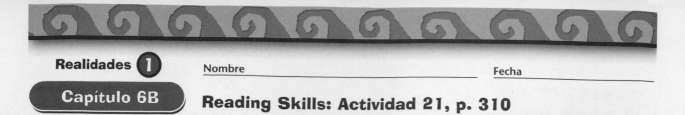

Synthesizing Information from Multiple Sources to Draw Conclusions

Often readers are asked to look at two or more reading passages and make connections between the different passages. When readers synthesize information, they are forming new ideas based on what they have read in the different reading passages.

Tip

When synthesizing information from various sources, readers benefit when they read actively. While they read, active readers are constantly formulating ideas about how information from various sources relate to each other. Active readers often show these relationships in charts, tables, or graphs.

1. Review **Actividad 21** "*¿Qué casa están buscando?*" on page 310 in your textbook, and then fill out the chart below.

	What would the house buyer like about Casa Venezia?	What would the house buyer dislike about Casa Venezia?
José Guzmán		
Alejandro Lara		
Dora Peña		

Sample question:

2. Based on the descriptions about the three house buyers and the description of Casa Venezia, which statement below is true?

   A José Guzmán's wife would not like the kitchen at Casa Venezia.

   B Alejandro Lara needs a house like Casa Venezia with its three levels.

   C Dora Peña would have no need for Casa Venezia's carpets in the bedrooms.

   D Casa Venezia seems more suitable for Dora Peña than it does for José Guzmán.

Communication Workbook

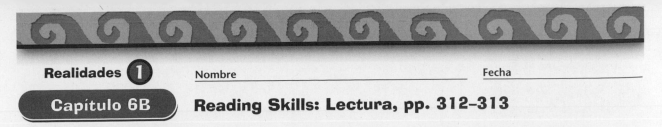

Analyzing the Effectiveness of Complex Elements of Plot

When reading stories, it is important for readers to identify the protagonist, or main character, of the story. The protagonist usually has a goal in the story, and it is the protagonist's attempt to reach that goal that moves along the plot of the story. The plot can be summed up as all the actions that occur as the protagonist attempts to reach his or her goal. While attempting to reach his or her goal, the protagonist encounters problems or conflicts that must be resolved. The climax of the story is the point when it becomes clear to the reader that the protagonist will or will not reach his or her goal. Good readers can explain how various elements of the plot such as the protagonist's goals or conflicts affect the outcome of the story.

Tip

1. One way that you can identify and understand various plot elements is to use a chart. After reviewing the **Lectura**, *Cantaclara* on pages 312 and 313 in your textbook, fill in the information required in the chart below.

Who is the protagonist?

_____
_____
_____
_____

What is his/her goal?

_____
_____
_____
_____

What conflicts does he/she encounter?

_____
_____
_____
_____

What is the outcome of each conflict?

_____
_____
_____
_____

When is the climax of the story?

_____
_____
_____
_____

Sample question:

2. How would the outcome of the story have been different if Cantaclara had a nice stepmother but a poor singing voice?

   A Cantaclara would have had to let her sisters go with her to *La estrella del futuro*.

   B Cantaclara would have had to clean the kitchen before going to *La estrella del futuro*, but she would not have been a winner.

   C Cantaclara would not have had to clean the kitchen, but she would not have been a winner on *La estrella del futuro*.

   D Cantaclara's mother would have introduced Cantaclara to a handsome prince who would have told Cantaclara that he loved her even without a beautiful singing voice.

Integrated Performance Assessment
Unit theme: ¿Cómo es tu casa?

Context for the Integrated Performance Assessment: You usually do chores around the house to help your parents. Now you find yourself in the position of needing money for your personal expenses. You want to convince your parents to give you money and you are willing to do more chores in order to earn money. However, you need some help in planning how to convince your parents.

Interpretive Task: Watch the *Videohistoria: Los quehaceres de Elena* from *Realidades 1, DVD 3, Capítulo 6B* (without the words displayed) to see how Elena negotiates with her little brother, Jorgito. Listen to the chores that Elena does and write down any that you are willing to do.

Interpersonal Task: Discuss your situation with a friend in Spanish class. Explain the extra chores you are willing to do. Ask your friend to suggest additional chores and to help you decide how much money you are going to ask your parents to give you.

Presentational Task: Make an oral presentation to a group of 3 or 4 students in order to rehearse what you plan to say to your parents. Mention at least four chores you are willing to do.

Interpersonal Task Rubric

	Score: 1 Does not meet expectations	Score: 3 Meets expectations	Score: 5 Exceeds expectations
Language Use	Student uses little or no target language and relies heavily on native language word order.	Student uses the target language consistently, but may mix native and target language word order.	Student uses the target language exclusively and integrates target language word order into conversation.
Vocabulary Use	Student uses limited and repetitive language.	Student uses only required acquired vocabulary.	Student uses both recently and previously acquired vocabulary.

Presentational Task Rubric

	Score: 1 Does not meet expectations	Score: 3 Meets expectations	Score: 5 Exceeds expectations
Amount of Communication	Student mentions fewer than four chores that he/she is willing to do.	Student mentions four chores that he/she is willing to do.	Student mentions more than four chores that he/she is willing to do.
Accuracy	Student's accuracy with vocabulary and structures is limited.	Student's accuracy with vocabulary and structures is adequate.	Student's accuracy with vocabulary and structures is exemplary.
Comprehensibility	Student's ideas lack clarity and are difficult to understand.	Student's ideas are adequately clear and fairly well understood.	Student's ideas are precise and easily understood.
Vocabulary Use	Student uses limited and repetitive vocabulary.	Student uses only recently acquired vocabulary.	Student uses both recently and previously acquired vocabulary.

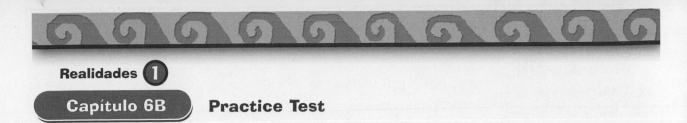
Mi segunda casa es ... ¡una cueva!

1 ¡Hola! Me llamo Macarena y soy española.
Vivo con mis padres y tres hermanos en un
apartamento grande y bonito en Granada,
que está en el sur de España. Pero tenemos
otra casa y es... ¡una cueva! Nuestra casa-
cueva está cerca de Guadix, un pueblo pin-
toresco de unos 20.000 habitantes. Guadix
está a 60 kilómetros de Granada, y es famoso
por sus casas-cueva.

2   Más de un cuarto de la población del
pueblo vive en estas casas subterráneas.
Tradicionalmente sólo para los pobres y arte-
sanos, hoy día las casas-cueva son la segunda
residencia de muchas familias de la clase
media. ¡Me encanta pasar tiempo con mi
familia en nuestra casa-cueva!

3 ¿Qué tienen de atractivo las casas-cueva?

- La temperatura se mantiene constante
  (20 grados centígrados) durante todo el
  año.
- Si la familia necesita más espacio, sólo
  hay que excavar otro cuarto.

- Tienen todas las comodidades de una
  casa moderna: dormitorios, cocina,
  cuarto de baño, sala, comedor, chime-
  nea, electricidad y conexiones para
  Internet y fax.
- De la puerta hay una magnífica vista.
  (¡Pocas cuevas tienen ventanas!)

4   Si quieres vivir en un ambiente original,
íntimo y rústico, o si simplemente prefieres
vivir en otra casa durante el fin de semana o
durante las vacaciones de verano, las casas-
cueva son perfectas para ti.

Una casa en el Barrio de las cuevas

Answer questions 1–6. Base your answers on the reading *"Mi segunda casa es...*
¡una cueva!"

1. According to the reading, which of the following statements is false?

   A   Cave houses have all the conveniences of a modern home.

   B   Cave houses are not only for artisans and the poor.

   C   Macarena's family has two homes.

   D   Cave houses offer wonderful views from the windows.

2. From Macarena's description of her family's second home, the reader can conclude that

   F   it gets too hot in Granada during the summer.

   G   her parents are artisans.

   H   she enjoys spending time in the cave.

   J   she doesn't like living in an apartment.

3. In paragraph 4, what does the word *ambiente* mean?

   A   countryside

   B   cave

   C   atmosphere

   D   city

4. Which of the following is <u>not</u> mentioned as an advantage of living in a cave house?

   F   There's a great view from the door.

   G   It's easy to make more furniture from the rocks.

   H   The houses maintain an even temperature all year.

   J   It's easy to add more space to the home.

5. Make a list of buildings, vehicles, or places that could be used as homes. Describe the advantages or disadvantages of each one.

6. ¿Te gustaría vivir en una casa-cueva? Explica por qué.

                                                               Communication Workbook

Nombre ______________________ Fecha ______________

Capítulo 6B

Practice Test Answer Sheet

1 Ⓐ Ⓑ Ⓒ Ⓓ 2 Ⓕ Ⓖ Ⓗ Ⓙ 3 Ⓐ Ⓑ Ⓒ Ⓓ

4 Ⓕ Ⓖ Ⓗ Ⓙ

5

READ
THINK
EXPLAIN

6

READ
THINK
EXPLAIN

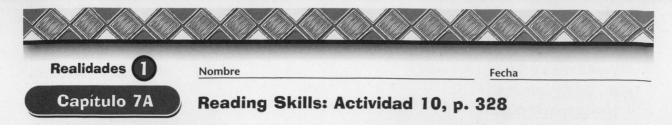

Interpreting Diagrams, Graphs, and Statistical Illustrations

When good readers encounter a diagram, a graph, or any statistical information, they are able to make meaning from what they see. They are able to translate the information that is presented graphically or statistically into useful information. Readers are often asked to make comparisons involving the information in the diagrams, graphs, or statistics.

Tip

One strategy that helps students make meaning from diagrams, graphs, and statistics is to practice translating graphic or statistical information into sentences. In describing relationships that you observe in the diagrams, graphs, or statistics, you should become familiar with making statements with the following words or expressions of comparison:

more than → most   less than → least → fewer than
greater than → larger → largest   smaller → smallest
bigger → biggest   equal → same → different

1. Review **Actividad 10** on page 328 in your textbook. Look at the foreign currency exchange rate data below and then answer the questions that follow.

Foreign Exchange Rates Compared to the U.S. Dollar

Country	Currency	$1 U.S. =	Country	Currency	$1 U.S. =
Argentina	peso	3.0050	Peru	nuevo sol	3.414
Colombia	peso	2274.50	Uruguay	nuevo peso	24.4350
Mexico	peso	10.4730	Venezuela	bolivar	2147.30

Would the shoes in **Actividad 10** that cost 1,820 Uruguayan pesos cost more or less in U.S. dollars? Why?

_____

Are 1,820 Uruguayan pesos worth more or less than 1,820 Mexican pesos? Why?

_____

Which peso (from Argentina, Colombia, Mexico, or Uruguay) could be purchased with the smallest amount of U.S. currency? Why?

_____

Sample question:

2. Based on the information presented in the Foreign Exchange Rate chart above, which statement below is true?
   A When exchanging for U.S. dollars, the Uruguayan nuevo peso is nearly equal in value to the Colombian peso.
   B The number of pesos you would receive in Mexico for 10 U.S. dollars is more than the number of pesos you would receive in Argentina for the same amount of U.S. dollars.
   C One Venezuelan bolivar is equal to 2147.30 U.S. dollars.
   D You would need more Argentinian pesos than Peruvian nuevo soles to buy $1 U.S. dollar.

Locates, Gathers, Analyzes, and Evaluates Written Information

By showing that they can locate, gather, analyze, and evaluate information from one or more reading passages, good readers demonstrate that they know how to conduct research. On a test, readers are often asked to locate, gather, analyze, and evaluate information from a reading passage and then show how to put that information to good use.

Tip

Readers who conduct research are skilled at organizing information from their reading. For many, the outline is an excellent way to organize information gathered from research. With an outline, you begin by organizing information into broad categories and then gradually narrow your focus to more specific details.

1. Review the **Lectura,** *Tradiciones de la ropa panameña* on pages 336 and 337 in your textbook and then fill in the missing blanks of the outline below.

Traditional Panamanian Clothing
I _____
   A *Montuna*
   B *De* _____
      1 _____
      2 It costs a lot.
         a _____
         b _____
         c _____
      3 Something that is very important in the city of Las Tablas.

II *La blusa de molas*
   A Made by the Kuna Indians from the San Blas Islands.
   B Molas are decorative panels on the fronts and backs of the blouses.
      1 _____
      2 _____
      3 *Molas* can be found in museums as works of art.

Sample question:

2. If you were interested in making your own samples of traditional Panamanian clothing, all of the following statements would be helpful to you EXCEPT which one?
   A You will need a lot of jewels to decorate a *pollera de gala*.
   B You can show your individual talent and expression with your *molas*.
   C You will discover that the *pollera de gala* is most important in the city of Las Tablas.
   D A *pollera de gala* could require as many as seven months to make by hand.

Integrated Performance Assessment
Unit theme: ¿Cuánto cuesta?

Context for the Integrated Performance Assessment: You are planning on going to a special event and want to buy some new clothes to wear.

Interpretive Task: Watch the *Videohistoria: Una noche especial* from *Realidades 1, DVD 4, Capítulo 7A* (without words displayed) as Teresa shops for clothes for a special event. Make a list of the clothes she looks at.

Interpersonal Task: Describe your special event and the new clothes you want to buy to a friend in Spanish class. Ask his/her opinion on the clothes. Then ask him/her for the names of some stores where you should shop for the new clothes.

Presentational Task: Write an e-mail to a friend describing your special event, the new clothes you want to buy, and where you plan to shop. Invite your friend to go with you.

Interpersonal Task Rubric

	Score: 1 Does not meet expectations	Score: 3 Meets expectations	Score: 5 Exceeds expectations
Language Use	Student uses little or no target language and relies heavily on native language word order.	Student uses the target language consistently, but may mix native and target language word order.	Student uses the target language exclusively and integrates target language word order into conversation.
Vocabulary Use	Student uses limited and repetitive language.	Student uses only recently acquired vocabulary.	Student uses both recently and previously acquired vocabulary.

Presentational Task Rubric

	Score: 1 Does not meet expectations	Score: 3 Meets expectations	Score: 5 Exceeds expectations
Amount of Communication	Student gives limited or no details about the special event, the clothes, and the shops.	Student gives adequate details about the special event, the clothes, and the shops.	Student gives consistent details about the special event, the clothes, and the shops.
Accuracy	Student's accuracy with vocabulary and structures is limited.	Student's accuracy with vocabulary and structures is adequate.	Student's accuracy with vocabulary and structures is exemplary.
Comprehensibility	Student's ideas lack clarity and are difficult to understand.	Student's ideas are adequately clear and fairly well understood.	Student's ideas are precise and easily understood.
Vocabulary Use	Student uses limited and repetitive vocabulary.	Student uses only recently acquired vocabulary.	Student uses both recently and previously acquired vocabulary.

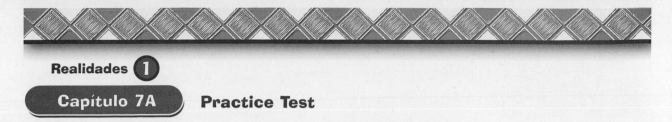

A Culture as Seen Through Its Textiles

1 On July 26, 1925, archaeologists made a dramatic discovery in the desert of the Paracas peninsula, approximately 150 miles south of the Peruvian capital of Lima. In the desert off the Pacific coast they found an underground network of tombs from the Paracas and Nazca cultures that dated back to the fourth century B.C. Such a group of elaborately interconnected tombs is sometimes called a <u>necropolis</u>, a Greek word meaning "city of the dead." The Paracas necropolis contained beautiful, richly decorated gold objects, along with hundreds of perfectly preserved human bodies carefully wrapped in intricately woven, embroidered cloth that was as well preserved as the bodies it contained.

2   Woven cloth, or textiles, has of course played both a practical and a ceremonial role in world cultures for thousands of years. The textiles found at Paracas were probably specially made for use in burials and almost surely revealed the social status of the people buried there.

3   Images woven into garments or added to them were a form of communication in ancient cultures. Whether painted, embroidered, or decorated with metal or brightly colored feathers, many textiles contained important symbolic information. The most common images found on the Paracas textiles were those of birds, cats, snakes, rodents, llamas, and fish. By showing the animals that were native to

the region, these pictures represented in one way or another the three basic realms of nature that daily affected the people who made the pictures: the sky, the earth, and the sea. Human forms were also shown. These pictures no doubt reflected concepts important to the culture, such as nature gods, the individual's ancestors, or the individual's social status.

4   Today, people in Peru and neighboring Bolivia continue to weave ponchos, tunics, and hats that use some of the same designs found in their people's textiles over 2,000 years ago.

Answer questions 1–6. Base your answers on the reading *"A Culture as Seen Through Its Textiles."*

1 What is Paracas?

    A   another name for Peru

    B   a Peruvian peninsula and the name of a people who once lived there

    C   the capital of Peru

    D   a type of Peruvian textile

2 What is a <u>necropolis</u>?

    F   a desert in Peru

    G   a place for storing ancient gold objects

    H   a vast underground burial site

    J   a type of Greek city

3 Which one of the following statements is <u>not</u> true?

    A   The modern textiles of Peru are totally different from those found in ancient tombs.

    B   The people of Peru still use many of the same design elements that their ancestors did.

    C   Weaving is a practice that dates back to ancient times.

    D   The tombs in Paracas were discovered in the twentieth century.

4 Why were images included in the textiles of ancient peoples?

    F   for purely religious reasons

    G   to communicate information of some sort

    H   to preserve the body of the person around whom it was wrapped

    J   to impress visitors to the tombs

5 "Woven cloth, or textiles, has . . . played both a practical and a ceremonial role in world cultures for thousands of years." Make a list of three "Practical" and three "Ceremonial" uses of textiles today.

6 Choose any well-known person and describe the textile that you would design to represent him or her. Describe the symbols (colors, objects, figures) that you would use and explain why you chose them.

Nombre ______________________ Fecha ______________

Practice Test Answer Sheet

1 Ⓐ Ⓑ Ⓒ Ⓓ   2 Ⓕ Ⓖ Ⓗ Ⓙ   3 Ⓐ Ⓑ Ⓒ Ⓓ

4 Ⓕ Ⓖ Ⓗ Ⓙ

5 READ THINK EXPLAIN

6 READ THINK EXPLAIN

Drawing Conclusions

To draw a conclusion is to form an opinion based on evidence. Sometimes the evidence presented to readers is very limited, but they must ensure that their evidence-based opinions make sense.

Conclusion statements are rarely right or wrong. They are often presented as believable or not. If you are successful at drawing conclusions from your reading, then you likely are skilled at finding evidence in your reading that supports your conclusions.

Conclusions are only as strong as the evidence on which they are based. Conclusions based on little evidence are not as believable as conclusions based on a lot of different kinds of evidence. You must also be willing to change your conclusions as more evidence becomes available in the reading passage.

Tip

One strategy that helps students as they draw conclusions is to use "If-Then" statements with their evidence and conclusions. If a conclusion does not make logical sense, then it will become obvious when presented in an "If-Then" statement. As more evidence is presented in the "If" statements, the conclusions in the "Then" statements will also likely change.

1. On page 358 of your textbook, review **Actividad 17 "Una lección de historia,"** and then complete these statements. Can you draw more than one possible conclusion for the evidence presented below?
   A If in 1848 President James K. Polk paid $15 million dollars to Mexico according to the Treaty of Hidalgo, **and**
   B If in 1898 President William McKinley helped Cuba and Puerto Rico declare their independence from Spain, **then** one could conclude that

   _____

   or

   _____.

   Now add this third piece of evidence:
   C If in 1904 President Theodore Roosevelt began building the Panama Canal, **then** based on points **A, B,** and **C,** one could conclude that American presidents

   _____

   _____.

Sample question:

2. If Columbus discovered the Dominican Republic in 1492 and if Juan Ponce de León explored Florida in 1513, then one could conclude that
   A both Columbus and de León were motivated by the desire to find gold.
   B the Dominican Republic and Florida would have a lot in common during the 1500's.
   C Spain was active in exploration of the Americas in the late fifteenth and early sixteenth centuries.
   D neither Columbus nor de León would discover the fountain of youth in the New World.

Determining the Main Idea

To determine the main idea of a reading passage, the reader must be able to describe what a reading passage is mostly about. He or she should be able to summarize the main idea of the reading passage in one sentence. A common problem for students when working with this skill is confusing an important detail in the reading passage with the main idea. Just because something is mentioned in the reading passage does not mean it is the main idea of the passage. Many times the main idea is not even stated in the reading passage. This is often called an implied main idea. No matter if the main idea is stated or implied, the basic question remains the same: "What is this reading passage mostly about?"

Tip

One common mistake that students make with main-idea questions is that they often choose main-idea statements that are either too broad or too narrow. When you are too broad in your thinking, you are too general and do not recognize what is unique about the particular reading passage. When you are too narrow, you focus too much on isolated details without looking at the whole picture.

1. Review the **Lectura, *¡De compras!*** on page 364 of your textbook. Then read the main-idea statements listed below and indicate if they are too broad, too narrow, or just right.

    _____ Little Havana is the heart of the Cuban community in Miami.

    _____ Shopping is a fun activity.

    _____ United States cities with large Hispanic communities offer interesting shopping opportunities.

    _____ Hispanic residents of the United States love to go shopping.

    _____ Olvera Street is the oldest street in Los Angeles and the place to see Mexican culture.

    _____ One can find inexpensive and unique things to buy in the Hispanic neighborhoods of American cities.

Sample question:

2. Another good title for the reading passage "**¡De compras!**" would be
   A "Guava Paste on Miami's Eighth Street."
   B "Shopping Adventures in America's Hispanic Neighborhoods."
   C "Trying to Find Original Products at Good Prices."
   D "What to Buy in Los Angeles and San Antonio."

Integrated Performance Assessment
Unit theme: ¡Qué regalo!

Context for the Integrated Performance Assessment: A group of students from Colombia is coming to spend three weeks in your school. They want to know where to shop and what to buy in your community so that they can buy gifts for friends and family.

Interpretive Task: Read the *Lectura: ¡De compras!* on pages 364–365 of *Realidades 1* to see how the shops and shopping areas of four cities are described. As you read, think about the shops and shopping areas in your community. Write down the names of four shops in your community and a brief description of what each shop sells.

Interpersonal Task: Discuss your ideas about the shops and what they sell with your partner. Working together, select three shops that you think the students from Colombia would like.

Presentational Task: Send an e-mail to one of the students from Colombia describing the three shops that you and your partner selected. Tell him/her what each shop sells and why you think he/she will like each shop.

Interpersonal Task Rubric

	Score: 1 Does not meet expectations	Score: 3 Meets expectations	Score: 5 Exceeds expectations
Language Use	Student uses little or no target language and relies heavily on native language word order.	Student uses the target language consistently, but may mix native and target language word order.	Student uses the target language exclusively and integrates target language word order into conversation.
Vocabulary Use	Student uses limited and repetitive language.	Student uses only recently acquired vocabulary.	Student uses both recently and previously acquired vocabulary.

Presentational Task Rubric

	Score: 1 Does not meet expectations	Score: 3 Meets expectations	Score: 5 Exceeds expectations
Amount of Communication	Student gives limited or no details about the three shops, what they sell, and why the visiting student would like the shops.	Student gives adequate details about the three shops, what they sell, and why the visiting student would like the shops.	Student gives consistent details about the three shops, what they sell, and why the visiting student would like the shops.
Accuracy	Student's accuracy with vocabulary and structures is limited.	Student's accuracy with vocabulary and structures is adequate.	Student's accuracy with vocabulary and structures is exemplary.
Comprehensibility	Student's ideas lack clarity and are difficult to understand.	Student's ideas are adequately clear and fairly well understood.	Student's ideas are precise and easily understood.
Vocabulary Use	Student uses limited and repetitive vocabulary.	Student uses only recently acquired vocabulary.	Student uses both recently and previously acquired vocabulary.

Necesito comprar ropa

¿Te gusta ir de compras, pero no te gusta estar con muchas personas?
Lee este artículo de la solución de Margarita para este problema.

1   Margarita, una joven argentina de dieciséis años, tiene un problema. Necesita comprar ropa para sus vacaciones en Chile, pero está muy ocupada. No le gusta ir al centro comercial porque siempre hay muchas personas por allí. Decide visitar uno de los sitios en el Internet para buscar la ropa que necesita.

2   Primero, Margarita busca un sitio donde se especializan en ropa para jóvenes. El sitio que más le gusta tiene un catálogo con mucha variedad de ropa moderna. En la página principal, hay información sobre cómo seleccionar el departamento donde quiere comprar unos artículos. Esa página indica cómo pagar por lo que compra y cómo comunicarse con la compañía. También incluye información sobre garantías, descuentos y qué opciones tiene si no le gusta lo que compra.

3   Margarita selecciona dos jeans, tres camisetas de diferentes colores, dos pantalones cortos, un suéter negro, una sudadera morada, una chaqueta y unos zapatos. También compra el especial de la semana, una minifalda azul que cuesta sólo veinte pesos. ¡Perfecto!

4   Luego, Margarita tiene una pregunta: "¿Cómo puedo determinar si esta ropa y estos zapatos me van a quedar bien?" Decide consultar la página donde hay información para ayudar a los clientes a determinar esto.

5   Después, Margarita decide pagar por toda la ropa con su tarjeta de crédito, pero tiene otra pregunta: "¿Garantiza este sitio la protección de mi información personal?" Consulta otra página donde informan a los clientes que sí hay protección.

6   Cuando la ropa llega a su casa, Margarita está muy contenta. Toda la ropa que compró le queda bien y los colores son brillantes.

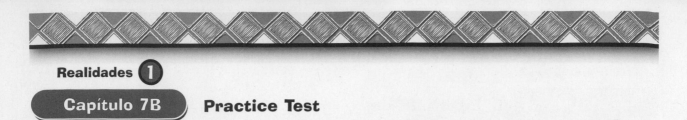
Answer questions 1–6. Base your answers on the reading *"Necesito comprar ropa."*

1. What is Margarita's problem?

    A She needs clothes for her vacation but doesn't have enough money to buy them.

    B She needs clothes for her vacation but doesn't like to shop in crowded malls.

    C She needs to replace the clothes that she lost during her vacation.

    D She needs to buy vacation clothes before the stores close.

2. What type of information is <u>not</u> mentioned on the main page of the Web site that Margarita consults?

    F how to pay for your purchases

    G how to choose the department you're interested in

    H which items are discounted

    J which items are no longer available

3. According to the article, why is Margarita concerned about ordering from an online catalog?

    A She's worried that she won't receive the items on time.

    B She's worried that her personal information might not be protected.

    C She's worried that she can't return the items if she's unhappy with them.

    D She's worried that the items might look different from the way they look in the catalog.

4. How does Margarita feel after the package arrives?

    F unhappy because it didn't arrive on time

    G unhappy because the clothes did not fit well

    H happy because the clothes fit well and the colors were bright

    J happy because the company included a special gift in the package

5. ¿Prefieres ir de compras en un centro comercial o en el Internet? ¿Por qué?

6. Imagina que vas a crear un sitio en el Internet para ropa deportiva para jóvenes. Inventa un nombre para el sitio, decide qué tipo de información vas a incluir en la página principal, qué tipos de fotos o dibujos vas a incluir y cuánto cuesta cada artículo de ropa. En tu hoja de papel, dibuja la página principal de tu sitio. Debes dibujar una página atractiva que a los estudiantes de tu escuela les gustaría visitar.

Nombre ____________________ Fecha ____________

Practice Test Answer Sheet

1 Ⓐ Ⓑ Ⓒ Ⓓ   2 Ⓕ Ⓖ Ⓗ Ⓙ   3 Ⓐ Ⓑ Ⓒ Ⓓ

4 Ⓕ Ⓖ Ⓗ Ⓙ

5

READ
THINK
EXPLAIN

6

READ
THINK
CREATE

Analyzing the Validity and Reliability of Information

When good readers analyze information for validity and reliability, one of the most important questions that they ask themselves about what they have read is: "How do I know that I can trust that this information is true or accurate?" After answering this question, readers need to determine how such information can be used.

Tip

One way readers check information in a reading passage for validity and reliability is to ask, "How could I verify that this information is accurate or true?" Some ways to verify this include: observing, taking measurements, conducting experiments, getting advice from experts in that particular field, and interviewing people with firsthand experience.

1. On page 381 of your textbook, review **Actividad 9 "¿Quieres aprender a bucear?"** Then read the statements below from this activity and explain how, if at all, you could verify their truth or accuracy.

   ¡Aprende a bucear en sólo tres cursos!

   _____
   _____

   Practica un deporte interesante y divertido.

   _____
   _____

   Pasa tiempo en un lugar fantástico.

   _____
   _____

   Hay un lenguaje especial que permite a los buzos comunicarse en el agua con señales.

   _____
   _____

   En los cursos de buceo, puedes aprender estas señales.

   _____
   _____

Sample question:

2. If you were using the brochure for *Escuela de buceo "Flor del mar"* for a research project about scuba diving in the Dominican Republic, which information seems least reliable?
   A Scuba diving is an interesting and fun sport.
   B You can learn hand signals in the diving courses, and this will help you as a diver.
   C You can learn to scuba dive after only three classes.
   D One of the most important hand signals for scuba divers is "Danger!"

Strategies to Analyze Words: Context Clues

It is impossible to know the meaning of every word in a language. Good readers develop strategies to determine the meanings of unknown words as they read without having to look them up in the dictionary. Good readers examine the sentences surrounding new vocabulary words looking for context clues that might help them guess the meaning of the new word.

Tip

Good readers pay attention to the punctuation marks next to unusual vocabulary words because they know that writers will often place a comma after an unusual word and then describe or define that word in a parenthetical expression. This expression could be a one-word description, a descriptive phrase, or an even longer relative clause. Look at how this works with the unusual word, **vitamina:**

One-word description: We drank a *vitamina*, a smoothie, and it gave us energy.

Descriptive phrase: We drank a *vitamina*, a fruity milkshake with oatmeal and honey in it.

Relative clause: We drank a *vitamina*, which is a hearty drink consisting of yogurt, ice, bananas, strawberry, honey, and oatmeal.

Notice that when these parenthetical expressions are used in the middle of a sentence, a comma comes both before and after the expression. If the expression comes at the end of the sentence, a period will often follow the expression.

1. After reviewing the **Lectura** in your textbook on pages 390–391, *Álbum de mi viaje a Perú,* record the description or definition given in the **Lectura** for the terms listed below. For each term, tell if the parenthetical expression after it is an one-word description, descriptive phrase, or relative clause.

	Definition/Description	Type
Cuzco		
Lima		
Machu Picchu		
Hiram Bingham		

Sample question:

2. Read the sentence below and then choose the best meaning for the underlined word.

Viewed from above, *las líneas de Nazca* resemble the <u>hieroglyphics</u>, picture writing, of the ancient Egyptians.

A geometric figures
B a language system that uses symbols or drawings as words
C giant bird figures sketched in the sands of the Peruvian desert
D cave paintings found throughout North Africa and Europe

Integrated Performance Assessment
Unit theme: De vacaciones

Context for the Integrated Performance Assessment: Your school's Spanish Club is going to Costa Rica for a week. Your sponsor wants to know what the members of the club would like to see and do there. He/she also wants to know what questions you have about the trip.

Interpretive Task: Watch the *Videohistoria: ¿Qué te pasó? from Realidades 1, DVD 4, Capítulo 8A.* Take notes on what there is to see and do in Costa Rica.

Interpersonal Task: Work with a group of 2 or 3 members of the Spanish Club. Discuss what you would like to see and do in Costa Rica until the group agrees on 4 activities. Also discuss questions that you have about the trip and prepare 3 questions to ask your club's sponsor.

Presentational Task: Make an oral presentation to the members of the Spanish Club describing what your group would like to see and do in Costa Rica. In addition, ask the club's sponsor the 3 questions from your group.

Interpersonal Task Rubric

	Score: 1 Does not meet expectations	Score: 3 Meets expectations	Score: 5 Exceeds expectations
Language Use	Student uses little or no target language and relies heavily on native language word order.	Student uses the target language consistently, but may mix native and target language word order.	Student uses the target language exclusively and integrates target language word order into conversation.
Vocabulary Use	Student uses limited and repetitive language.	Student uses only recently acquired vocabulary.	Student uses both recently and previously acquired vocabulary.

Presentational Task Rubric

	Score: 1 Does not meet expectations	Score: 3 Meets expectations	Score: 5 Exceeds expectations
Amount of Communication	Student gives limited or no details about what the group wants to do in Costa Rica. He/she asks fewer than three questions.	Student gives adequate details about what the group wants to do in Costa Rica. He/she asks three questions.	Student gives consistent details about what the group wants to do in Costa Rica. He/she asks more than three questions.
Accuracy	Student's accuracy with vocabulary and structures is limited.	Student's accuracy with vocabulary and structures is adequate.	Student's accuracy with vocabulary and structures is exemplary.
Comprehensibility	Student's ideas lack clarity and are difficult to understand.	Student's ideas are adequately clear and fairly well understood.	Student's ideas are precise and easily understood.
Vocabulary Use	Student uses limited and repetitive vocabulary.	Student uses only recently acquired vocabulary.	Student uses both recently and previously acquired vocabulary.

Spanish Missions in Texas

1 Since the earliest days of Spanish exploration in the Americas, a highly successful mission system was put in place. In the southeastern United States, it extended from Florida up to North Carolina, and in the southwest from Texas to California. Through this system, Catholic priests received financial and military support from the Spanish Crown to build missions where the priests could convert the indigenous people not only to the Catholic faith, but also to the Spanish way of life. The priests were protected by

San José Mission

Spanish soldiers as new lands were claimed, although very often these two groups disagreed about the best way to treat the new converts. The priests were the protectors of the indigenous and taught them religion as well as valuable vocational skills.

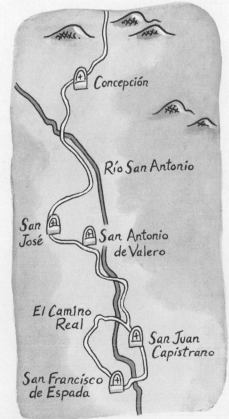

2 In 1690, the first Spanish mission in Texas was founded: San Francisco de los Tejas. Several other missions were established shortly thereafter and in close proximity to each other. All were in East Texas, an area that was plagued by disease, drought, constant attacks from indigenous inhabitants who rejected the Spaniards' presence, and threats from the French who fought for power in the same region. For these reasons, the missions were closed and four were relocated along the San Antonio River in what is now the city of San Antonio. By 1731, there were five missions established around this area: San Antonio de Valero (1718), San José (1720), San Juan Capistrano (1731), Concepción (1731), and San Francisco de Espada (1731). The dirt road that linked all the missions was known as *El Camino Real*, a route that began in Mexico City and continued up through the northernmost territories of Nueva España, as Mexico was then called. Today these territories are the west and southwest regions of the United States.

3 The oldest and best known of these missions is San Antonio de Valero, named for the Spanish viceroy of Mexico, el marqués de Valero. It is also known as the Alamo, one of the most famous landmarks in Texas history. The original building was made of sticks and straw, but these flimsy

Spanish Missions in Texas (*continued*)

building materials made it an easy victim of attacks. Subsequent construction of this and other missions was made with sturdier materials, such as sandstone, which could be cut into slabs for floors and walls, or certain clay soils, which were made into tiles and bricks. Although some of the missions were more elaborate than others, their overall architectural style was simple and practical.

4   The mission of San José was the best fortified and most successful and soon became an important social and cultural center. It was also considered the most beautiful. San José was founded by Fray Antonio Margil de Jesús, a Franciscan priest who was born in 1657 in Valencia, Spain. While still in his early teens, Margil expressed interest in becoming a Franciscan and at the age of twenty-five he was ordained. Soon thereafter, he was on his way to the New World as a missionary. After serving in Costa Rica, Guatemala, and Mexico, he went on to help establish missions in East Texas. These missions are considered the cornerstone from which other missions in Texas grew.

5   As protectors of the indigenous inhabitants, the Franciscans opened workshops in the missions in order to teach them trades. Under the priests' guidance, they learned such skills as carpentry and masonry in order to enhance the construction of the missions, as well as blacksmithing, which was needed to repair farm tools. The mission of San Juan Capistrano became a major supplier of agricultural products in the region, along with wood, iron, cloth, and leather goods that the indigenous inhabitants produced in the mission's workshops.

6   The mission of Concepción (full name: Misión Nuestra Señora de la Purísima Concepción de Acuna) is the best preserved of the San Antonio missions, with 45-inch thick walls. It has what many consider

to be the oldest fully preserved church building in the United States. Concepción was well-known for its religious celebrations.

7   The mission of Espada is unique because of its irrigation system, the oldest still in use in the United States. Missions depended on a steady harvesting of crops for the survival of their residents. Because rainfall was irregular in this part of Texas, an irrigation system was a top priority. Irrigation was so important that settlers measured the farmland in suertes, which is the amount of land that they could water in a day.

8   Today, the Alamo is a visitor's center and museum. The other four missions—San José, San Juan, Concepción, and Espada—are functioning Catholic parishes and are open to the public. All are popular tourist destinations.

San Francisco de Espada Mission

Communication Workbook

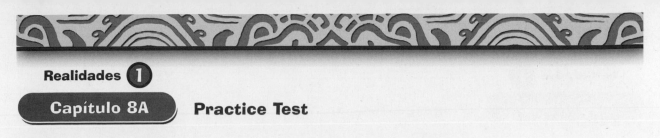

Answer questions 1–6. Base your answers on the reading, *"Spanish Missions in Texas."*

1 Which of the following trades was <u>not</u> taught to the indigenous in the missions?

   A   masonry

   B   blacksmithing

   C   printing

   D   carpentry

2 In the early 1700s, what was the name of the land that today is Mexico?

   F   San Antonio

   G   El Camino Real

   H   Nueva España

   J   San Francisco de los Tejas

3 In paragraph 4, what does the word <u>cornerstone</u> mean?

   A   end

   B   foundation

   C   adobe

   D   building material

4 In paragraph 7, what are *suertes*?

   F   a kind of farming system

   G   luck

   H   a kind of land measurement

   J   crops

5 Why do you think the missions are so popular with tourists? Use information from the reading and your own ideas to support your answer.

6 Father Margil was in his early teens when he made his commitment to become a priest. What personal qualities do you think are necessary for a person that young to make a commitment that is so serious? Do you think that it would be much more difficult today for a person so young to make such a decision and commitment? Why or why not?

❶   Ⓐ   Ⓑ   Ⓒ   Ⓓ   ❷   Ⓕ   Ⓖ   Ⓗ   Ⓙ   ❸   Ⓐ   Ⓑ   Ⓒ   Ⓓ

❹   Ⓕ   Ⓖ   Ⓗ   Ⓙ

❺

READ
THINK
EXPLAIN

❻

READ
THINK
EXPLAIN

Communication Workbook

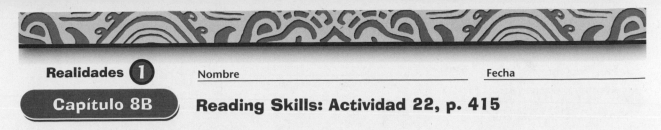

Recognizing Cause-Effect Relationships

To recognize cause-effect relationships in fiction, nonfiction, drama, or poetry, readers should be aware of why things happen (causes) as well as the consequences or results of actions (effects) in a reading passage.

Tip

Good readers can recognize when effects are presented in a reading passage. They also make predictions while they read and can predict the outcomes or effects of an action even if the effects are not explicitly written in a reading passage.

To gain practice with predicting outcomes, you should find places in the reading passage where you can stop and ask a "What if . . . ?" question. Sometimes the answer to your "What if . . .?" question will be stated right in the reading passage. Other times, your question might be hypothetical and the acceptable answer will be one that makes sense, even if it is not stated in the reading passage.

1. In your textbook on page 415, review **Actividad 22 "Las tortugas tinglar."** Then answer the "What if . . . ?" questions that follow. After answering each question, tell if the answer was in the reading passage or if you had to arrive at the answer logically.

   What if the tinglar turtle were not so big?

   _____

   _____

   What if the tinglar turtle were not in danger of extinction?

   _____

   _____

   What if volunteers from different countries did not go to the beaches of Culebra Island?

   _____

   _____

   What if, after hatching from eggs, tinglar turtles went immediately to swim in the ocean?

   _____

   _____

Sample question:

2. What effect have volunteers had on the population of tinglar turtles on Culebra Island?
   A Their camping on the beaches has destroyed vital habitat for the tinglar turtle.
   B They have taught the turtles how to lay and hatch eggs.
   C They have helped newly hatched turtles progress to life in the ocean.
   D Their patrols on the beaches have saved the turtles from hunters.

Determining the Author's Purpose

To determine the author's purpose for writing a book, a story, an article, or any other text, the reader must figure out why the author wrote that particular book, story, article, or text. Some common purposes for writing are to inform, to entertain, to persuade, or to describe. Readers should also be able to explain why the author uses different techniques or includes different features within a text.

Tip

When presented with a multi-paragraph text, good readers will often "chunk" the text into different sections to improve their understanding. The chunk might be a paragraph itself. In longer texts, a chunk is more likely to include several paragraphs. When you chunk a text, you are able to identify both the main idea of that chunk and the author's purpose for including that chunk in the text.

1. On page 416 in your textbook, re-read the **Lectura**, *Hábitat para la Humanidad Internacional*. Examine below how the text has been separated into six different chunks. Identify the main idea for each chunk and author's purpose for including that chunk in the text.

	Main Idea	Author's Purpose
1 "Hábitat es una..."		
2 "Guatemala tiene quince..."		
3 "Ayer fue mi..."		
4 "La mayoría del..."		
5 ¿Sabes que el...?"		
6 "Es una experiencia..."		

Sample question:

2. What was the author's purpose in the fourth paragraph for including the quotation from a lady of the Baja Verapaz community?
   A to entertain readers with a humorous story about volunteers
   B to provide a real life example of a type of person mentioned in the previous paragraph
   C to provide background information for the subsequent paragraph that mentions former President Jimmy Carter
   D to explain how money for Habitat for Humanity is collected and spent

Integrated Performance Assessment
Unit theme: Ayudando en la comunidad

Context for the Integrated Performance Assessment: The members of your Spanish Club have decided to raise money for *Hábitat para la Humanidad Internacional*. The sponsor needs your help as he prepares to go to the principal and ask his/her permission. Your sponsor wants to know why you support raising the money and how the members plan to raise the money.

Interpretive Task: Read the *Lectura: Hábitat para la Humanidad Internacional* on pages 416-417 of *Realidades* 1 to learn more about the organization. Take notes on information about the organization's goals and accomplishments.

Interpersonal Task: Work with a group of 2 or 3 other students. Discuss what you learned about the organization's goals and accomplishments. Listen to the other students, and based on what they have to say, add more information to your notes. Discuss at least 2 possible ways of raising money.

Presentational Task: Write a note to the sponsor of the Spanish Club explaining why you think it is a good idea to raise money for *Hábitat para la Humanidad Internacional*. In your note, suggest two ways that the club can earn the money.

Interpersonal Task Rubric

	Score: 1 Does not meet expectations	Score: 3 Meets expectations	Score: 5 Exceeds expectations
Language Use	Student uses little or no target language and relies heavily on native language word order.	Student uses the target language consistently, but may mix native and target language word order.	Student uses the target language exclusively and integrates target language word order into conversation.
Vocabulary Use	Student uses limited and repetitive language.	Student uses only required acquired vocabulary.	Student uses both recently and previously acquired vocabulary.

Presentational Task Rubric

	Score: 1 Does not meet expectations	Score: 3 Meets expectations	Score: 5 Exceeds expectations
Amount of Communication	Student gives limited or no explanation why it is a good idea to raise money and suggests fewer than two ways to do so.	Student gives an adequate explanation why it is a good idea to raise money and suggests two ways to do so.	Student gives a very good explanation why it is a good idea to raise money and suggests more than two ways to do so.
Accuracy	Student's accuracy with vocabulary and structures is limited.	Student's accuracy with vocabulary and structures is adequate.	Student's accuracy with vocabulary and structures is exemplary.
Comprehensibility	Student's ideas lack clarity and are difficult to understand.	Student's ideas are adequately clear and fairly well understood.	Student's ideas are precise and easily understood.
Vocabulary Use	Student uses limited and repetitive vocabulary.	Student uses only recently acquired vocabulary.	Student uses both recently and previously acquired vocabulary.

¡Bienvenidos a la calle Olvera!

1   Si vas a Los Ángeles, debes visitar la calle Olvera, que está en el centro viejo de la ciudad y que tiene una atmósfera totalmente mexicana. En el año 1930, esta calle se transformó en un mercado mexicano donde puedes comprar toda clase de productos mexicanos y comer platos mexicanos auténticos. Los fines de semana muchas personas comen en los restaurantes y los mariachis tocan música en la plaza cerca de esta calle.

2   La calle Olvera lleva el nombre de Agustín Olvera, quien vivió en una casa delante de la plaza en el <u>siglo</u> XIX y fue uno de los primeros oficiales de la ciudad. Esta calle es una de las más viejas de la ciudad y tiene mucho interés histórico. Allí están muchos de los lugares más viejos como Casa Pelanconi,

en donde está situado el Café La Golondrina, el primer restaurante en Los Ángeles de comida mexicana auténtica.

3   Si estás en la calle Olvera en un día de fiesta mexicana, puedes observar tradiciones y ceremonias muy importantes de la cultura mexicana. Algunos de los días de fiesta mexicana más populares se celebran en la plaza cerca de la calle Olvera. El Cinco de Mayo conmemora la victoria de los mexicanos sobre los franceses en Puebla en 1862. El 16 de septiembre se celebra el Día de la Independencia de México porque ése fue el día en 1810 en que los mexicanos declararon su independencia de España. El dos de noviembre se celebra el Día de los Muertos, el día en que las familias mexicanas van a los cementerios para conmemorar a sus familiares muertos. Cada noche del 16 al 24 de diciembre se celebran las posadas, una fiesta que

conmemora los nueve días cuando la Virgen María y San José buscaron un lugar para descansar con el Niño Jesús.

4   Hoy la calle Olvera forma parte del Monumento Histórico del Pueblo de Los Ángeles. Si la visitas, vas a tener una experiencia muy interesante. Casi dos millones de personas visitan la calle Olvera cada año para participar en las actividades culturales, comer en los restaurantes y aprender más sobre la historia de Los Ángeles.

Capítulo 8B   **Practice Test**

Answer questions 1–6. Base your answers on the reading *"¡Bienvenidos a la calle Olvera!"*

1 In the article, three of the following are mentioned as ways in which Olvera Street resembles a community in Mexico. Which one is <u>not</u> mentioned?

    A   Vendors sell Mexican products.

    B   Restaurants serve authentic Mexican food.

    C   Mariachis provide entertainment.

    D   Visitors bargain for the products they would like to buy.

2 What does *siglo* mean in paragraph 2?

    F   address

    G   number

    H   century

    J   building

3 Three of the following statements are false. Which one is true?

    A   Olvera Street was named in honor of Agustín Olvera, Los Angeles County's first official.

    B   Olvera Street is the oldest street in Los Angeles.

    C   Olvera Street is the site of some of the oldest buildings in Los Angeles.

    D   Olvera Street is located just outside of Los Angeles.

4 Which of the following statements best describes how the celebration of *las posadas* differs from the other celebrations mentioned?

    F   It takes place over a period of several days and commemorates a religious event.

    G   It commemorates a famous event in Mexican history.

    H   It commemorates a famous tradition celebrated in Mexico.

    J   It takes place only once a year.

5 ¿Qué impacto crees que las diversas comunidades de los Estados Unidos tienen en lo que llamamos "la cultura estadounidense"? Usa detalles e información del artículo en tu respuesta.

6 Piensa en un lugar en tu comunidad o en otra comunidad que es similar a la calle Olvera. ¿Qué hacen las personas de esa comunidad para celebrar su cultura?

1 Ⓐ Ⓑ Ⓒ Ⓓ   **2** Ⓕ Ⓖ Ⓗ Ⓙ   **3** Ⓐ Ⓑ Ⓒ Ⓓ

4 Ⓕ Ⓖ Ⓗ Ⓙ

5

READ
THINK
EXPLAIN

_____
_____
_____
_____
_____
_____
_____

6

READ
THINK
EXPLAIN

_____
_____
_____
_____
_____
_____
_____
_____
_____

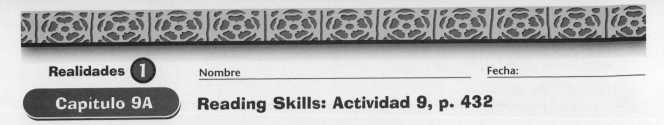

Determining the Author's Point of View

To determine the author's point of view in a reading selection, the reader must figure out how the author feels about a subject in the reading selection. To begin with, you should be able to identify when an author feels positive, negative, or neutral toward a subject. As you gain more practice with this skill, you should then be able to identify a wide range of emotions or attitudes shown by authors. Some of these emotions or attitudes might include admiration, nostalgia, sarcasm, surprise, and sympathy.

To figure out the author's point of view toward his or her subject, try to locate words, phrases, or sentences in which the author expresses an emotional reaction or an opinion. It helps to know how to distinguish facts from opinions.

1. Review **Actividad 9 ¿Qué dicen los críticos?** on page 432 in your textbook. Pay special attention to the movie reviews **"En nuestra opinion."** Now examine the excerpts from the movie reviews listed below. Identify each as a fact or opinion. Describe what the opinions express about the author's feelings or attitude toward his or her subject.

	Fact or Opinion	Feelings Expressed by Opinions
"Esta película, de dos horas y media, es similar a las viejas fórmulas de las telenovelas..."	_____	_____
"Recomendable para personas que no tienen nada que hacer."	_____	_____
"Una producción... que combina elementos de comedia y ciencia ficción."	_____	_____
"Es tan fascinante y cómica que no puedes creer que estás en el cine por más de tres horas."	_____	_____

Sample question:

2. The movie critic's point of view toward the film *Mis padres son de otro planeta* could best be described as
   A disappointed with the movie's length.
   B cautious about recommending it for an audience of adults.
   C incredulous that anyone would pay money to see this film.
   D enthusiastic about the movie's content.

Identifying Methods of Development and Patterns of Organization

Good readers understand the tools and techniques of authors. To identify the methods of development used by an author in a text, good readers must first determine the author's purpose by asking, "Why was this text written?" After determining the author's purpose, readers next ask, "What techniques did the author use to achieve his or her purpose?" These techniques are known as methods of development and could include, among other things, the organization pattern, the word choice, or the sentence structure used in the text.

Tip

One common pattern of organization for writers is the problem-solution essay. Readers can expect a problem-solution essay to address, but not be limited to such sub-topics as: a description of the problem, its causes and effects, statistics about real-life examples, and its possible solutions.

1. On pages 440–441 of your textbook, review the **Lectura**, *Una semana sin televisión.* Then look at the chart below and fill out information from the reading passage that relates to one of the sub-topics.

Sub-Topics About the Problem	Information from *"Una semana sin televisión"*
Description:	
Causes:	
Effects:	
Statistics:	
Possible solutions:	

Sample question:

2. All of the following issues related to the problem of excessive television viewing are addressed in the reading passage *Una semana sin televisión* EXCEPT:
   A causes of the problem
   B effects of the problem
   C statistics about the problem
   D possible solutions to the problem

Integrated Performance Assessment
Unit theme: El cine y la televisión

Context for the Integrated Performance Assessment: The principal of your school has received a notice from the Department of Education inviting his/her students to participate in a program called "No TV for One Month!" The students in your Spanish class have to decide if they want to participate or not.

Interpretive Task: Read the Lectura: *Una semana sin televisión* on pages 440–441 of *Realidades 1, Capítulo 9A*. Take notes on the effects of watching too much television on students and on the benefits to students who watch little or no television. Decide if you can go for one month without watching TV and make a list of reasons that explain your decision.

Interpersonal Task: Find a student who agrees with you. Discuss your opinions and your reasons. If your partner has reasons that did not occur to you and you agree with them, add them to your list.

Presentational Task: Make an oral presentation to the class explaining whether you are willing to go for one month without TV or not, and say why or why not. You should have at least 5 reasons to support your decision.

Interpersonal Task Rubric

	Score: 1 Does not meet expectations	Score: 3 Meets expectations	Score: 5 Exceeds expectations
Language Use	Student uses little or no target language and relies heavily on native language word order.	Student uses the target language consistently, but may mix native and target language word order.	Student uses the target language exclusively and integrates target language word order into conversation.
Vocabulary Use	Student uses limited and repetitive language.	Student uses only required acquired vocabulary.	Student uses both recently and previously acquired vocabulary.

Presentational Task Rubric

	Score: 1 Does not meet expectations	Score: 3 Meets expectations	Score: 5 Exceeds expectations
Amount of Communication	Student gives fewer than five reasons to support his/her decision.	Student gives five reasons to support his/her decision.	Student gives more than five reasons to support his/her decision.
Accuracy	Student's accuracy with vocabulary and structures is limited.	Student's accuracy with vocabulary and structures is adequate.	Student's accuracy with vocabulary and structures is exemplary.
Comprehensibility	Student's ideas lack clarity and are difficult to understand.	Student's ideas are adequately clear and fairly well understood.	Student's ideas are precise and easily understood.
Vocabulary Use	Student uses limited and repetitive vocabulary.	Student uses only recently acquired vocabulary.	Student uses both recently and previously acquired vocabulary.

Spanish-Language Television in the United States

1 Spanish-language television was first broadcast in the United States in New York City and San Antonio in the mid-1940s, at approximately the same time as English-language television. The Spanish-language programs were shown in various time slots on certain English-language channels. The first full-fledged Spanish-language station, KCOR-TV in San Antonio, began broadcasting in 1955. Among its early shows was *Buscando estrellas,* a talent show that brought young entertainers from Mexico to Texas.

2 Today there is a large, well-established audience for Spanish-language broadcasting in the United States. Viewers can enjoy *telenovelas* and other entertainment shows from Mexico, Argentina, Venezuela, and Spain, as well as from such U.S. cities as New York and Miami. International sporting events are broadcast by satellite from around the globe, with commentary and play-by-play coverage in Spanish.

3 Because Hispanic populations in the United States represent many different countries and cultures, it has been a challenge to create programs that will appeal to this diverse market. One major success was a *telenovela* entitled *Angélica, mi vida,* produced in Puerto Rico in the 1980s. Its subplots dealt with love, tragedy, and power among families of Puerto Rican, Cuban, and Mexican origin.

4 Today's programs include the most-watched talk show in the world, Miami-based *Cristina,* and the longest-running show on Spanish-language television, *Sábado gigante,* which began broadcasting from Miami in 1986. Cuban-born Cristina Saralegui, who hosts her own show, engages her guests and audiences in lively debates on topical issues. *Sábado gigante* is hosted by Chilean-born Mario Kreutzberger, who uses the pseudonym Don Francisco on his show, which features

Cristina Saralegui

celebrity guests, contests, games, comedy, and interviews on topics of interest to the Hispanic community. Popular programs originating from outside the United States include *Bailando por un sueño* (Mexico), *Informe semanal* (Spain), and *La fea más bella* (Colombia).

5 English-language shows dubbed into Spanish are also shown on Spanish-language TV channels. Among the longest-running of these are cartoon series, such as *The Pink Panther* (*La Pantera rosa*) and *Spiderman* (*El Hombre araña*).

Don Francisco

Answer questions 1–5. Base your answers on the reading *"Spanish-Language Television in the United States."*

1 Where were the first full-time, regularly scheduled U.S. Spanish-language television programs broadcast from?

    A   Florida

    B   Mexico

    C   New York

    D   Texas

2 Why was *Buscando estrellas* an appropriate name for that particular show?

    F   It highlighted Mexican entertainers.

    G   It was trying to find up-and-coming young entertainers.

    H   It was one of the first shows on KCOR-TV.

    J   It was broadcast regularly.

3 What do Cristina Saralegui and Mario Kreutzberger have in common?

    A   They were both born in South America.

    B   They both broadcast from Florida.

    C   They both use pseudonyms.

    D   Neither of them invites audience participation.

4 Which one of the following statements is <u>not</u> true?

    F   Cultural differences can make programming for Spanish-speaking audiences difficult.

    G   Some of the most popular Spanish-language programs are broadcast from Miami.

    H   *Telenovelas* are always filmed in Puerto Rico with actors from many countries.

    J   Many English-language programs are also broadcast on Spanish-language television using a Spanish soundtrack.

5 Based on the article, in what ways would you say that Spanish-language and English-language television programs are similar? In what ways are they different?

Realidades 1

Nombre ______________________ Fecha ______________

Capítulo 9A

Practice Test Answer Sheet

1 Ⓐ Ⓑ Ⓒ Ⓓ   2 Ⓕ Ⓖ Ⓗ Ⓙ   3 Ⓐ Ⓑ Ⓒ Ⓓ

4 Ⓕ Ⓖ Ⓗ Ⓙ

5

READ
THINK
EXPLAIN

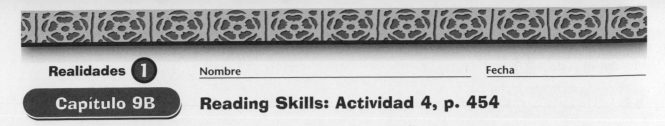

Drawing Conclusions

To draw a conclusion is to form an opinion based on evidence. Sometimes the evidence presented to readers is very limited, but they must ensure that their evidence-based opinions make logical sense.

Conclusion statements are simply right or wrong. They are often presented as believable or not. If you are successful at drawing conclusions from your reading, then you likely are skilled at finding evidence in your reading that supports your conclusions.

Conclusions are only as strong as the evidence on which they are based. Conclusions based on little evidence are not as believable as conclusions based on a lot of different kinds of evidence. You must also be willing to change your conclusions as more evidence becomes available in the reading passage.

Tip

Readers must be flexible in their thinking if drawing conclusions from multiple and varied pieces of evidence. When the pieces of evidence are similar or the amount of evidence is limited, drawing conclusions is not difficult.

1. On page 454, review the quiz *"La computadora y tú"* in **Actividad 4.** Below you will find excerpts from the test questions that will serve as pieces of evidence. For each set of evidence, draw a conclusion that makes logical sense.

   Easy
   • Ana communicates most often with people by visiting chat rooms.
   • When she writes reports, Ana most often finds information by downloading documents from the Internet.
   • Ana knows how to design her own Web page.
   Conclusion about Ana: _____

   More difficult
   • Henry goes to the library to get books when he needs information to write a report.
   • Henry uses computers to play interactive games.
   • Henry communicates most often with people by e-mail.
   • Henry does not know how to write a composition using the computer.
   Conclusion about Henry: _____

Sample question:

2. Which conclusion below is LEAST credible about a person who would choose letter *A* responses for all the questions on the test titled *"La computadora y tú"*?
   A Such a person might prefer human contact to interaction with a computer.
   B Such a person will need training to become comfortable using a computer.
   C Such a person will never acquire computer skills.
   D Such a person might not like working with computers.

Recognizing the Use of Comparison and Contrast

To recognize comparison and contrast in a reading passage, good readers can point out how items or ideas in the reading passage are similar to or different from each other. Sometimes writers will directly state that they are comparing or contrasting items in a reading passage. Other times readers might recognize items in a reading passage that could be compared or contrasted even though the writer might not have presented the information for that purpose.

Tip

One common way that comparison and contrast appears in a reading passage is in the form of a debate. A debate usually involves an argument over a controversial issue. When you should encounter a debate in a reading passage, you should identify the two sides of the issue, known commonly as the pro (in favor of) and the con (against) positions.

1. Review the **Lectura**, *La invasión del ciberspanglish* on pages 464–465 in your textbook. Then fill in the blanks of the chart below.

   The issue debated in the **Lectura**, *La invasión del ciberspanglish* is

   _____

   _____.

Arguments supporting the PRO position	Arguments supporting the CON position
_____	_____
_____	_____
_____	_____
_____	_____
_____	_____

Sample question:

2. Which is NOT a reason given to support the idea that it is acceptable to mix English and Spanish?
   A It makes communication easier.
   B Spanish is a language as rich as English.
   C Expressing technical terms in Spanish is too complicated.
   D If a computer word has an English origin, it makes little sense to translate it to Spanish.

Integrated Performance Assessment
Unit theme: La tecnología

Context for the Integrated Performance Assessment: A group of students from Spain is coming to spend three weeks in your school. Each student in your class will be a buddy for one of the Spanish students. One of the criteria for matching a Spanish student with a buddy is knowledge of technology. Your Spanish teacher needs information about your ability to use technology

Interpretive Task: Watch the *Videohistoria: ¿Cómo se comunica?* from *Realidades 1, DVD 4, Capítulo 9B.* Write all the uses of technology mentioned in the video in one of 2 columns: *Yo puedo...* or *Yo no puedo....*

Interpersonal Task: Work with a partner. Using your notes, tell him/her what you can or cannot do with technology. Listen to your partner as he/she reads his/her notes. Ask each other questions about other uses of technology that were not mentioned in the video, including how you use technology in school. Keep track of what you can and cannot do.

Presentational Task: Write a note to your Spanish teacher giving him/her a detailed description of what you can and cannot do with technology.

Interpersonal Task Rubric

	Score: 1 Does not meet expectations	Score: 3 Meets expectations	Score: 5 Exceeds expectations
Language Use	Student uses little or no target language and relies heavily on native language word order.	Student uses the target language consistently, but may mix native and target language word order.	Student uses the target language exclusively and integrates target language word order into conversation.
Vocabulary Use	Student uses limited and repetitive language.	Student uses only required acquired vocabulary.	Student uses both recently and previously acquired vocabulary.

Presentational Task Rubric

	Score: 1 Does not meet expectations	Score: 3 Meets expectations	Score: 5 Exceeds expectations
Amount of Communication	Student gives limited or no details or examples of what he/she can do with technology.	Student gives adequate details or examples of what he/she can do with technology.	Student gives consistent details or examples of what he/she can do with technology.
Accuracy	Student's accuracy with vocabulary and structures is limited.	Student's accuracy with vocabulary and structures is adequate.	Student's accuracy with vocabulary and structures is exemplary.
Comprehensibility	Student's ideas lack clarity and are difficult to understand.	Student's ideas are adequately clear and fairly well understood.	Student's ideas are precise and easily understood.
Vocabulary Use	Student uses limited and repetitive vocabulary.	Student uses only recently acquired vocabulary.	Student uses both recently and previously acquired vocabulary.

Música latina en la televisión

¿Te gusta ver los videos musicales de Ricky Martin, Marc Anthony, Gloria Estefan, Jennifer Lopez y otros artistas latinos? Pues, la siguiente información te va a interesar.

1 *MTV Latino* es un canal de televisión por cable que empezó en 1993 y que da programas musicales las 24 horas del día. Es el canal favorito del 50 por ciento de los jóvenes latinos en los Estados Unidos. A ellos les fascina porque en este canal dan toda clase de videos musicales, noticias sobre música, artistas, bandas, conciertos y películas y entrevistas con los artistas más populares. También los jóvenes pueden llamar por teléfono y pedir su video favorito.

Ricky Martin canta y baila al ritmo latino.

Gloria Estefan canta con Justin Timberlake y JC Chasez de *NSync.

2 *MTV en Telemundo* también da programas musicales para los jóvenes. Este programa de televisión por cable, que empezó en septiembre de 1999, es una colaboración entre Telemundo, una de las compañías más grandes de programación en español, y MTV Latinoamérica. Los viernes a las once y media de la noche y los sábados a las once de la noche, los jóvenes pueden ver los diez videos musicales más populares de la semana y también los bailes más populares del mundo latino.

Answer questions 1–5. Base your answers on the reading *"Música latina en la televisión."*

1 According to the reading, which of the following statements is true?

    A   Listeners can email their requests to *MTV Latino*.

    B   *MTV Latino* offers less musical programming than *MTV en Telemundo*.

    C   There are online surveys for both channels.

    D   Telemundo is a major television broadcasting company.

2 Which of the following statements is <u>not</u> true?

    F   Both *MTV Latino* and *MTV en Telemundo* got started in the 1990s.

    G   *MTV Latino* is the favorite channel of half of the young Latinos in the United States.

    H   *MTV en Telemundo* offers musical programs for young people on Sundays only.

    J   Both *MTV Latino* and *MTV en Telemundo* are on cable.

3 According to the reading, which of the following is <u>not</u> one of the reasons why teens watch *MTV Latino?*

    A   It offers a variety of musical programming.

    B   It presents news about and interviews with their favorite recording artists.

    C   It allows them to call in and request their favorite videos.

    D   It doesn't cost anything to receive it.

4 How does *MTV en Telemundo* differ from *MTV Latino?*

    F   It offers musical programming, but not on a 24-hour basis.

    G   It's available on cable television.

    H   It's older than *MTV Latino*.

    J   It presents music videos.

5 ¿Por qué crees que la música latina es tan popular entre los jóvenes latinos de los Estados Unidos?

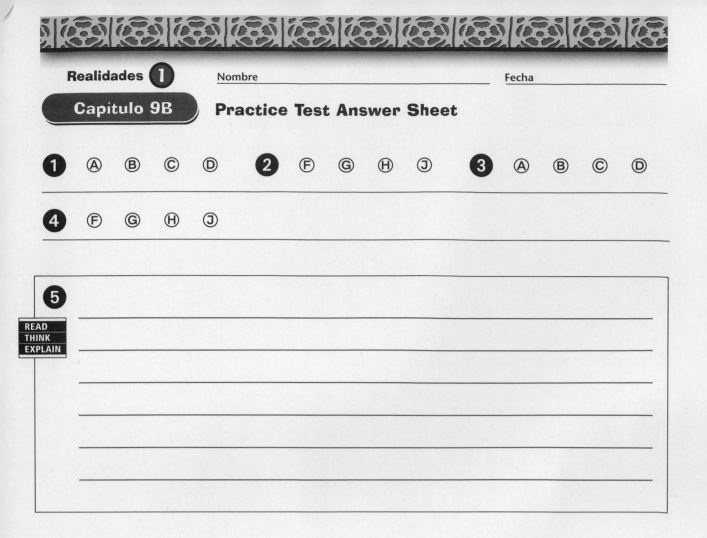

1 Ⓐ Ⓑ Ⓒ Ⓓ   2 Ⓕ Ⓖ Ⓗ Ⓙ   3 Ⓐ Ⓑ Ⓒ Ⓓ

4 Ⓕ Ⓖ Ⓗ Ⓙ

5

READ
THINK
EXPLAIN

_____

_____

_____

_____

_____

_____

Communication Workbook

Notes

Notes

Notes

Notes

Notes

Notes